AF575937

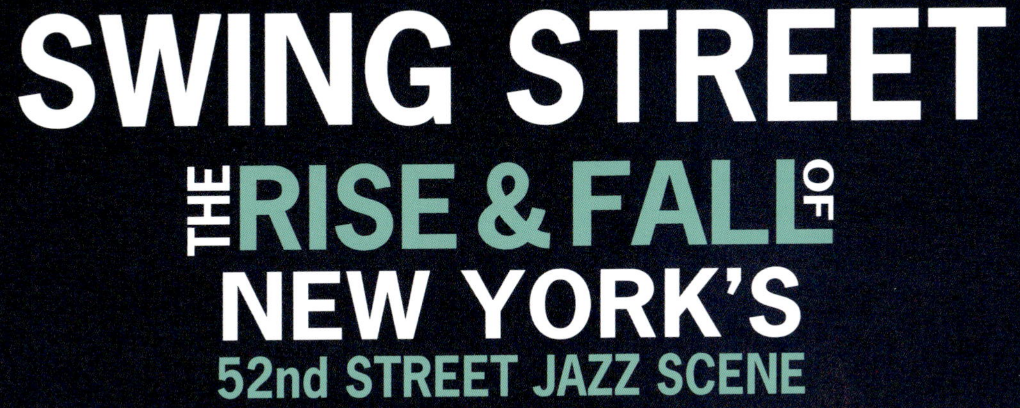

SWING STREET

THE RISE & FALL OF NEW YORK'S 52nd STREET JAZZ SCENE

AN ILLUSTRATED TRIBUTE, 1930–1950

Leo T. Sullivan

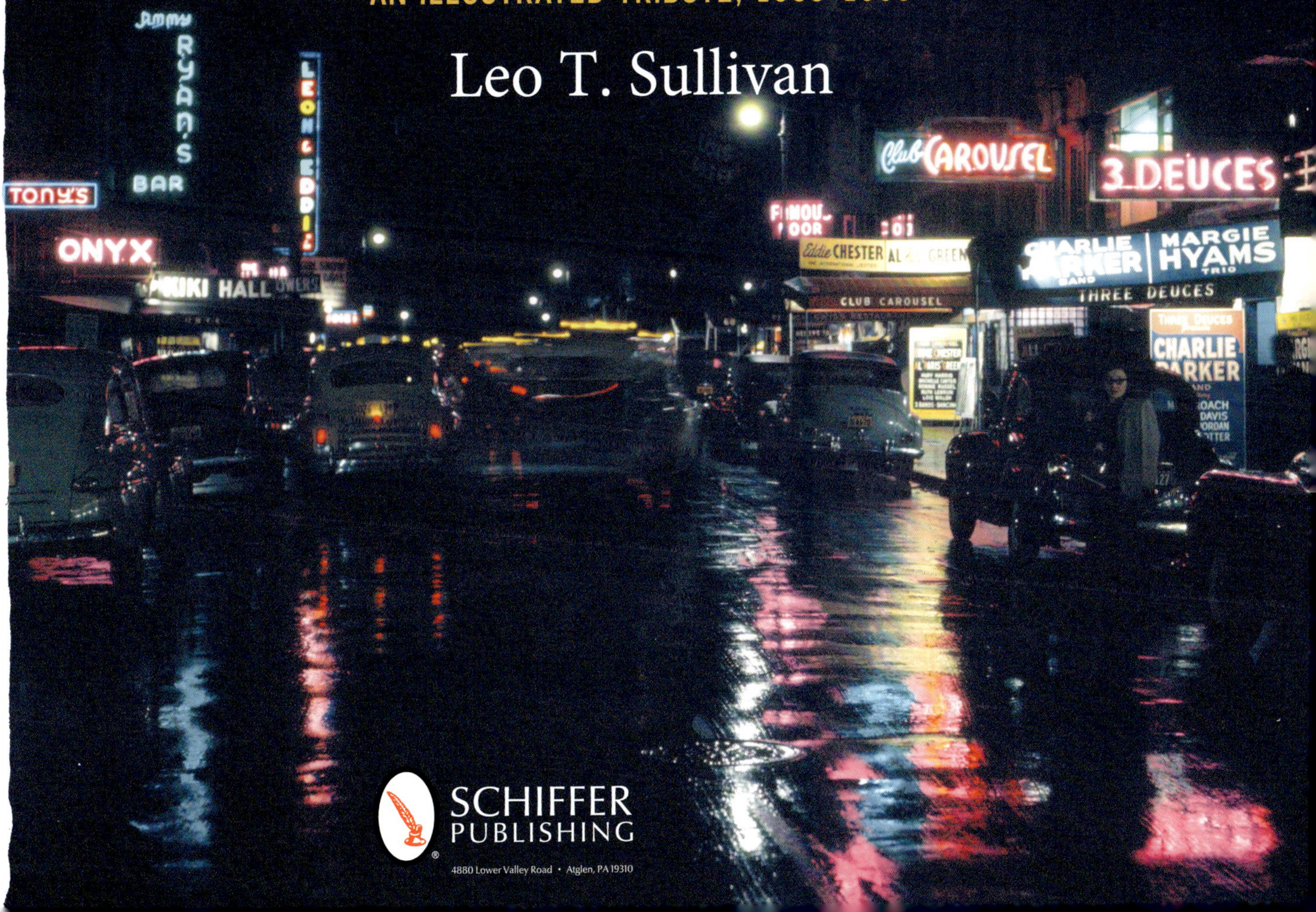

SCHIFFER PUBLISHING

4880 Lower Valley Road • Atglen, PA 19310

A special thanks to the Library of Congress for use of the William P. Gottlieb photographic images, and especially to the late William P. Gottlieb for capturing these iconic images of these legendary jazz artists over his many years visiting the jazz clubs on 52nd Street.

Also, a special thanks to senior editor Bob Biondi of Schiffer Publishing for his endless support and assistance.

This book is dedicated to my lovely wife, Shirley; son, Steven; daughter, Christine, and her husband, Shaun; and my adorable grandchildren, Tristan, Ashton, Avery, Kingsley, and Laughlin. Also, to my sister, Catherine; brother, Patrick, and Diane; and nephew, Sean, and his wife, Tanya, and children Jack and Chloe.

Other Schiffer Books by the Author:
Birdland, the Jazz Corner of the World: An Illustrated Tribute, 1949–1965, ISBN: 978-0-7643-5586-8

Library of Congress Control Number: 2019947901

Type set in Tandelle/Helvetica/Times

ISBN: 978-0-7643-5973-6
Printed in China

Published by Schiffer Publishing, Ltd.
4880 Lower Valley Road
Atglen, PA 19310
Phone: (610) 593-1777; Fax: (610) 593-2002
E-mail: Info@schifferbooks.com
Web: www.schifferbooks.com

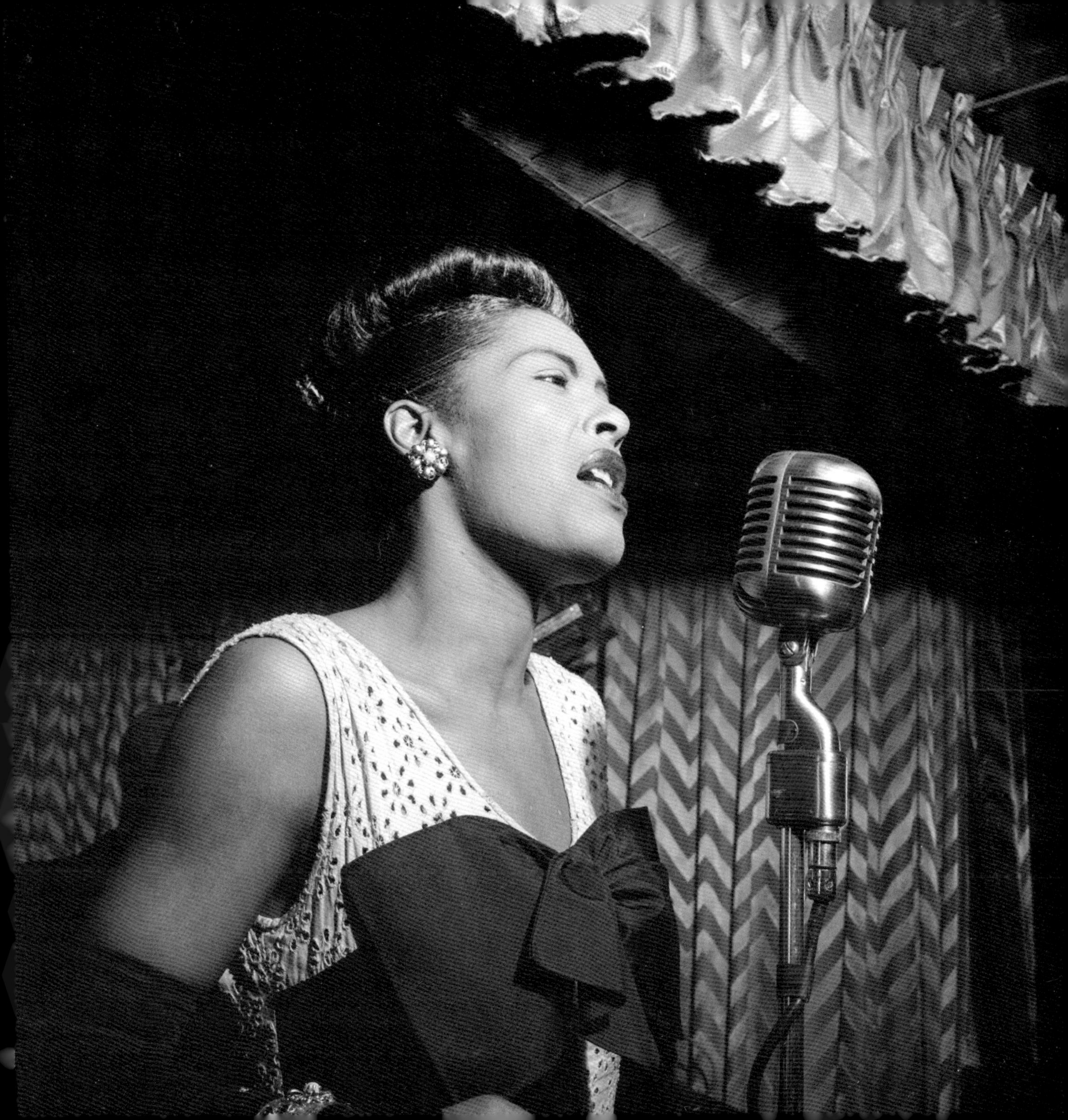

CONTENTS

INTRODUCTION

Swing Street is an illustrated tribute to a midtown Manhattan street from the late 1920s to the 1950s, built up of five-story Victorian brownstone buildings with street-level bar entrances, often leading into cramped interiors showcasing some of the world's greatest jazz artists. There were more nightclubs, bars, and cafés per square block on 52nd Street than anywhere else in world, featuring all styles of jazz music and entertainment. Between 5th and 6th Avenues, 52nd Street became known as "the Street" or "Swing Street," evolving and becoming recognized as "the Jazz Capital of the World."

52nd Street, from a musical perspective, came into existence when the Dixieland combos of the 1920s speakeasy era developed into the swing and big-band music of the thirties, leading to a smaller combo setting during the 1940s, which evolved into bebop, cool, and modern jazz.

Big bands such as Count Basie, Duke Ellington, and Dizzy Gillespie would often squeeze into the overcrowded clubs, but most of the time the clubs would hire groups of six musicians or fewer, such as groups led by Coleman Hawkins, Billie Holiday, Art Tatum, and Charlie Parker.

Imagine yourself stopping by Club Downbeat on 52nd Street for a late-night drink in the 1940s to catch a set of Dizzy Gillespie and his seventeen-piece big band, then crossing the street to Jimmy Ryan's to listen to trombonist Jack Teagarden with his Dixieland band, and later heading down the block to another basement club, the Three Deuces, to hear the Charlie Parker Quintet featuring Miles Davis until late into the evening. Afterward, head outside into the neon-lit street to enjoy the evening air while listening to a stream of musical stylings filtering from the many club doorways. And now to round off your perfect evening, you stop by Kelly's Stable to catch the last set of the Art Tatum Trio.

Swing Street is the story of how the music and musicians in Harlem came downtown to 52nd Street with such jazz legends as Duke Ellington, Art Tatum, Billie Holiday, Teddy Wilson, Stuff Smith, Benny Carter, Coleman Hawkins, "Hot Lips" Page, Roy Eldridge, Fats Waller, Erroll Garner, Lester Young, Mary Lou Williams, Dizzy Gillespie, Charlie Parker, Miles Davis, Maxine Sullivan, Sarah Vaughan, Ella Fitzgerald, and Count Basie, to name only a few.

"52nd St. was total friendship," says noted composer-arranger Alec Wilder. "It was the last time that an American street gave you a feeling of security and warmth, and the excitement of musical friendship." Jazz pianist Marian McPartland added, "On 52nd Street you could walk through the history of jazz. In several hours while nursing a few drinks, you could travel musically from New Orleans up to Harlem and Bop."

From the early 1930s onward, if you mentioned to a friend, "I'll see you on the Street tonight," he wouldn't have to ask you which street you meant, or if you flagged a cab and asked to be taken to the Street, you would be driven without hesitation to 52nd Street between 5th and 6th Avenues, known then and today as Swing Street.

CHAPTER ONE

SWING STREET

THE JAZZ CAPITAL OF THE WORLD

The genesis of nightlife on 52nd Street dates back to the 1920s, when the street operated a number of illegal speakeasies where white professional musicians jammed and mingled, but things really began to take off in 1926, when the New York City Board of Estimate passed a resolution lifting the residential restrictions on the brownstones between Fifth and Sixth Avenues, therefore allowing business rentals to operate within the brownstones. By the early 1930s, it was the core of a vibrant midtown entertainment district. This small strip of midtown nightspots on 52nd Street became an ideal location for new jazz clubs.

In December 1933, things changed for the better when alcohol became legal with the repeal of Prohibition and legal nightclubs opened on 52nd Street, featuring small combos both of black and white musicians. During the mid- to late 1930s, as swing music became the craze, audiences were drawn to 52nd Street's small venues, which drew both jazz lovers and the curious alike.

Since the clubs were operated out of the basements of past residential brownstones, they were unattractive and cramped, having low ceilings, long and narrow, with subdued lighting to create an atmosphere. The tables were small, with hardwood chairs, and there was nothing special about the clubs except the music. Miles Davis commented about his first impression when he saw the Three Deuces in 1944: "It had such a big reputation in the jazz scene that I thought it would be all plush and shit. The bandstand wasn't nothing but a little tiny space that could hardly hold a piano. I remember thinking that it wasn't nothing but a hole in the wall."

On 52nd Street, all styles of music existed together. Dixieland musicians played alongside swing musicians, who in turn played alongside bebop musicians. Clubs at that time were given more freedom to allow both integrated bands and audiences, which helped tear down the racial boundaries of jazz.

It was a never-ending block party on 52nd Street. You felt safe and secure, with everybody seeming to get along with each other. You could pop in and catch a set of Billie Holiday at Club Downbeat or drop by the Three Deuces and hear the Charlie Parker and Dizzy Gillespie play the new innovative jazz stylings of bebop. Either way, on Swing Street you were guaranteed to experience an evening of incredible jazz and entertainment on a nightly basis, seven nights a week, till the wee hours of the morning.

Since the clubs were only doors apart, there grew a strong sense of comradery among the musicians. After finishing a set at their respective clubs, musicians would often pop into other clubs to listen or sit in, therefore creating a healthy exchange of musical ideas. This interplay would help develop and create new innovative styles of music, as well as educate certain musicians to the possibilities at hand.

In the mid-1930s, 52nd Street created an uneasiness among black musicians at that time, since midtown Manhattan was mostly white. Billie Holiday complained about her treatment at the Famous Door in the mid-1930s, where she and pianist Teddy Wilson would play during the intermissions: "Black musicians were rare at the time, and they were told in no uncertain terms not to fraternize with white patrons. White musicians were swinging from one end of 52nd Street to the other, but there wasn't a black face in sight on the street except Teddy Wilson and me. Teddy played intermission piano at the Famous Door, and I sang. There was no cotton to be picked between Leon & Eddie's and the East River, but man, it was a plantation any way you looked at it. And we not only had to look at it, we had to live it. The minute we were finished with our intermission stint, we had to scoot out back to the alley, or go out and sit in the street. Swing Street, as they called it, was this new kind of music. They could get away with calling it new because millions of squares hadn't taken a trip to 113th Street in Harlem. Soon the plantation owners found they could make money off black artists and they couldn't afford their old prejudices. So, the barriers went down, and it gave jobs to a lot of great musicians."

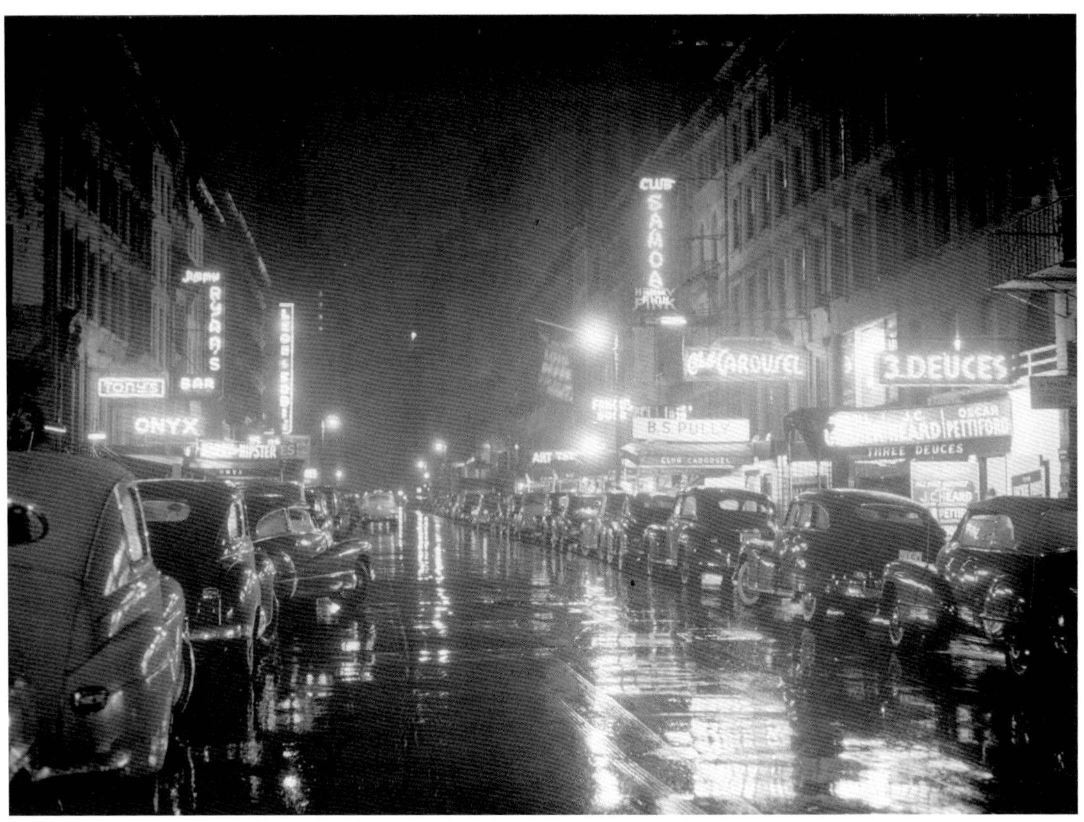

Swing Street. 52nd Street at night in the late 1940s.

Leonard Feather remembers, "I resented the exclusion of black people as customers. The clubs could not exclude black musicians with whom they were familiar. But, by and large, they tried to keep as white as possible. It was not until 1943–44 that the raised eyebrows began disappearing."

When it came to musicians getting paid on 52nd Street, black artists were paid much less than the white musicians during the early years, but that soon changed in the early 1940s, with Billie Holiday moving from $175 a week to making over $1,200, and Art Tatum grossing over $1,000 weekly.

World War II created a larger audience for Swing Street since the military on shore leave had money to burn after weeks at sea, and also given that the ships were docked only a short distance from the 52nd Street jazz scene. Down Beat reported in 1944 that "the war with its boom days and overtime payrolls is reviving the jazz interest on 52nd Street."

On the downside, the war created new restrictions on businesses that featured singing, dancing, or acting. In the spring of 1944, a 30 percent cabaret tax was leveed on clubs, forcing some clubs to limit their music to only instrumental music since it was exempt from taxes. This prompted clubs with instrumental music to place signs in their windows with a large "NO TAX" written on it.

Just when the clubs thought it couldn't get any worse, a nationwide curfew went into effect in early 1945, stating that all the nightclubs in the land would have to close at midnight to save fuel, manpower, and transportation. This read as a possible death sentence to 52nd Street, with some clubs laying off musicians and starting the night's entertainment at seven o'clock to counteract the loss of revenue, but the clubs would get back to business as usual in May 1945, when the curfew was finally lifted.

Radio broadcasts became an important medium for publicizing 52nd Street, and the most important radio personality on Swing Street in those days was disc jockey "Symphony" Sid Torin. His broadcasts from the Three Deuces on Sunday nights over WHOM were a big hit with black listeners in Harlem and abroad.

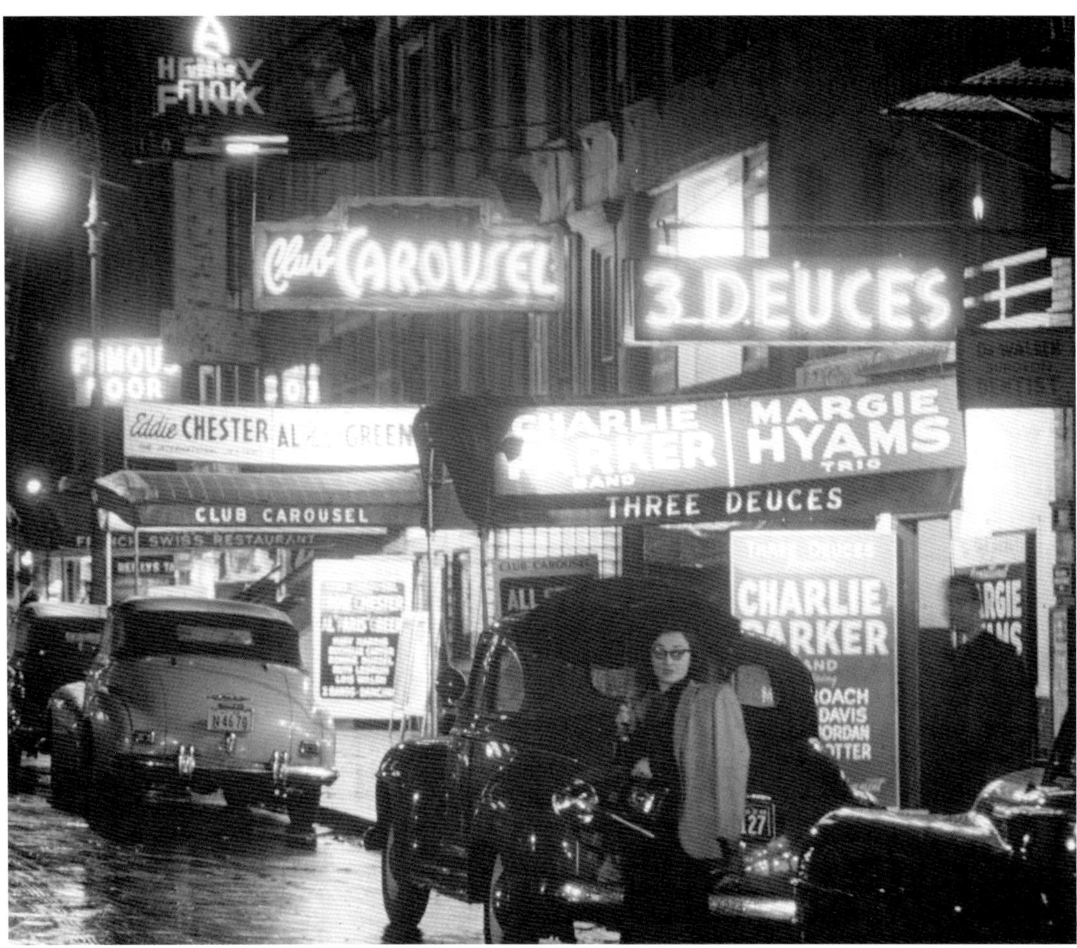

The south side of 52nd Street in 1948 between 5th and 6th Avenues, looking east. Crossing the street is jazz vibraphonist Margie Hyams, who was playing at the Three Deuces with her trio alongside the Charlie Parker Quintet featuring Miles Davis (trumpet), Duke Jordon (piano), Tommy Potter (bass), and Max Roach (drums).

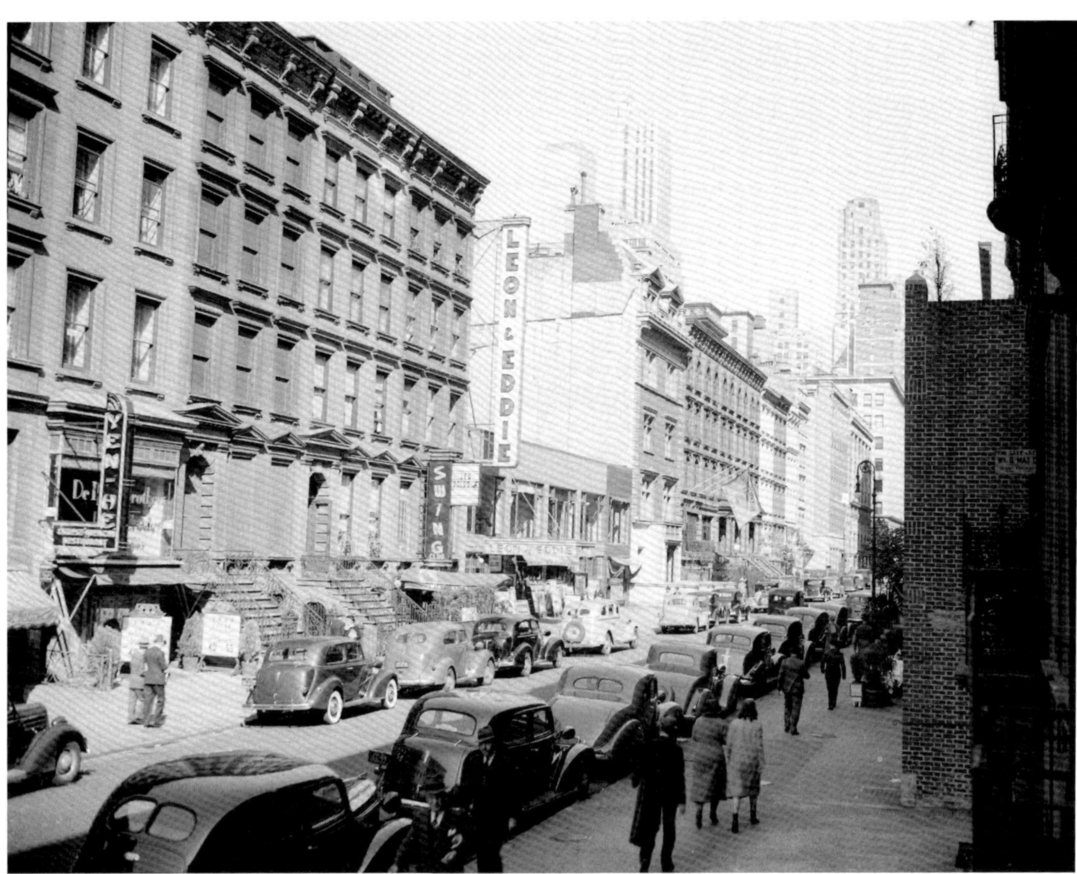

An afternoon on 52nd Street in 1937. Across the street on the north side are the Swing Club and Leon & Eddie's, and farther down with the flag banner is the 21 Club.

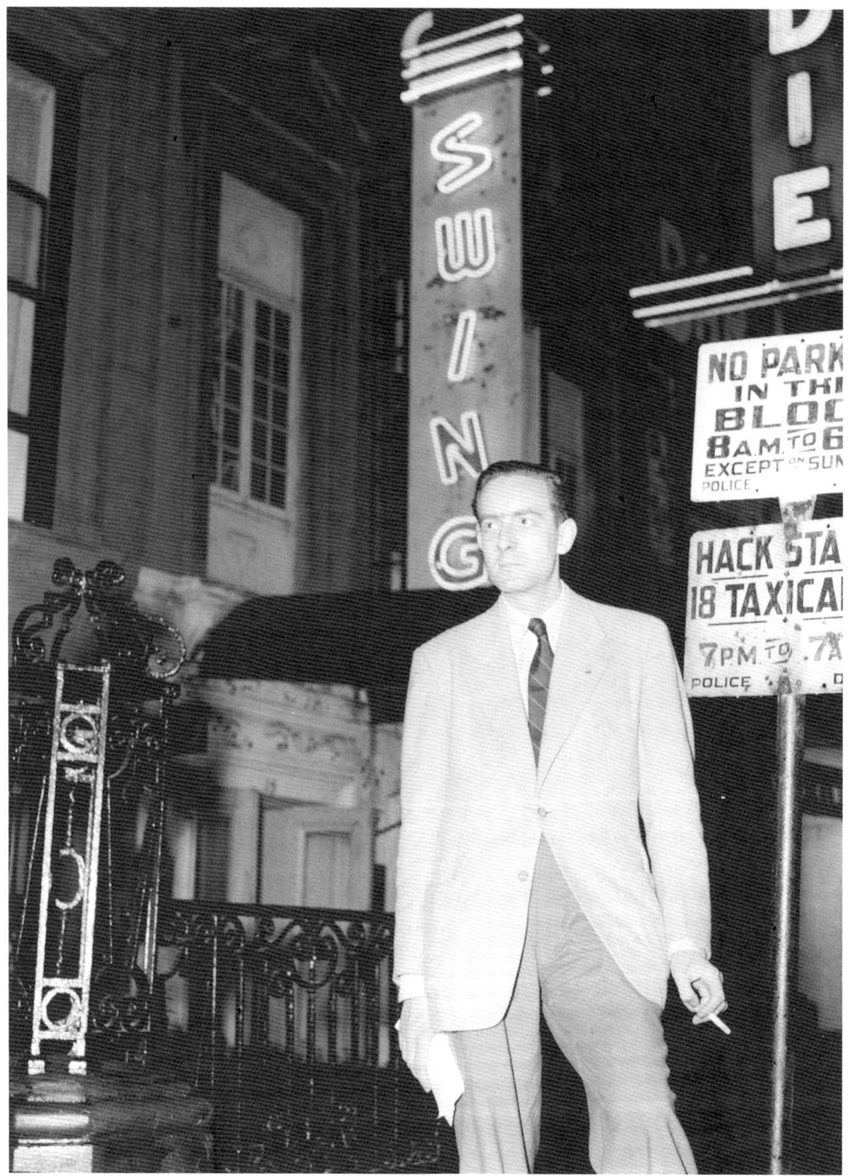

Charles Delaunay, a French author and cofounder of the Hot Club de France, standing in front of the Swing Club at 35 West 52nd Street in 1946

Nightclubs such as the Famous Door and the Onyx were the first on 52nd Street to provide instrumental jazz, with small combos proving to be profitable for the club owners. Once in a while they would squeeze a complete big band onto a small stage with the piano on the floor. The Famous Door became notable for being the location where the Count Basie Orchestra first performed to a New York audience in 1938. "Basie was a sensation—a total and absolute sensation. I don't think that New York has ever heard a jazz band quite like this ever before. It was with Basie in 1938 that 52nd Street got its reputation as the jumping-off place for jazz in New York," stated impresario John Hammond.

Many of the clubs on 52nd Street provided steady work for jazz musicians, while other clubs entertained their customers with elaborate floor shows, such as at Leon & Eddie's. Soon clubs began hiring small jazz combos and bringing in headliners, displaying their names on awnings and large wooden signs outside their club. The bigger the better.

In May 1945, *Metronome* magazine proclaimed that "Dizzy Keeps Street Alive" with his quintet at the Three Deuces, and in September 1947, *DownBeat* magazine reported that Charlie Parker (playing the Three Deuces) and Dizzy Gillespie (working Club Downbeat) were the two most popular acts on the street.

Jazz bassist Leonard Gaskin recalls the musicians he encountered from the 1930s to the 1950s on 52nd Street: "They were really joyous people to be around. There wasn't any animosity or any bad feelings. The feeling was one of warmth, one of sharing, one of enjoying themselves. And the camaraderie that existed was just outstanding. You know, back then I'd ask Pops [Louis Armstrong], How do you do this? Or Oscar Pettiford, How do you do this? Or Slam (Stewart), How do you do this? And they would painstakingly show you how to do the damn thing."

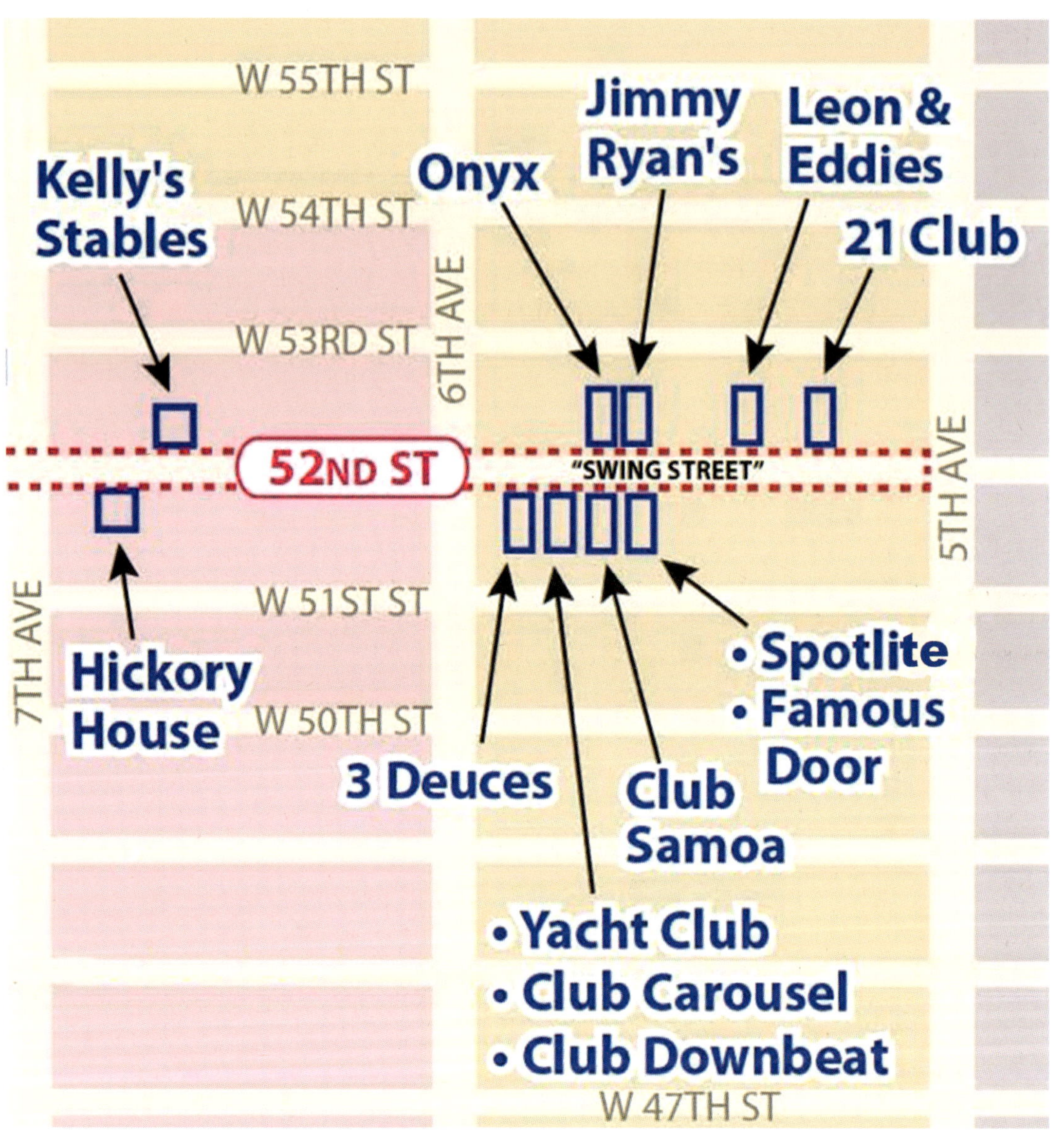

52nd Street map showing the popular jazz spots, including the multiple change of venues throughout the ages

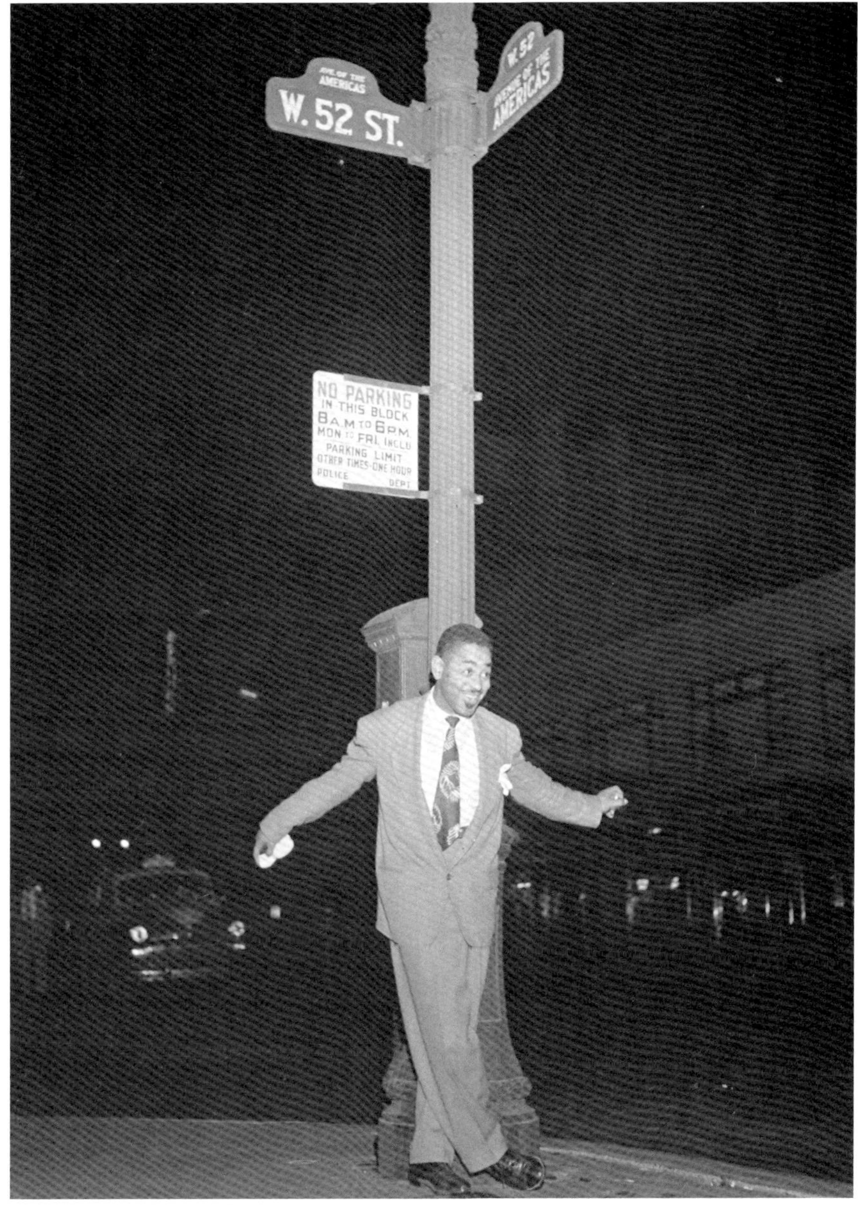

Jazz trumpeter Dizzy Gillespie at the corner of 52nd Street and 6th Avenue (Avenue of the Americas) in May 1946

Twelve months a year the entertainment overflowed from narrow shoebox interiors into the street, turning 52nd Street into an all-night event. All styles of jazz could be heard drifting through open doors, from such jazz artists as Charlie Parker, Dizzy Gillespie, Thelonious Monk, Fats Waller, Billie Holiday, Coleman Hawkins, and the Count Basie Orchestra.

Songwriter Johnny Mercer remembered 52nd Street as "the focal point of jazz for the influential musicians of the time. When they weren't playing, they wanted to listen."

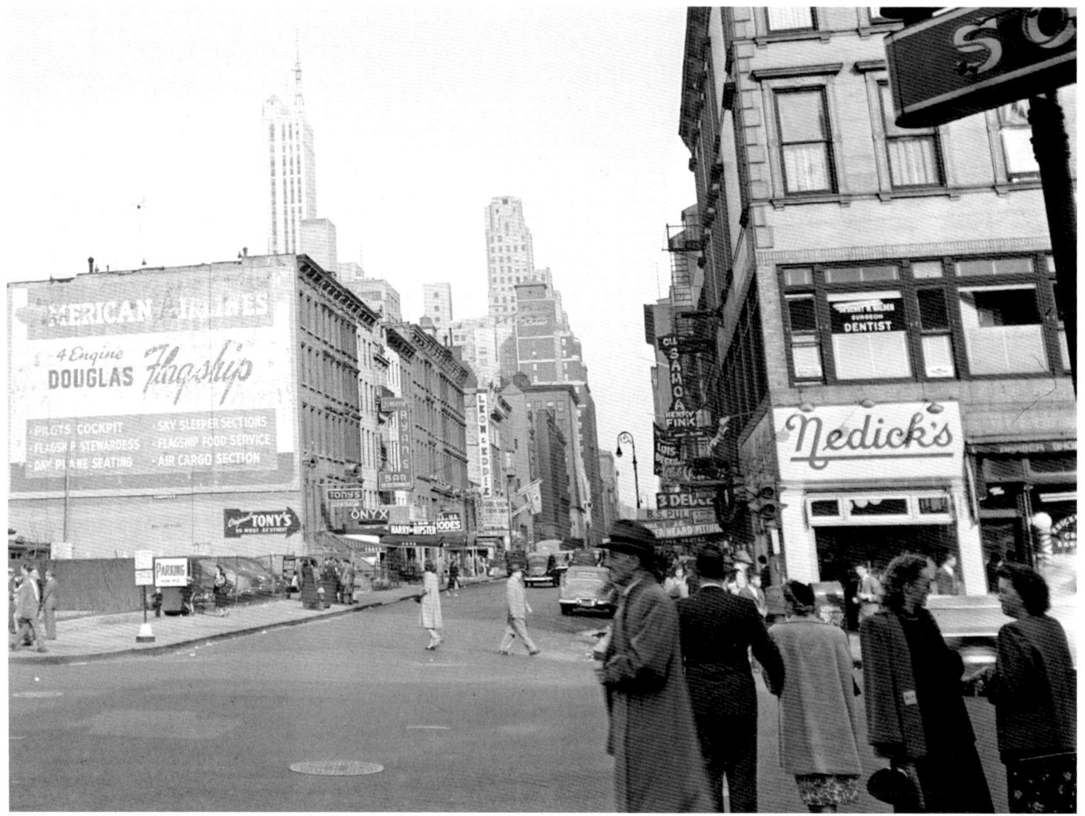

Looking west on 52nd Street in 1948. On the north side (*left*) you can see Tony's, the Onyx, Jimmy Ryan's, and Leon & Eddie's. On the south side (*right*) you can see the Three Deuces, Club Carousel, and Club Samoa.

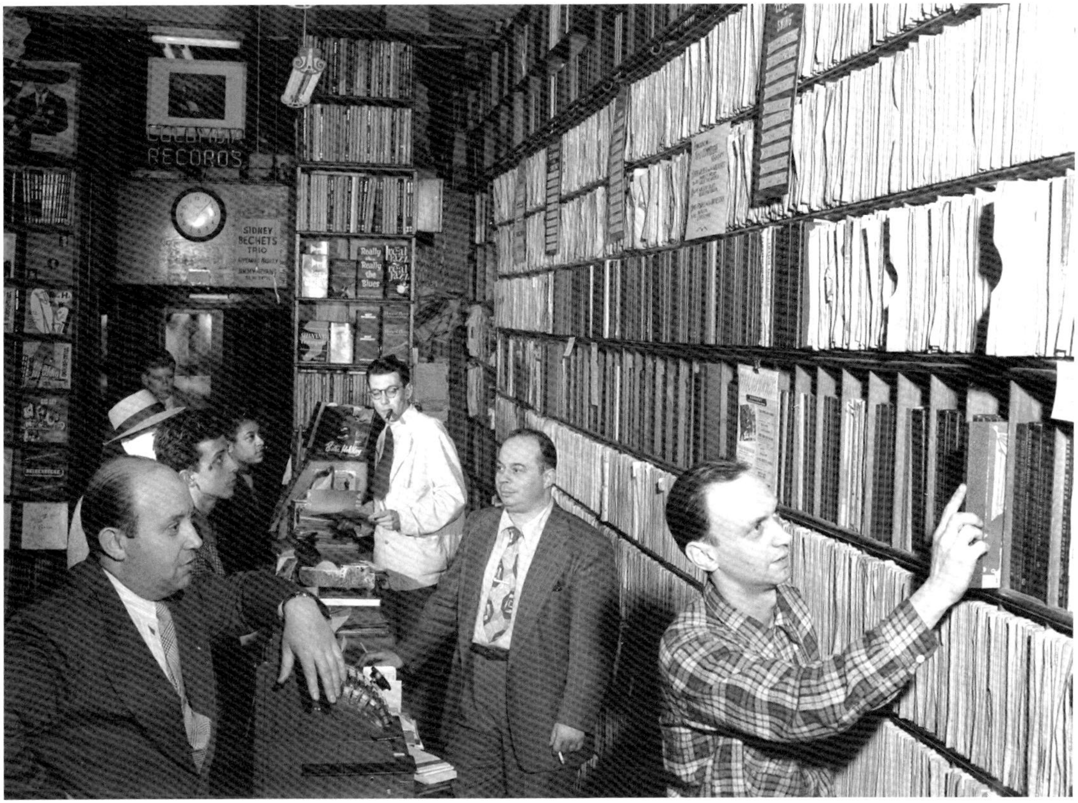

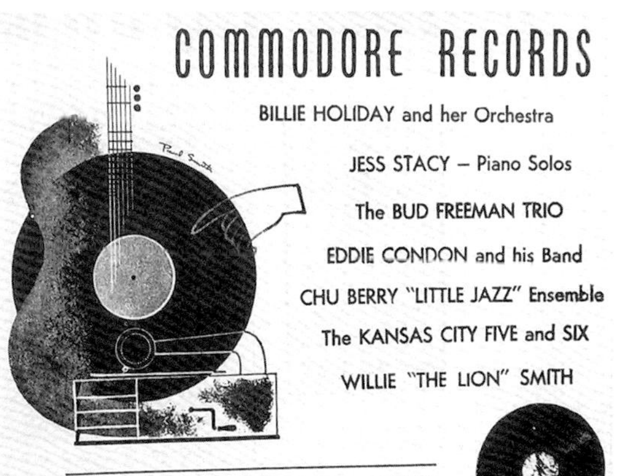

Left to right: Milt Gabler, Herbie Hill, Lou Blum, and Jack Crystal (actor Billy Crystal's father) at the Commodore Record Shop on 52nd Street in August 1947. Gabler, a musician and songwriter, leased the upstairs store at 46 West 52nd Street for three years during the late 1930s. He would be instrumental in starting successful jam sessions across the street at Jimmy Ryan's in 1938, creating his own handwritten circulars for the events. These jazz jams became the catalyst that started the beginning of commercial jazz concerts, which inspired impresario Norman Granz to launch his successful series of Jazz at the Philharmonic concerts.

Starting in 1944, the hipster movement started to become a recognized part of the 52nd Street theme, with their self-proclaiming coolness, zoot suit, beret, glasses, and goatee. They were emulating the symbol of hip at the time and bop pioneer Dizzy Gillespie. In 1946, the hipsters (or zombies as some called them) were taking over the street. Groups of hipsters would walk into a club wearing their hipster garb, using hipster jive talk, which eventually drove away any customers who were there for a night out.

An eccentric vocalist and virtuosic stride, boogie-woogie pianist Harry "the Hipster" Gibson became an overnight success with the hipsters on Swing Street. He noticed people were using the word "hip," so Harry coined the word "hipster." "Gather round, all you hipsters," he would say from the piano. Customers and musicians soon picked up on the new word and started to call him "the Hipster." He would write and sing a few hits such as "Handsome Harry, the Hipster" in the early 1940s, which solidified his hipster name and image. From 1939 to 1945 he worked full-time on "Swing Street," playing with Charlie Parker, Dizzy Gillespie, Billie Holiday, and Art Tatum, and starred in a few short films.

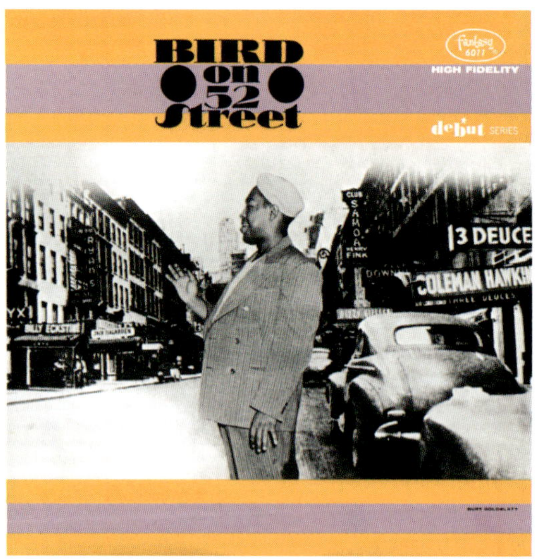

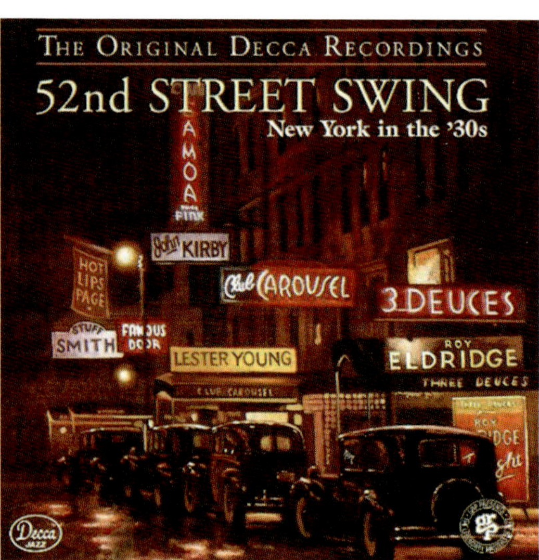

Almost every great jazz artist of the era performed at the clubs on 52nd Street, but by the late 1940s the jazz scene began moving elsewhere around New York City, and urban renewal began to take hold.

Journalist Leonard Feather wrote in *Metronome* in 1948, "The Street Is Dead. Fifty-Second Street, unless we are happily mistaken, is on its last legs, and looks like the end of an era. Both burlesque and drugs, with raids and arrests, and clubs ripping off customers added to its ultimate demise."

By the early 1960s, most of the jazz clubs were demolished or fell into disrepair. The 52nd Street of today shows little trace of its jazz history. But while it lasted, this midtown jazz scene on Swing Street was like nothing else in the history of jazz.

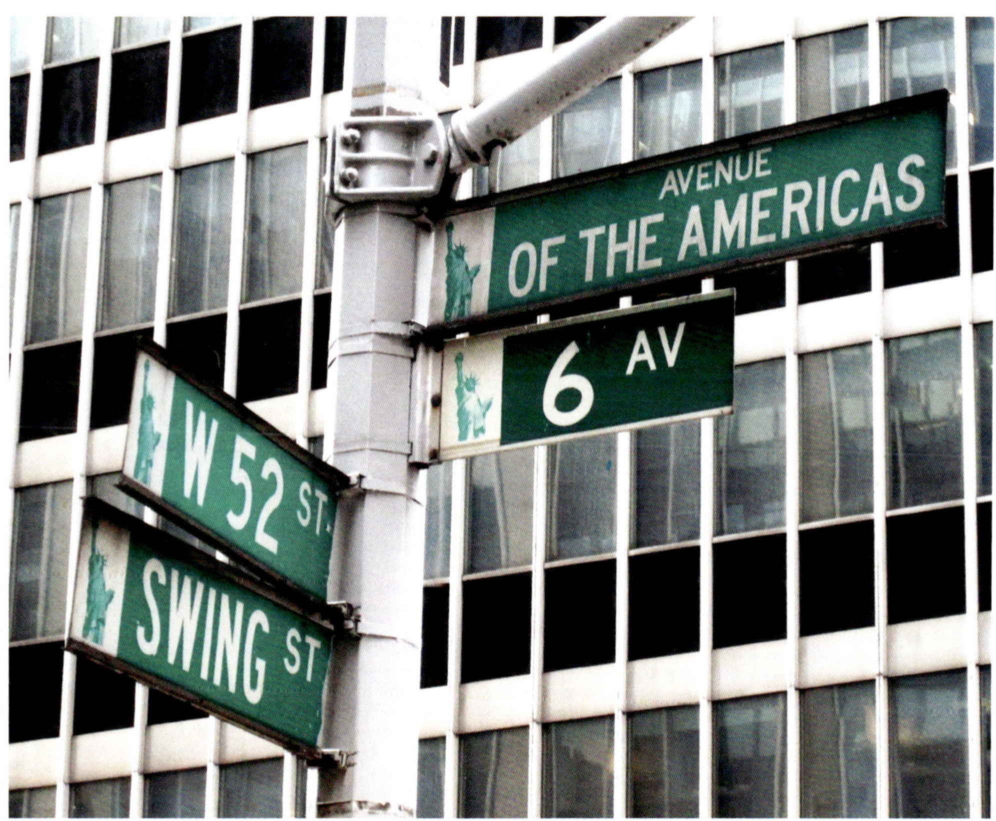

The block from 5th to 6th Avenues is formally conamed "Swing Street," and one block west is named "W. C. Handy's Place."

CHAPTER TWO

SWING STREET

52ND STREET JAZZ CLUBS

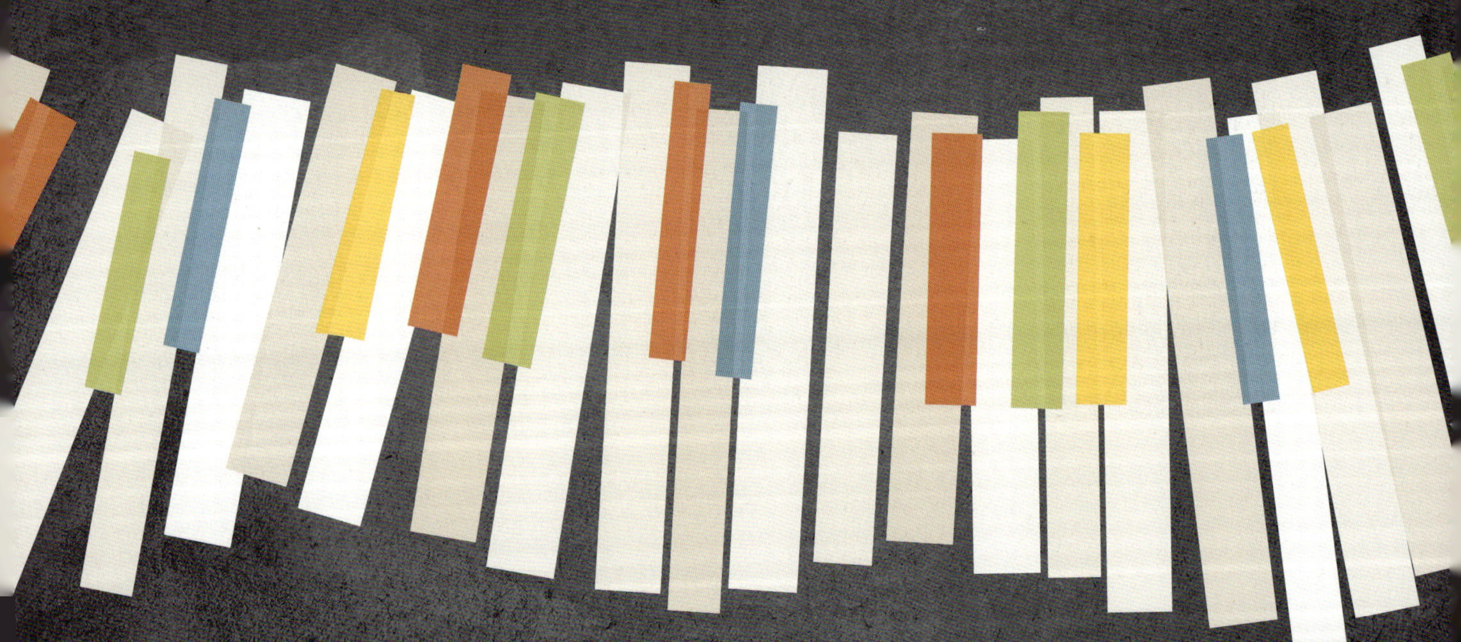

CLUB DOWNBEAT

Club Downbeat opened in May 1944 at 66 West 52nd Street, taking over the Yacht Club due to the latter's not being able to pay the 30 percent cabaret tax that was leveed on clubs that used singers or provided dancing during war times. Club Downbeat would operate for almost four years until closing in February 1948. Over their less than four-year stretch, Club Downbeat would employ the greatest names in jazz, such as Billie Holiday, Dizzy Gillespie, Coleman Hawkins, Thelonious Monk, Art Tatum, Ella Fitzgerald, Red Norvo, and Miles Davis, to name a few.

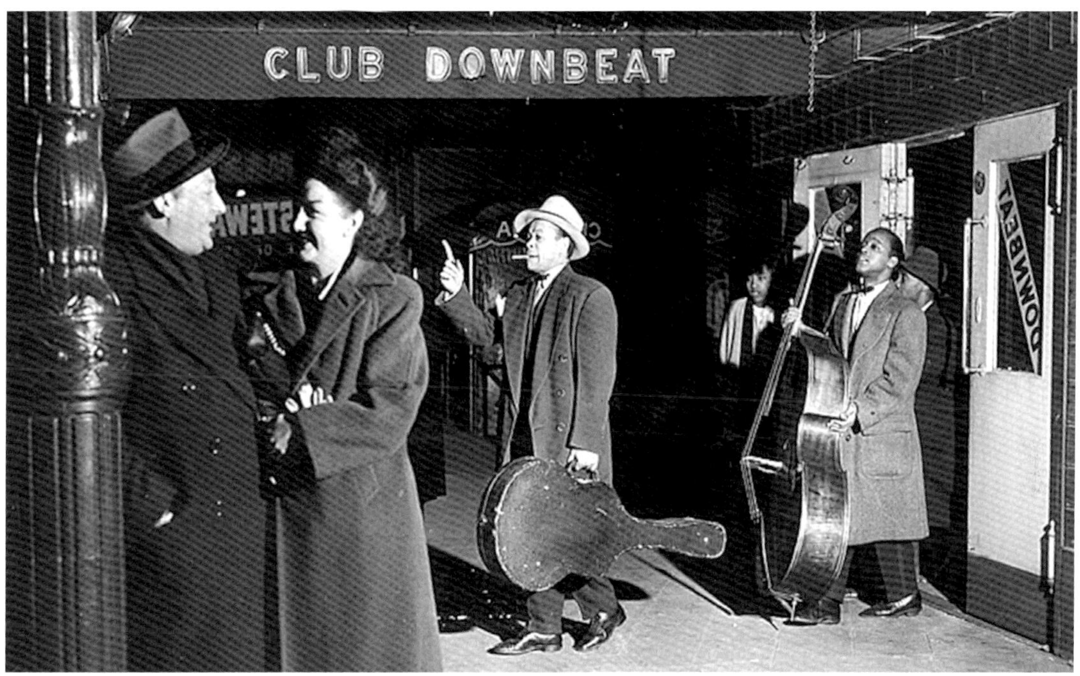

Unknown jazz musicians leaving Club Downbeat in the mid-1940s

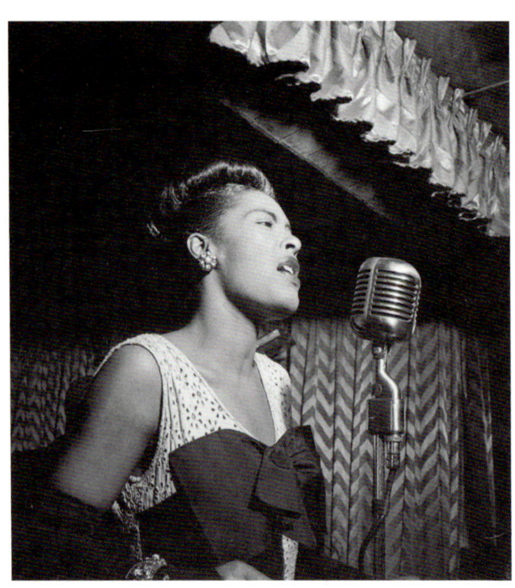

LEFT Billie Holiday on stage at Club Downbeat in February 1947

BOTTOM Billie Holiday and her pet boxer "Mister" in the dressing room at Club Downbeat in June 1946. Billie was a huge dog lover, always having them in her life, such as "Gypsy," a Great Dane; "Chiquita" and "Pepe," her beloved Chihuahuas; a terrier named "Bessie Mae Moocho"; and her soulmate, a boxer named "Mister."

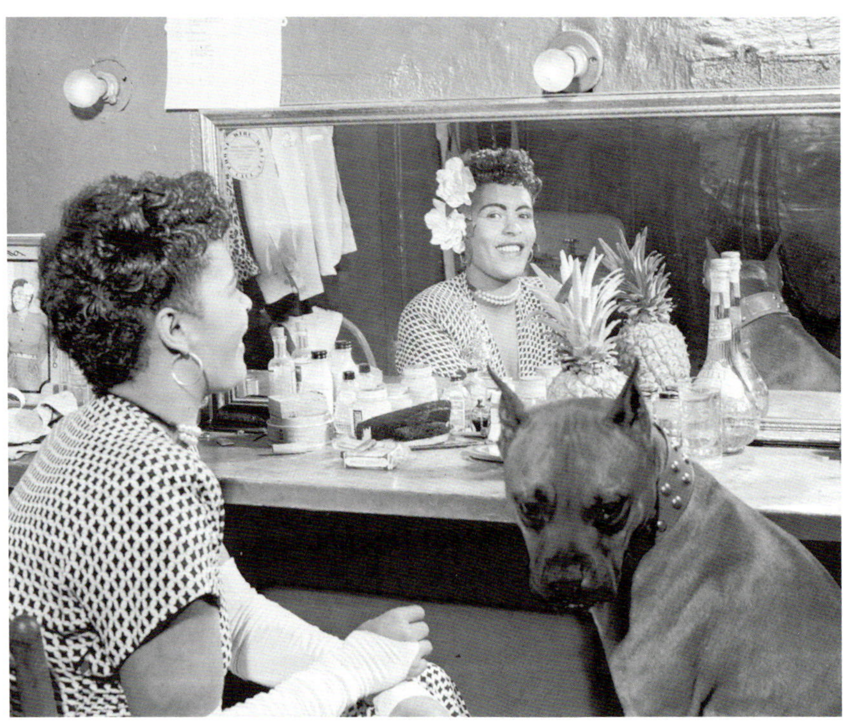

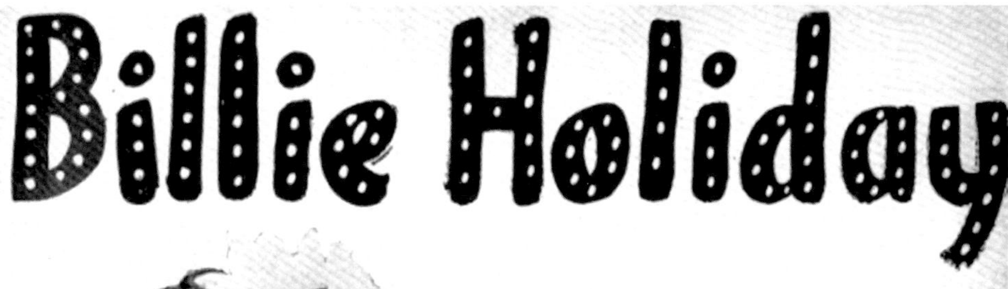

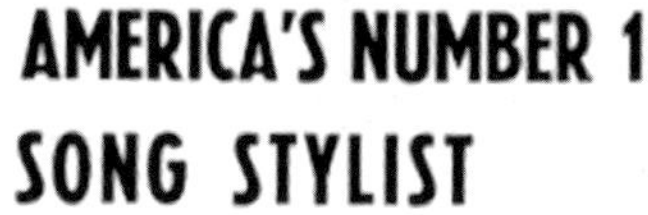

★WINNER ESQUIRE POLL 1944-1945

★"BILLIE HOLIDAY, THE THRUSH, IS BREAKING ALL 52ND STREET RECORDS AT THE DOWNBEAT."
★ —WALTER WINCHELL

★JUST CONCLUDED 12 SENSATIONAL WEEKS AT CLUB SAVOY, SAN FRANCISCO. NOW IN HER 7TH RECORD-BREAKING WEEK AT CLUB DOWNBEAT, NEW YORK.

DECCA RECORDS EXCLUSIVELY
LATEST RELEASE—LOVER MAN
#23391

ASSISTED BY BIG SID CATLETT
ESQUIRE'S ALL-AMERICAN DRUMMER MAN AND HIS SEXTET
and
AL CASEY
ESQUIRE'S ALL-AMERICAN GUITARIST AND HIS SENSATIONAL TRIO

BILLIE HOLIDAY AND HER BRAND NEW 15 PIECE ORCHESTRA AVAILABLE TO PLAY YOUR CITY STARTING ON TOUR SEPTEMBER 1ST.

ALL ABOVE MENTIONED ARTISTS UNDER EXCLUSIVE MANAGEMENT

A 1946 advert noting that Billie Holiday was breaking attendance records at Club Downbeat on 52nd Street after performing there for seven weeks

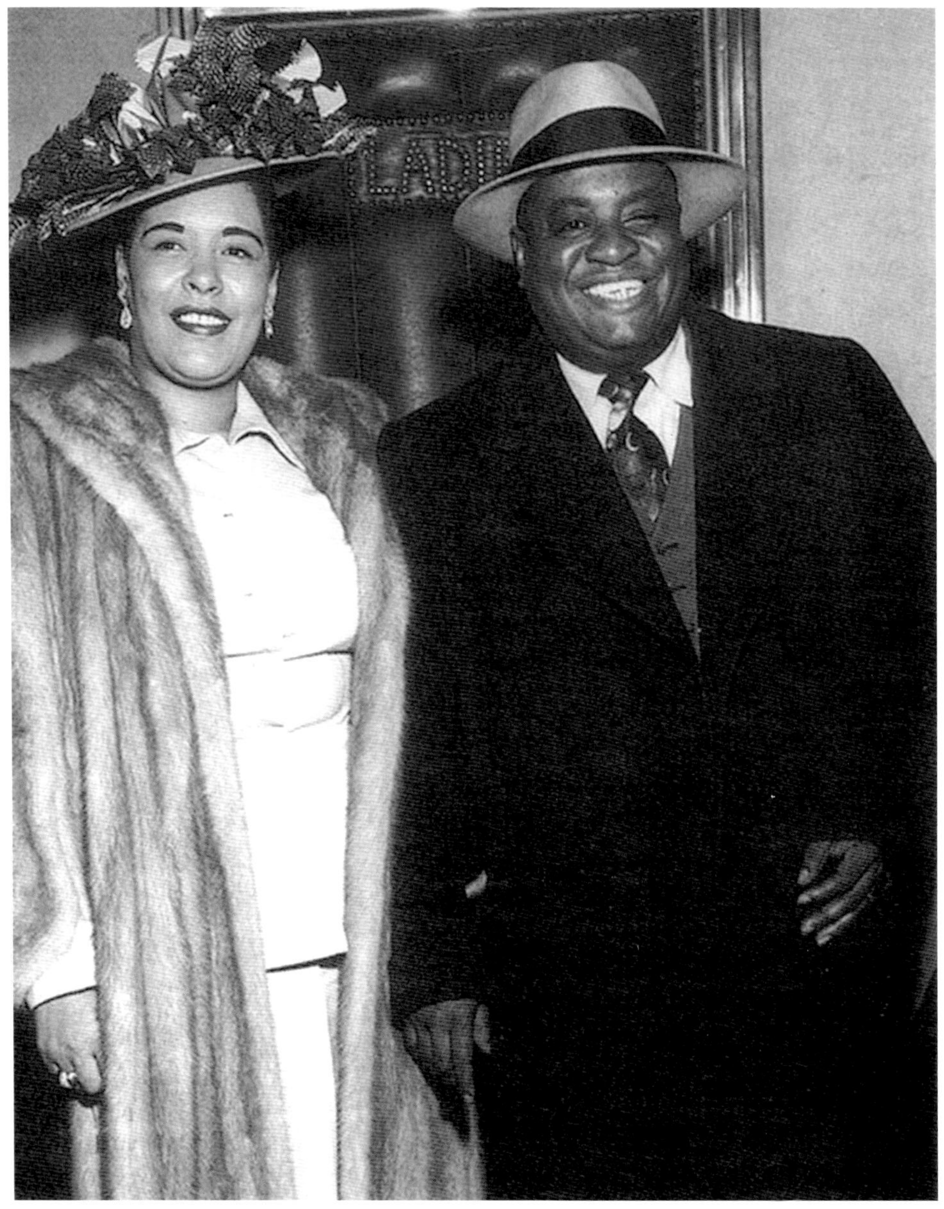

Billie Holiday and Art Tatum at Club Downbeat in December 1946. They were the featured artists in "America's Greatest Show," with the Lou Mel Morgan Trio and the Al Casey Trio.

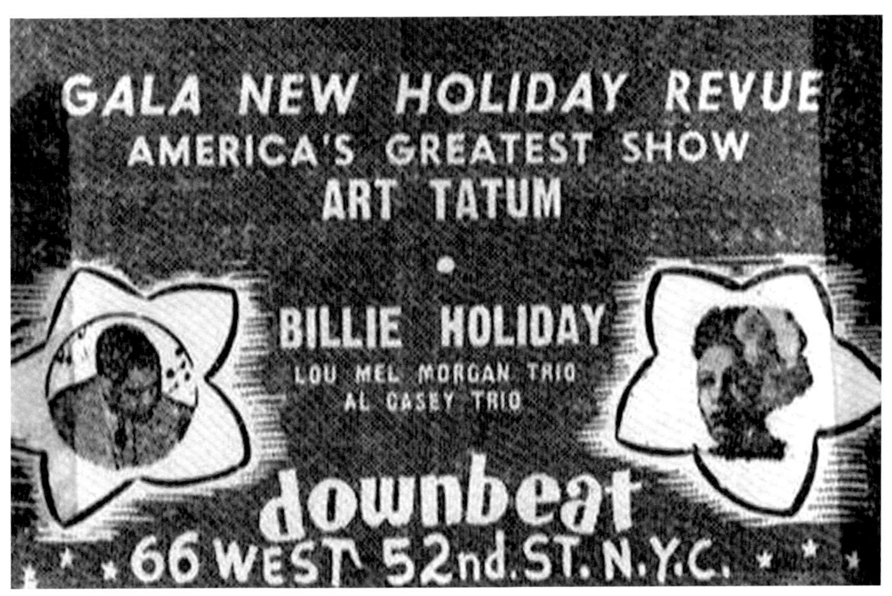

December 1946

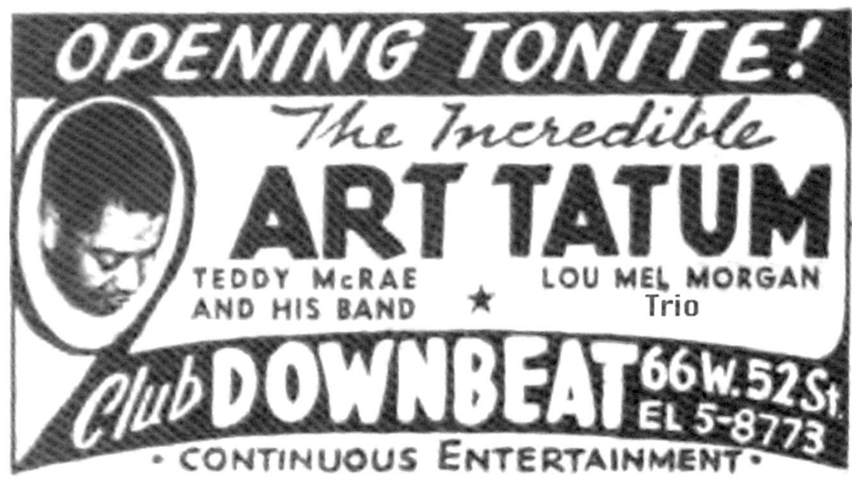

August 21, 1945

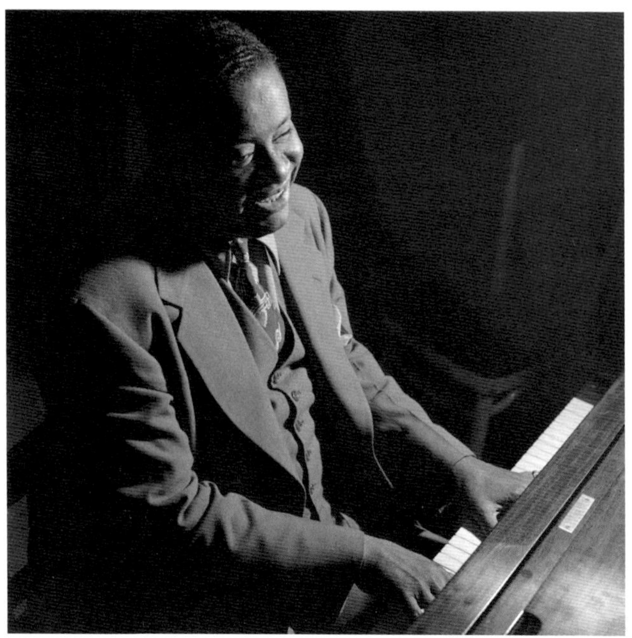

Art Tatum at Club Downbeat, May 1946. Tatum was a consistent drawing card at Club Downbeat. His virtuosic technique with incredible right-hand runs, being performed at seemingly impossible speeds, had jazz musicians and fans alike packing the club to watch this master of the keyboard. Even classical piano greats such as Vladimir Horowitz and Sergei Rachmaninoff after visiting Club Downbeat were astounded by his virtuosity. Pianist Fats Waller was performing on 52nd Street one night when Art Tatum walked in, and upon noticing him, Waller shouted out, "Ladies and gentlemen, I play the piano, but God is in the house."

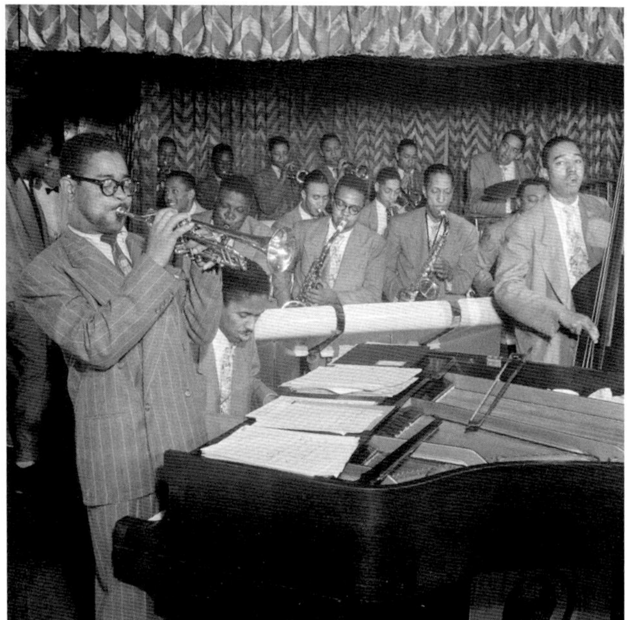

Jazz trumpeter Dizzy Gillespie leading his seventeen-piece big band at Club Downbeat during the summer of 1947. Band members: Dave Burns, Miles Davis, Elmon Wright, Matthew McKay, and Ray Orr (trumpets); Taswell Baird and Bill Shepard (trombones); John Brown and Howard Johnson (alto sax); James Moody and Joe Gales (tenor sax); Cecil Payne (baritone sax); John Lewis (piano); Ray Brown (bass); Joe Harris (drums); Milt Jackson (vibraphone); and Kenny "Pancho" Haygood (vocals).

Tracks on the album include originals by Dizzy Gillespie such as "Groovin' High," "Woody 'n' You," "Oo-Bop-Sh'Bam," and "Oop-Pop-a-Da." Also included on the album are a few original compositions by Tadd Dameron, such as "Hot House" and "Lady Bird."

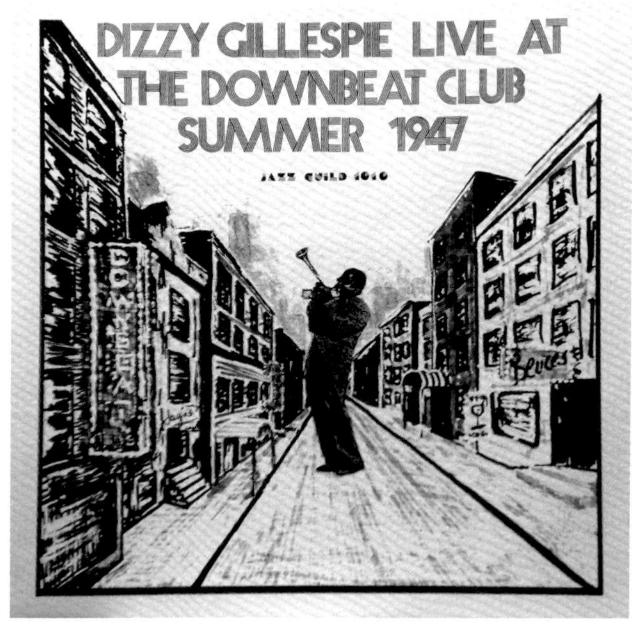

Dizzy Gillespie with his big band at Club Downbeat during the summer of 1947. Some of the musicians in view are Cecil Payne on baritone sax, James Moody on tenor sax, and Miles Davis in the rear trumpet section.

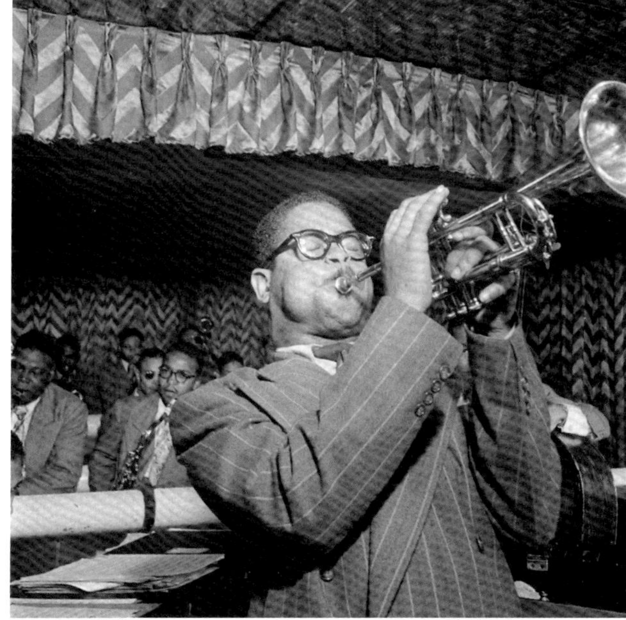

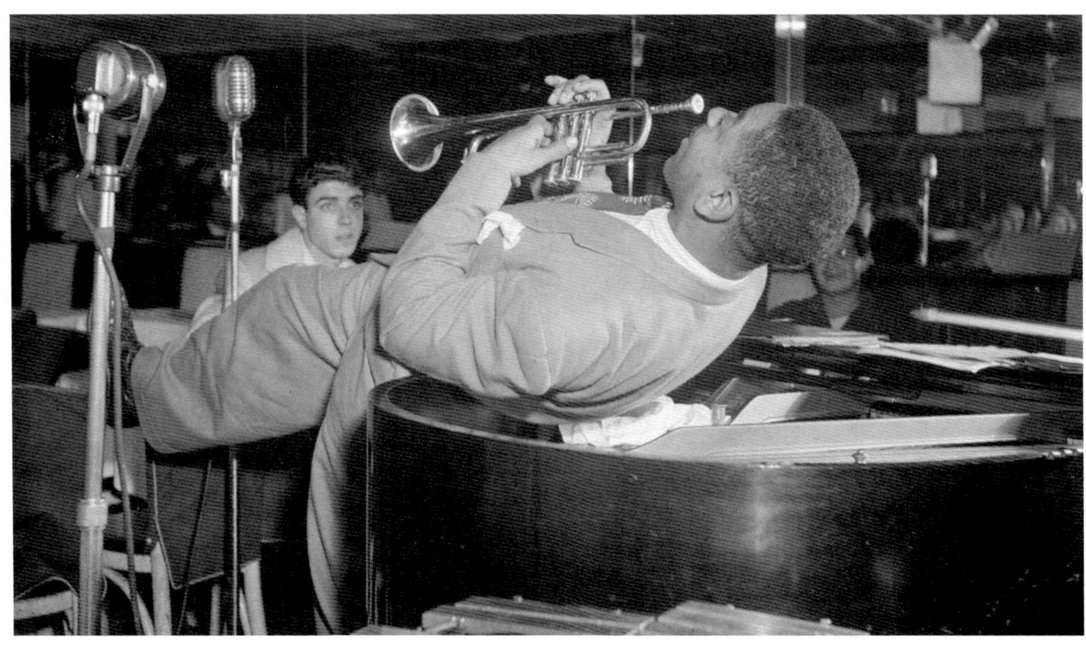

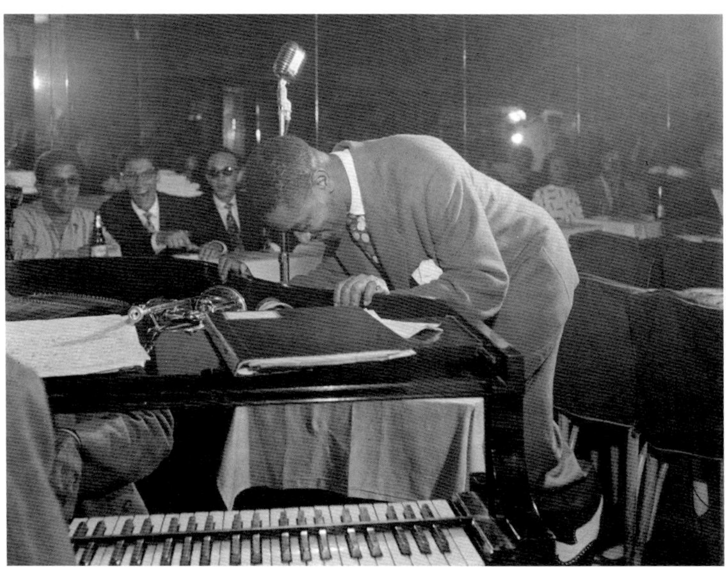

Dizzy Gillespie's crazy antics at Club Downbeat in August 1947

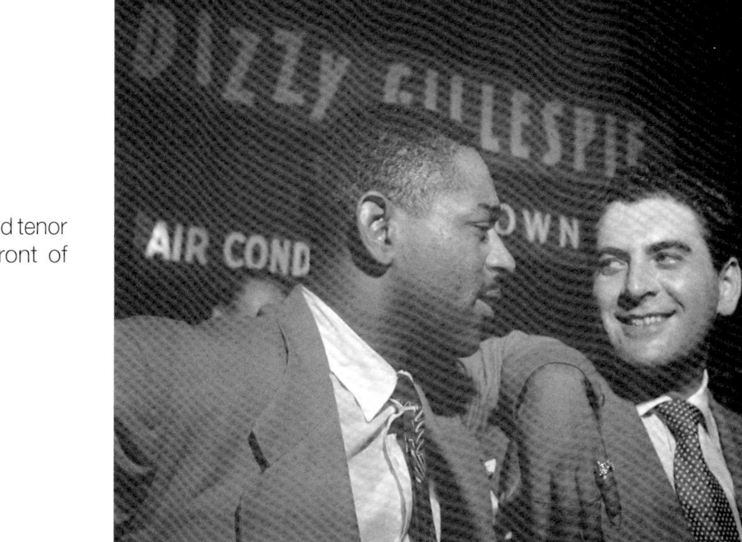

Dizzy Gillespie with bandleader and tenor saxophonist Georgie Auld in front of Club Downbeat in August 1947

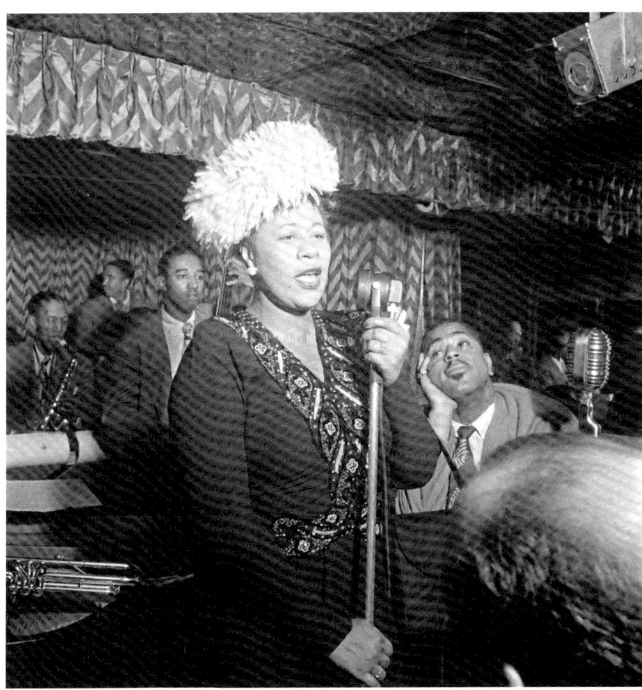

Ella Fitzgerald performing with Dizzy's big band at Club Downbeat in September 1947, as Dizzy looks on humorously. Ella would gross over $7,600 in her first week at Club Downbeat and later, in December, marry bassist Ray Brown (*seen behind Ella*).

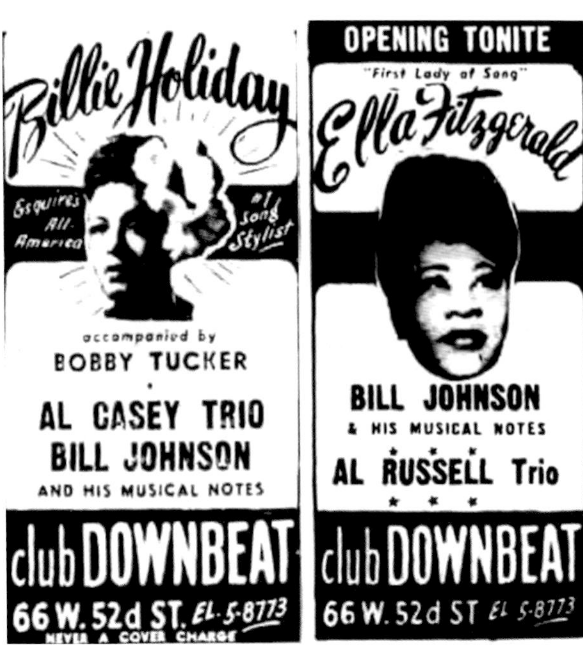

Billie Holiday and Ella Fitzgerald adverts for Club Downbeat in 1947. Billie was accompanied by her steady pianist Bobby Tucker, who started with her in 1946, later to quit in 1949 due to Billie's abusive lover threatening him. Ella Fitzgerald, "the First Lady of Song," would headline for five weeks with Dizzy Gillespie's seventeen-piece big band.

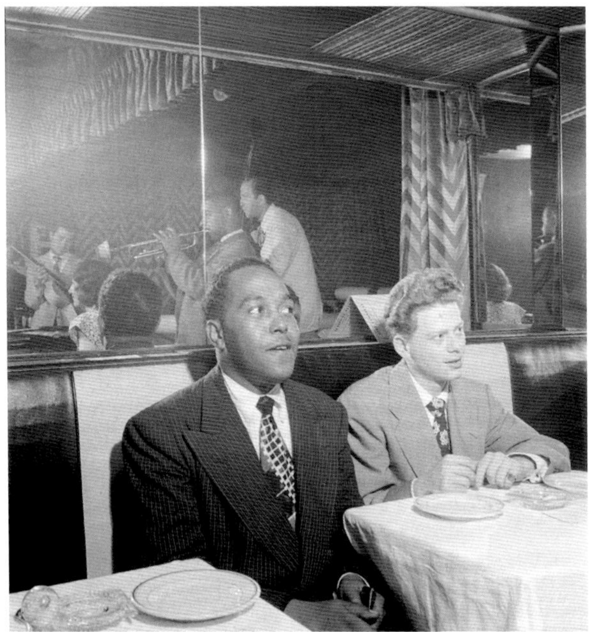

Charlie Parker and trumpeter Red Rodney checking out Dizzy Gillespie with the Barbara Carroll Trio—Barbara Carroll (piano), Chuck Wayne (guitar), and Clyde Lombardi (bass)—at Club Downbeat in July 1947. Charlie Parker Quintet was playing next door at the Three Deuces, and Rodney was working at Club Troubadour with the Georgie Auld band.

MONTE KAY & PETE KAMERAN

PRESENT

AN OPEN HOUSE JAM SESSION

STARRING

Coleman Hawkins

THE MASTER OF THE TENOR SAX

DON BYAS — BENNY HARRIS — DENZIL BEST

THELONIOUS MONK — EDDIE ROBINSON

CLYDE HART — JACK PARKER

BOB DORSAY — *LEN GASKIN*

and other famous Guest Stars

RAYMOND SCOTT — COSY COLE

BUSTER BAILEY — RAY NANCE

EARLE WARREN — LESTER YOUNG

 *Friday May 19th - 9 to 4* 

DOWNBEAT CLUB 66 W. 52ND ST. NEW YORK CITY

ELDORADO 5-8773

No Cover — No Minimum — No Cabaret Tax

1945 Club Downbeat handbill

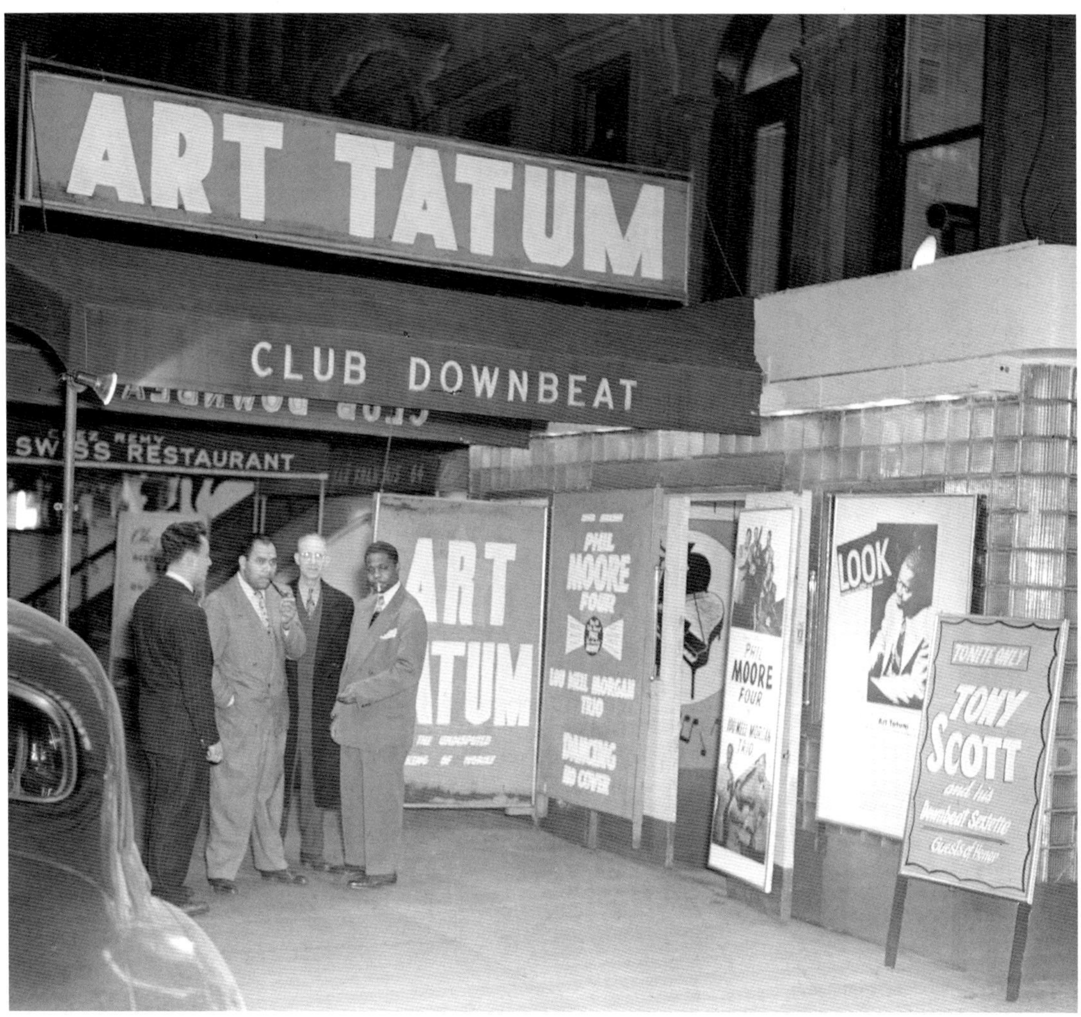

Jazz pianists Art Tatum (*far right*) and Phil Moore (*second from left*) having a smoke break outside Club Downbeat in 1948. Also at the club that evening was jazz clarinetist Tony Scott and his Downbeat Sextette alongside the Lou Mell Morgan Trio.

RIGHT Jazz tenor saxophonist, Arnett Cobb—"Wild Man of the Tenor Sax"—at Club Downbeat in 1948. A stomping Texas tenor player and originator of the "Southern Preacher" style of playing, he possessed the ability to build up a song and finish them off by blowing the roof off the place.

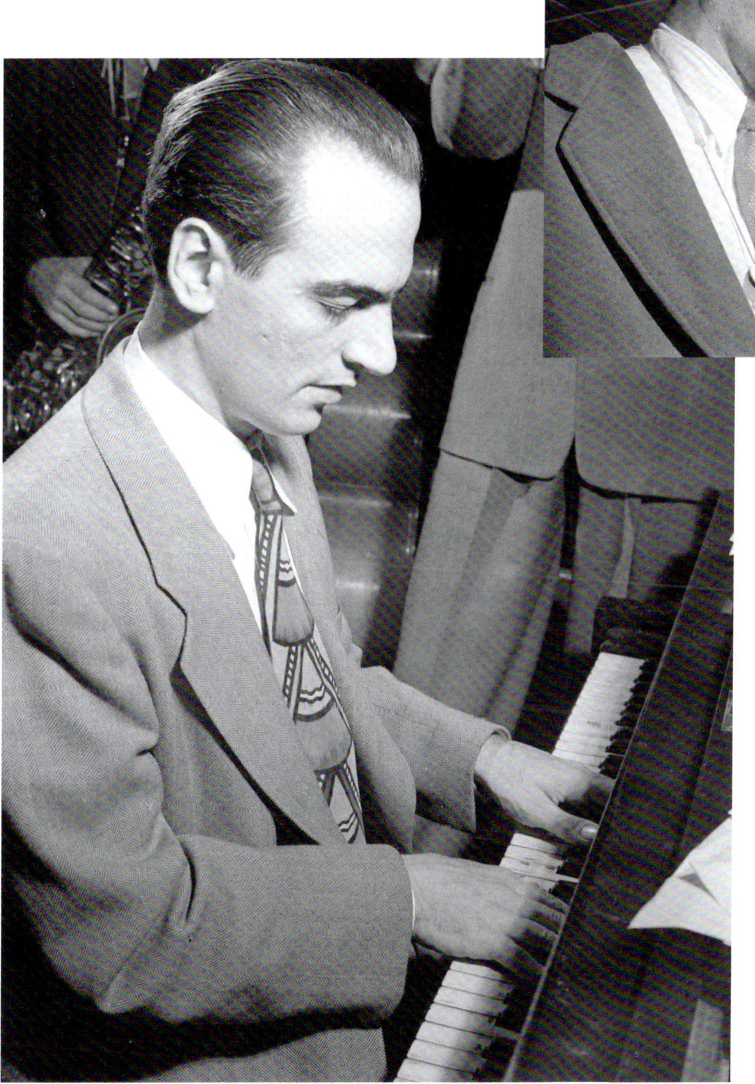

LEFT Jazz pianist Lennie Tristano at Club Downbeat in August 1947. Charlie Parker loved working with Tristano because of his harmonic approach and rhythmic complexity. A true trailblazer.

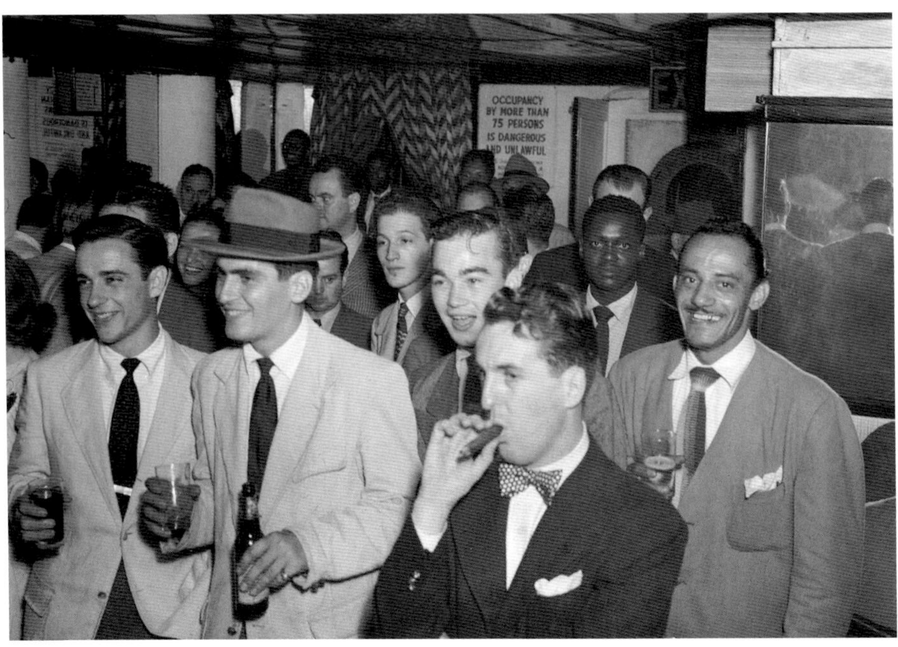

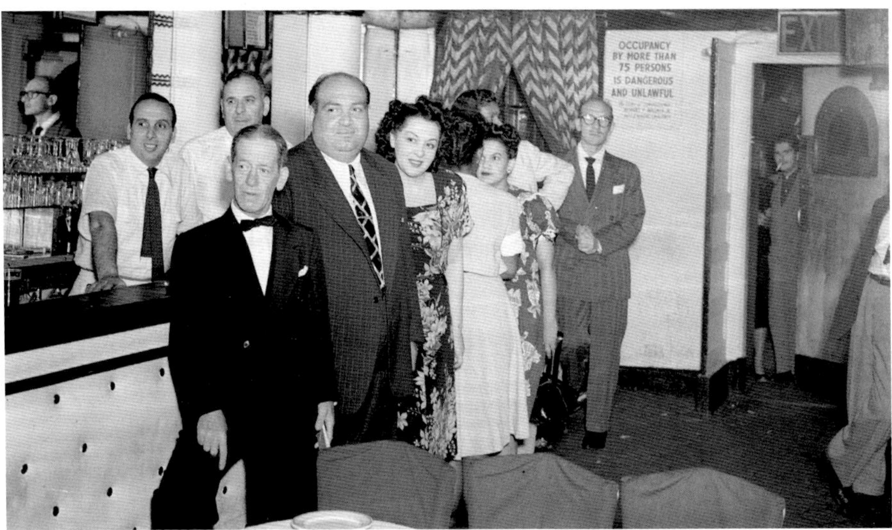

Jazz fans of all ages jammed into the cramped space at Club Downbeat in 1948, enjoying an evening of jazz in a nightclub with a maximum occupancy of seventy-five persons.

Opening Friday August 18

A NEW ALL STAR SHOW

STARRING

BILLIE HOLIDAY

ESQUIRE'S ALL AMERICAN SONG STYLIST
SINGING STRANGE FRUIT I'LL GET BY SOLITUDE
AND ALL HER OTHER FAVORITES

ALSO ESQUIRE'S ALL AMERICAN VIBRAHARPIST

RED NORVO SEXTET

AND THE BAND SENSATION OF 1944

BASCOMB BROS. Orchestra

PAUL BASCOMB TENOR SAX
DUD BASCOMB TRUMPET
FORMERLY FEATURED WITH ERSKINE HAWKINS

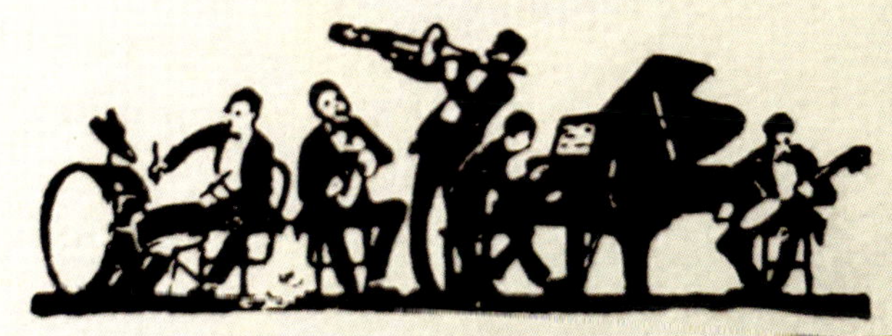

DOWNBEAT CLUB

Air Conditioned
No Cover Charge

66 West 52nd Street New York City

For Reservations Call ELdorado 5-8773

Friday, August 18, 1944, handbill

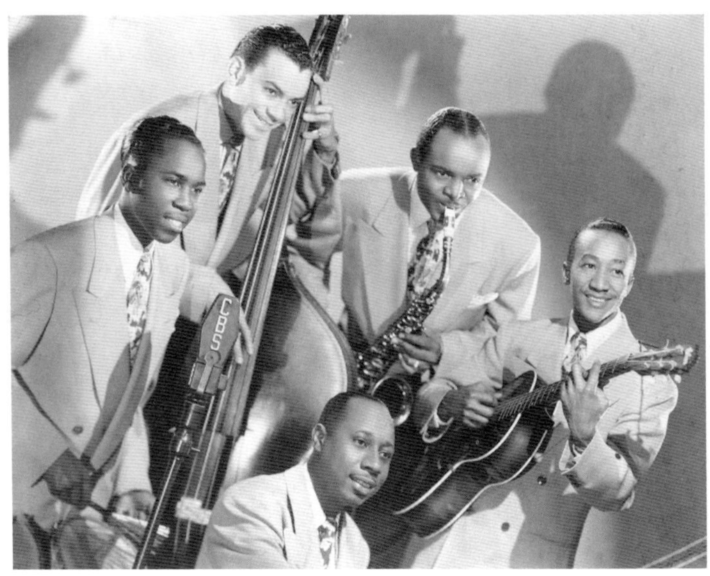

Bill Johnson & His Musical Notes performed alongside Ella Fitzgerald and Billie Holiday at Club Downbeat in 1947. Bill Johnson (alto sax), Egbert Victor (piano), Clifton "Skeeter" Best (guitar), Jimmy Robinson (bass), and Gus Gordon on drums. In 1939, Bill Johnson co-composed the song "Tuxedo Junction," which later became a number one hit for the Glenn Miller Orchestra in 1940.

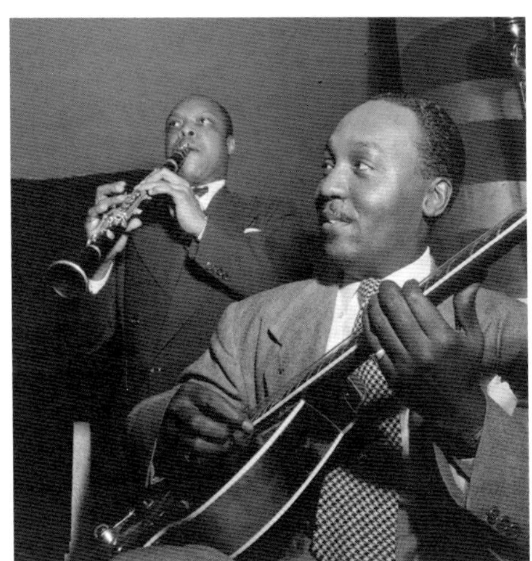

Swing guitarist Al Casey seen here at Café Society with clarinetist Eddie Barefield. They had a long residency at Club Downbeat with his trio, sharing many a bill there with the likes of Billie Holiday, Ella Fitzgerald, and many bebop musicians. Casey was best known for working with Fats Waller from 1933 until Fats's passing in 1943. Casey also played at the Onyx for eleven months before starting at Club Downbeat in 1945.

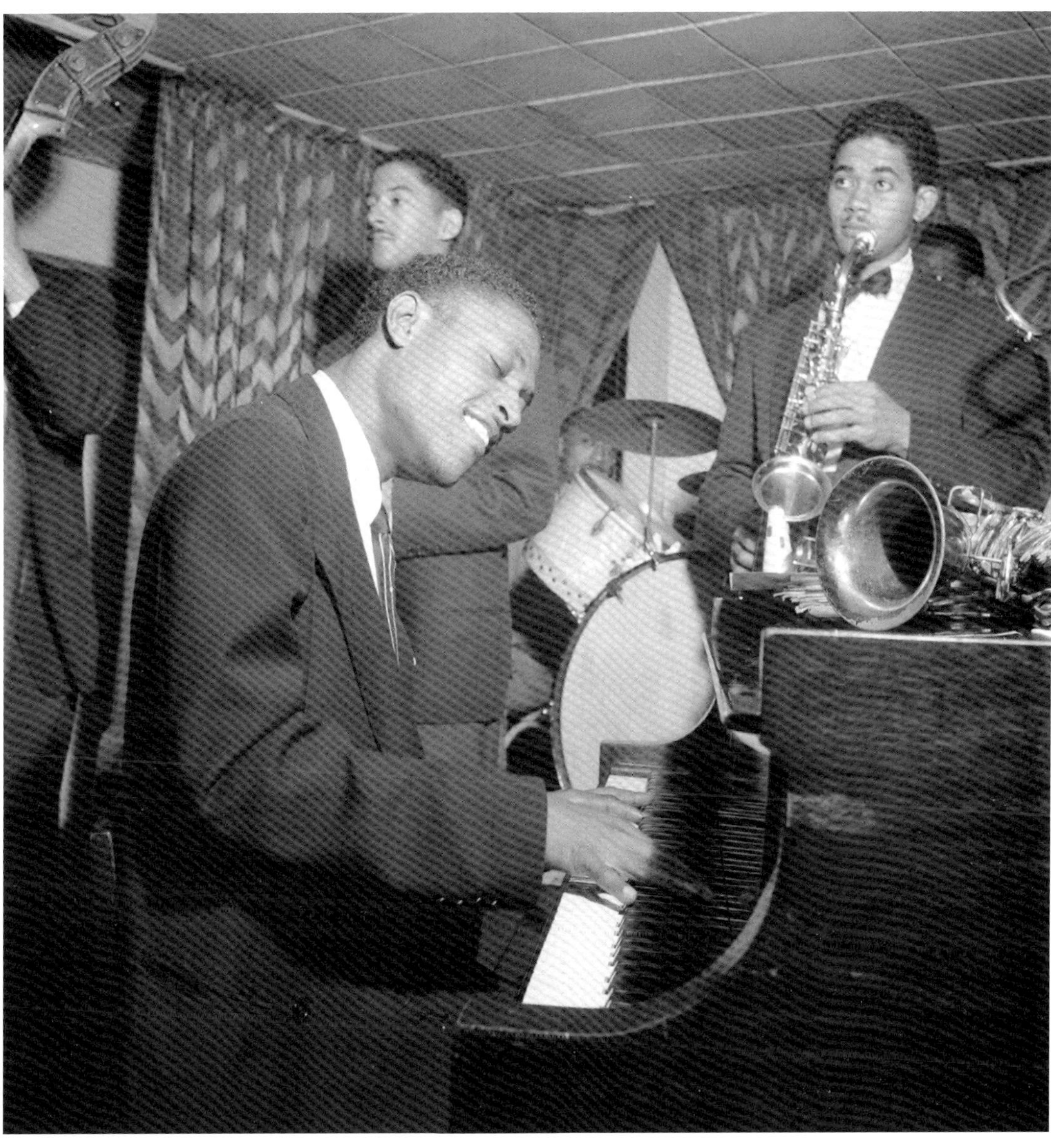

Jazz pianist Eddie Heywood and his sextet at Club Downbeat in July 1947 with Doc Cheatham (trumpet) and Lem Davis (alto sax). Not in view are Vic Dickenson (trombone), Al Lucas (bass), and Jack Parker (drums). Later that year, Heywood's hands would become paralyzed, forcing him to turn to composing and penning the hit song "Canadian Sunset."

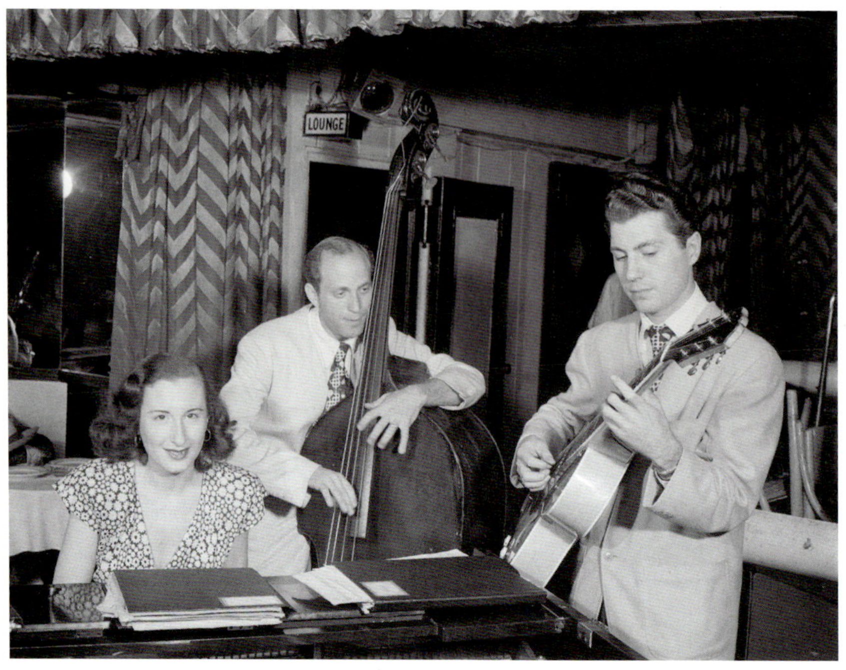

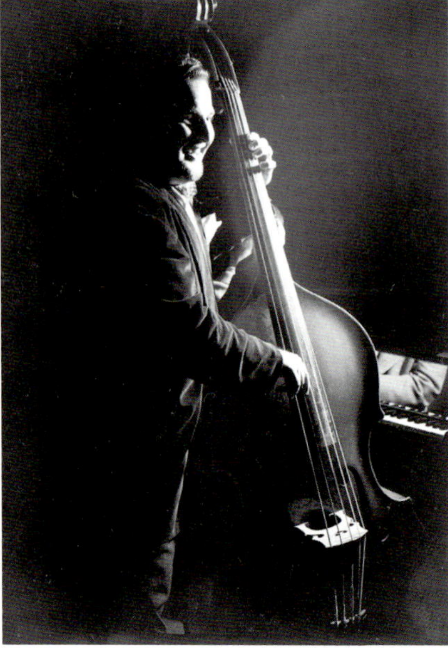

TOP Barbara Carroll (piano), Clyde Lombardi (bass), and Chuck Wayne (guitar) at Club Downbeat in September 1947. Carroll was dubbed by Leonard Feather as "the first girl to play bebop piano." In later life, Carroll would receive the Mary Lou Williams / Women in Jazz Lifetime Achievement Award.

LEFT Exuberant bassist Chubby Jackson at Club Downbeat in July 1946. In his earlier years, Chubby was the bassist with Woody Herman's "First Herd" for three years. He would later go on to host his own children's television show in Chicago for ten years, called "Chubby's Rascals."

THE FAMOUS DOOR

The Famous Door opened its doors at 35 West 52nd Street on March 1, 1935, to the music of Louis Prima and his New Orleans Gang playing their theme song, "Way Down Yonder in New Orleans." The whiskey drinks were fifty-five cents a shot, and beer cost thirty-five cents a glass. There was actually a door resting on a platform by the bar, inscribed with the signatures of the original investors of the club and numerous autographs of well-known musicians and personalities.

In its first year, musicians such as trumpeters Bunny Berigan and Bobby Hackett, vibraphonist Red Norvo, trombonist Georg Brunis, and Billie Holiday (for whom the Famous Door represented her first gig outside Harlem) helped establish its reputation. They were even able to secure blues singer Bessie Smith for a Sunday night in February 1936. It was one of Swing Street's most memorable moments.

Unfortunately, in May 1936 the Famous Door was forced into bankruptcy by four of its creditors due to the neglect of the club by its owners. But fortunately, the new Door would reopen its doors across the street at a new address, 66 West 52nd Street, in December 1937. Louis Prima and his band would again be the main attraction, with Art Tatum playing between sets in the new club, which had a capacity of sixty.

Broadcasts of Count Basie's band several nights a week from the club on CBS radio in 1938 helped popularize the band and catapult his career. The club would again close in 1940 for three months due to failure to pay the musicians.

In 1943, the Famous Door moved to 201 West 52nd Street, surviving until 1944, only to reopen in 1947 at 56 West 52nd Street. They would continue to hire the leading jazz artists of the day, such as Lester Young, Ben Webster, Jack Teagarden, and Dizzy Gillespie, until their final closure in 1950.

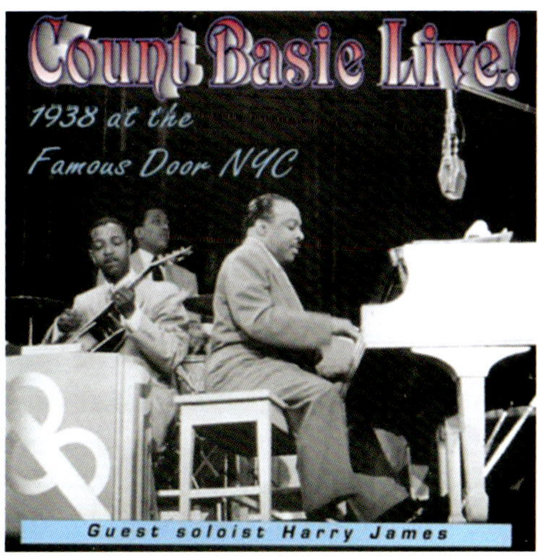

On July 11, 1938, at the Famous Door, the Count Basie Orchestra became the first big band to play on 52nd Street. Record producer John Hammond recalls Count Basie's performance that evening. "Basie was a total and absolute sensation. I don't think New York has ever heard a band like this. He had Lester Young on sax, Jo Jones on drums, Freddie Green on guitar, and saxes Herschel Evans and Earl Warren, and the great horns of Buck Clayton and Harry "Sweets" Edison. It was with the Basie in 1938 that 52nd Street got its reputation as the jumping-off place for jazz in New York City."

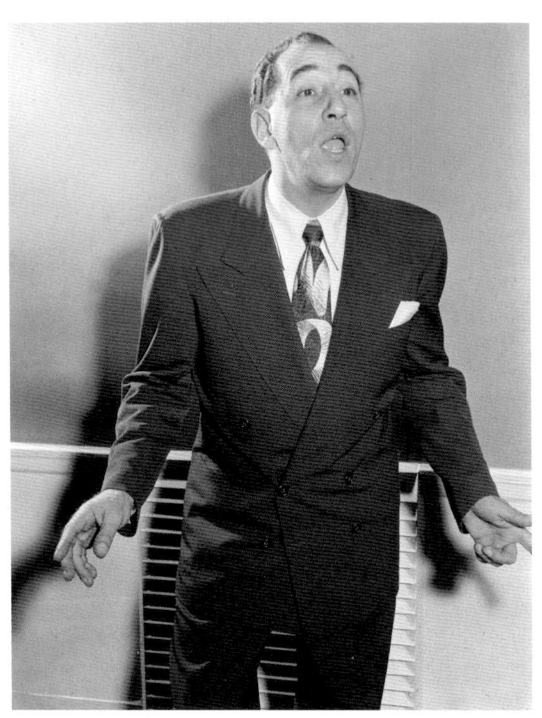

Louis Prima in New York City in June 1947. Prima and his band were one of the most entertaining acts on Swing Street during the early years.

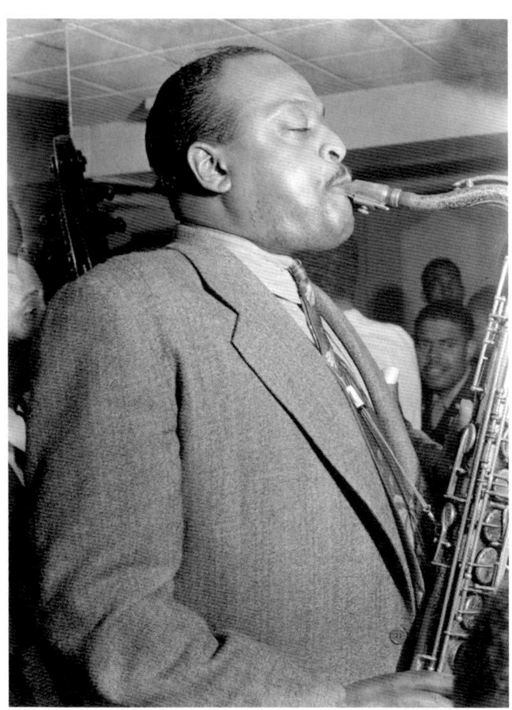

Tenor saxophonist Ben Webster at the Famous Door in October 1947

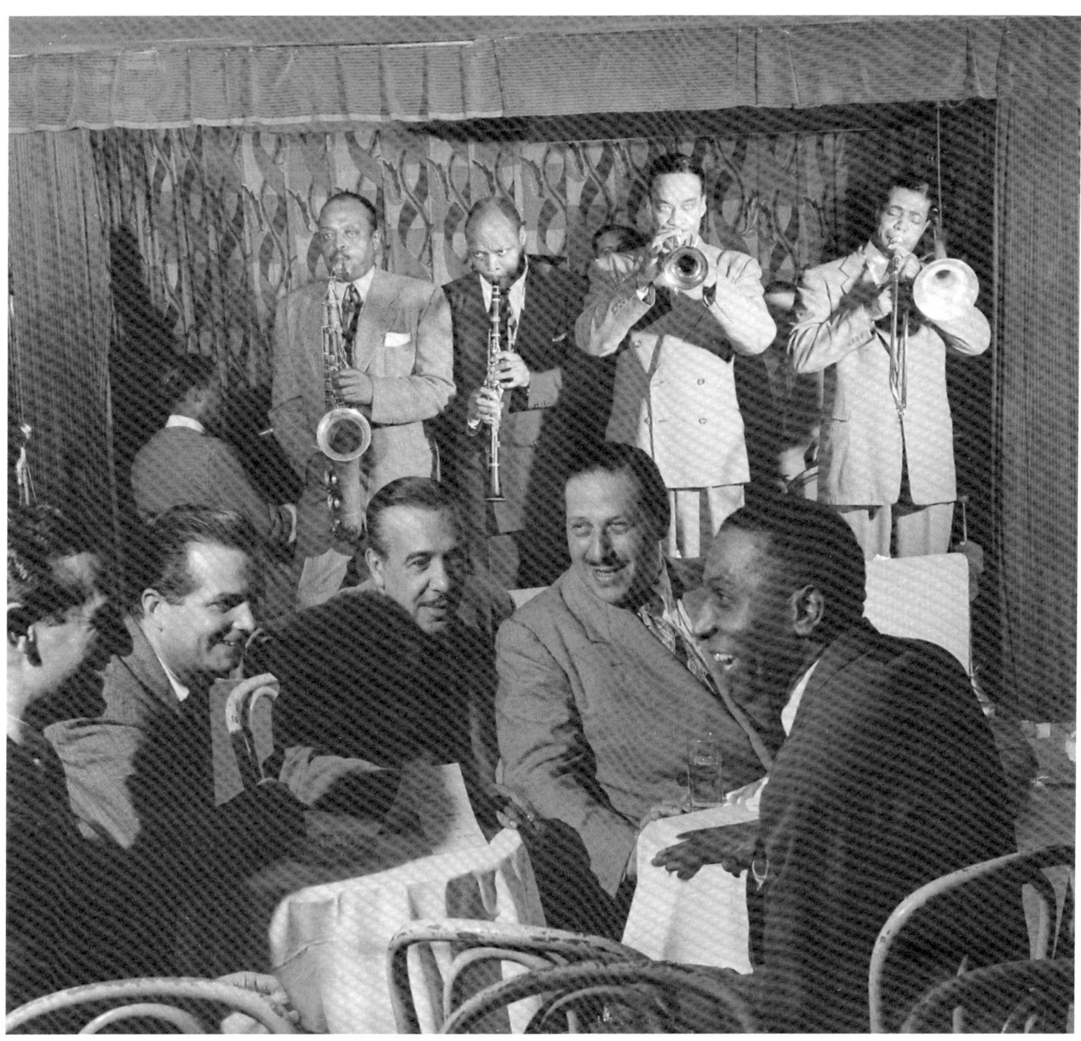

On stage (*left to right*): Ben Webster (tenor sax), Eddie Barefield (clarinet), Buck Clayton (trumpet), and Benny Morton (trombone) at the Famous Door in October 1947. At the table is clarinetist Joe Marsala (*second from the left*), and to the far right is drummer Cozy Cole.

Jack Teagarden ("Big T") would often head out of the Famous Door with his horn and sit in at the Three Deuces or Jimmy Ryan's in between sets. After a while, the manager of the Famous Door would say to Jack, "You're supposed to be appearing exclusively at the Famous Door; that's why your name is on the canopy, so that people who want to hear Jack Teagarden will patronize us." Jack would look at the furious manager with a slight smile on his face and say, "Just being neighborly."

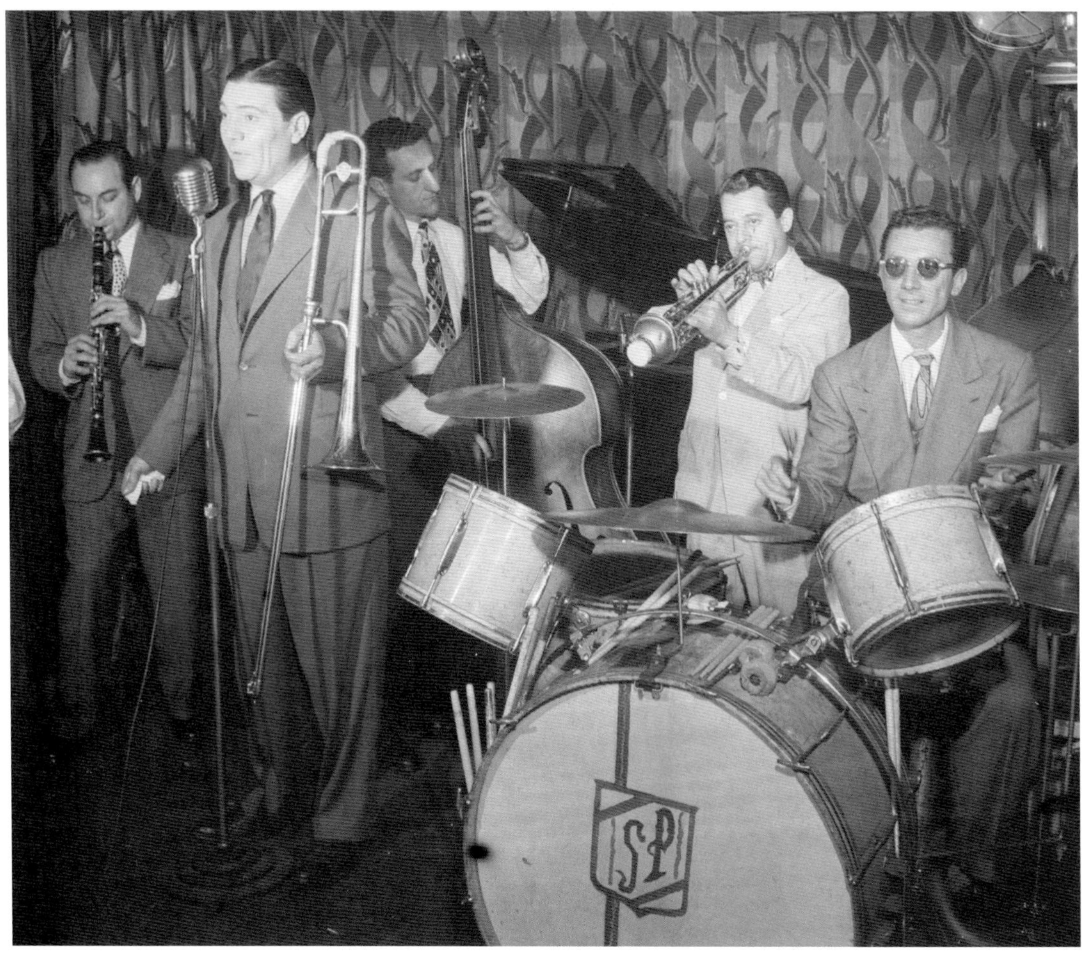

Jazz trombonist Jack Teagarden with his group at the Famous Door in July 1947: Peanuts Hucko (clarinet), Jack Lesberg (bass), and Max Kaminsky (trumpet). The drummer is unknown.

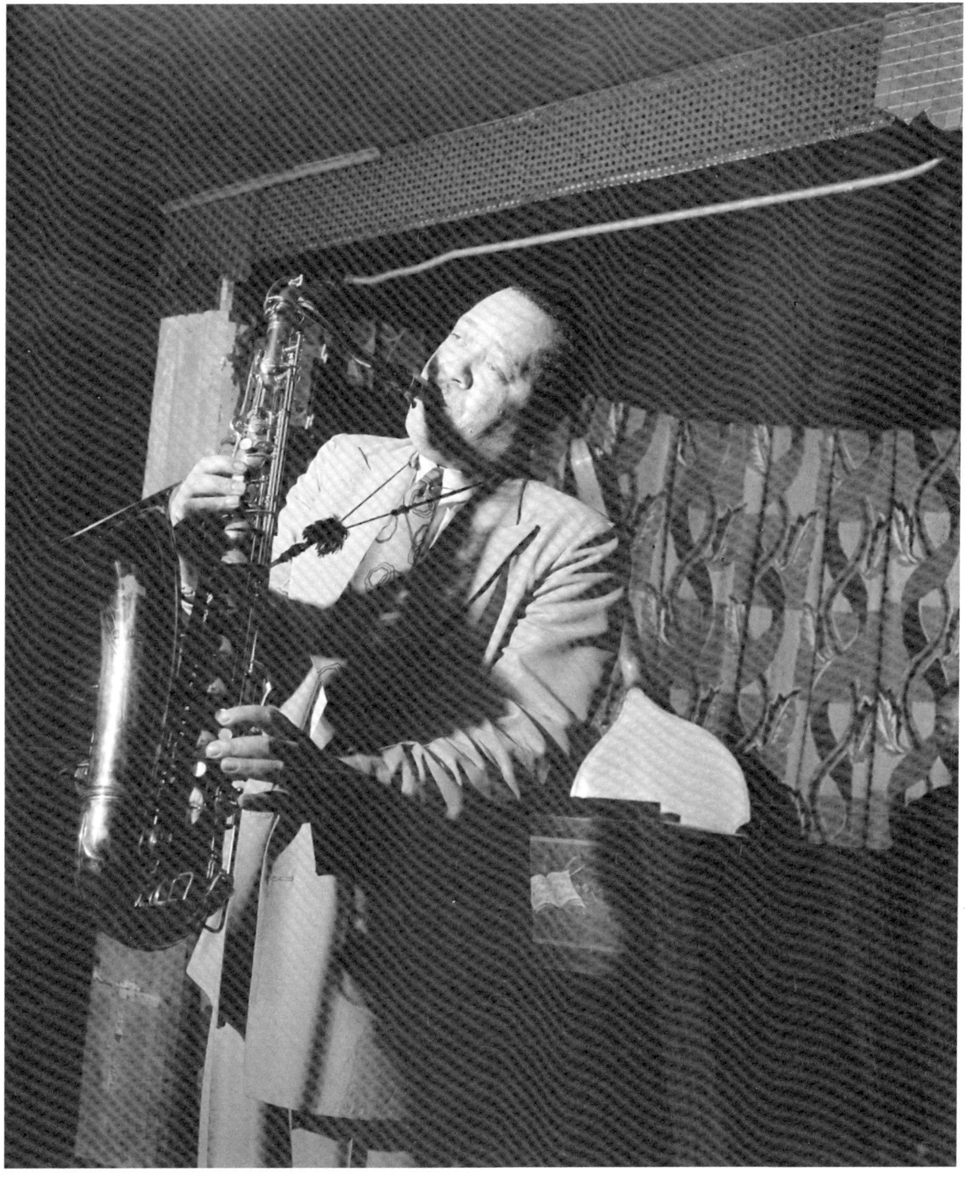

Lester "Prez" Young at the Famous Door in September 1946. Nicknamed "Prez" by Billie Holiday, Young's smooth, melodic flowing lines made him one of the most influential saxmen of the prebop era.

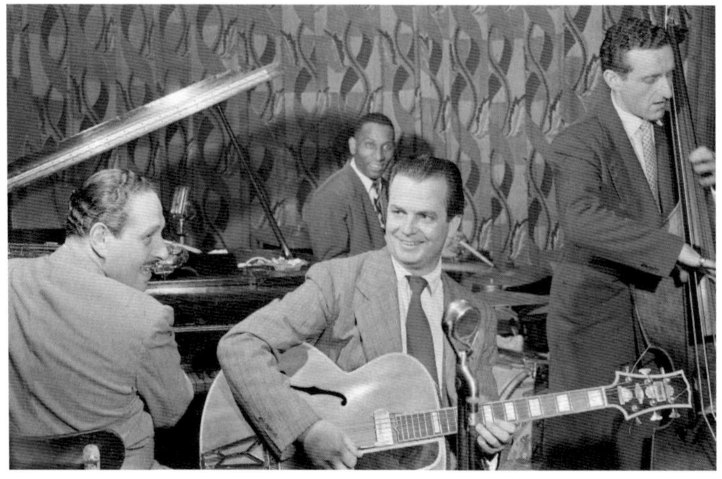

Left to right: Sanford Gold (piano), Cozy Cole (drums), Mike Bryan (guitar), and Jack Lesberg (bass) at the Famous Door in October 1947

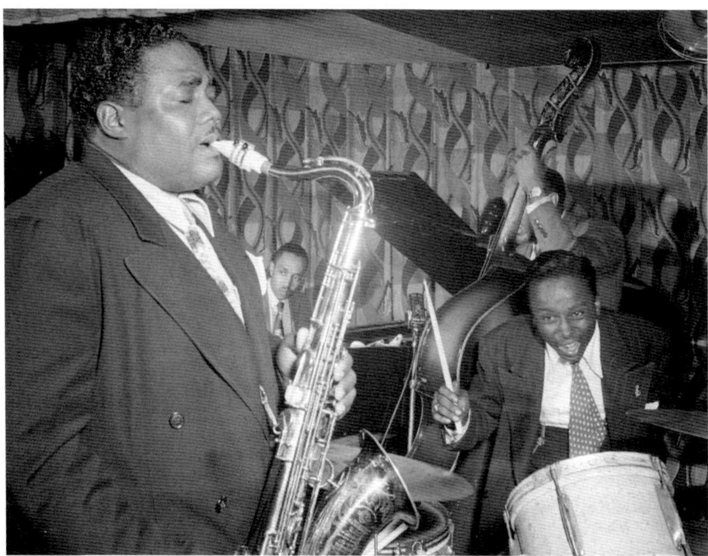

Texas tenor saxophonist John Hardee at the Famous Door with an unknown rhythm section in July 1947. In the 1950s, Hardee would retire from music and become a schoolteacher.

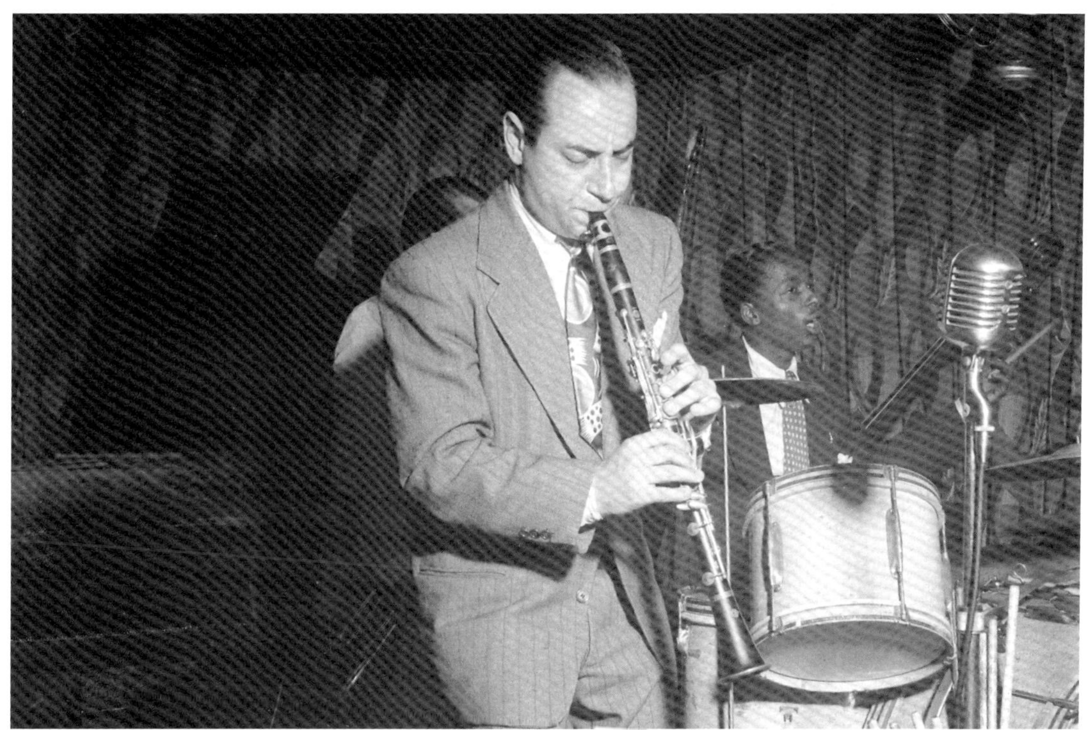

Jazz clarinetist Peanuts Hucko playing the Famous Door in the late 1940s. Peanuts's playing style was often compared to that of Benny Goodman's. He played in the bands of Glenn Miller, Benny Goodman, and Jack Teagarden during the 1940s, later joining the Louis Armstrong All-Stars in the late 1950s.

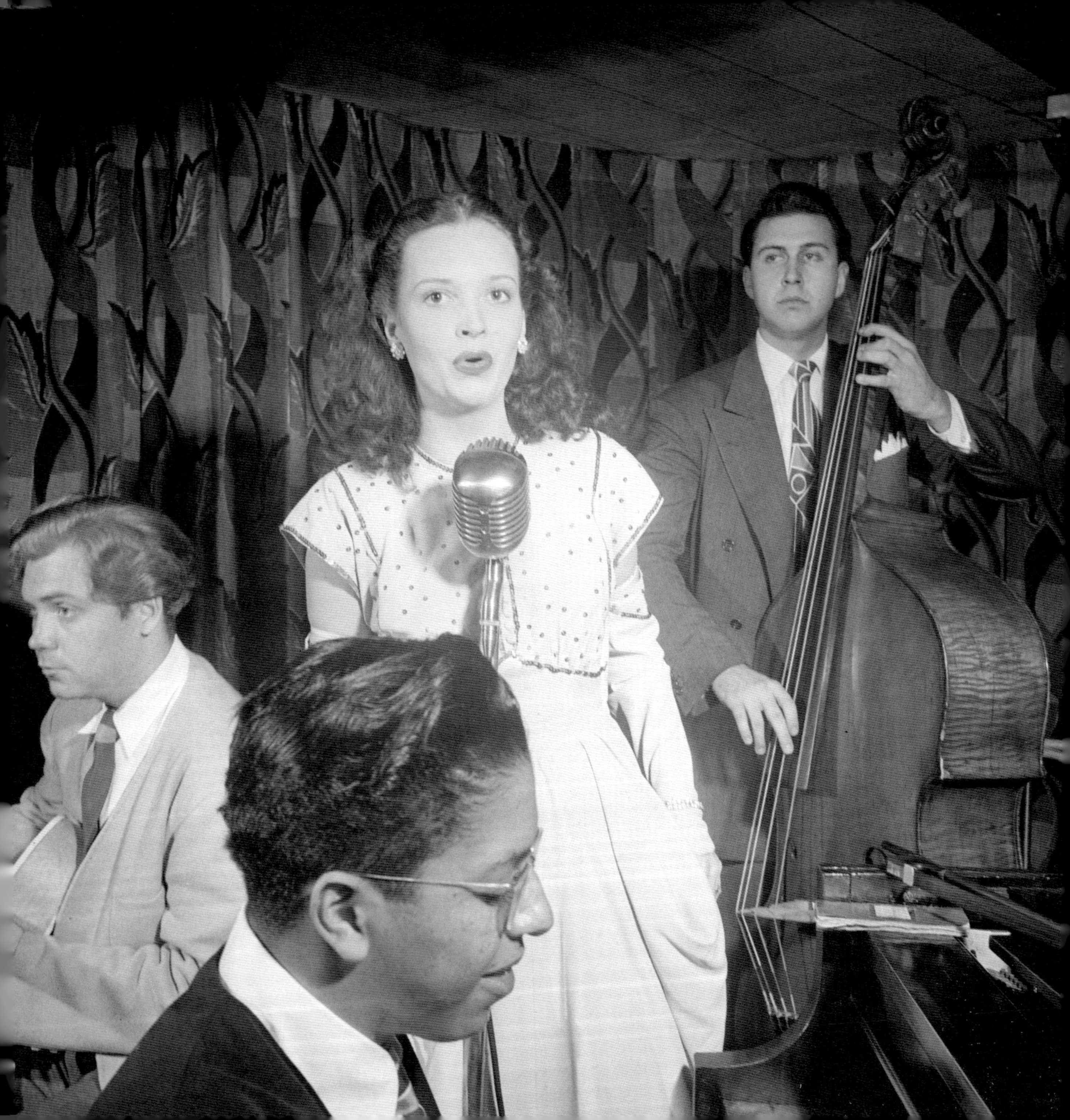

THE HICKORY HOUSE

The Hickory House opened its doors at 144 West 52nd Street in 1933 and remained in business for over thirty-five years. The owner, John Popkin, claimed that if all the jazz musicians who started their careers at the Hickory House were laid end to end, the line would reach well toward New Orleans, where Popkin first heard Louis Prima and persuaded him to move to New York.

The bandstand at the Hickory House was covered in a wooden canopy on a raised platform in the center of the bar. Jazz lovers who sat around this first-of-its-kind, huge, circular music bar, which seated seventy-five people, would have been entertained by the likes of Bix Beiderbecke, Artie Shaw, Buddy Rich, Frank Sinatra, Wingy Manone, Charlie Barnet, Joe Marsala, Red Norvo, Joe Venuti, Eddie Condon, and Sidney Bechet, to mention a few.

Hickory House also staked the claim to have originated the jam session and sitting-in before the local musicians' union clamped down, putting an end to such goings on. But it wasn't unusual on a Sunday afternoon to find Duke Ellington, Louis Armstrong, Frankie Laine, Benny Goodman, or the Dorsey Brothers sitting in just for kicks. Hickory House was also the first club to introduce jazz on the major networks.

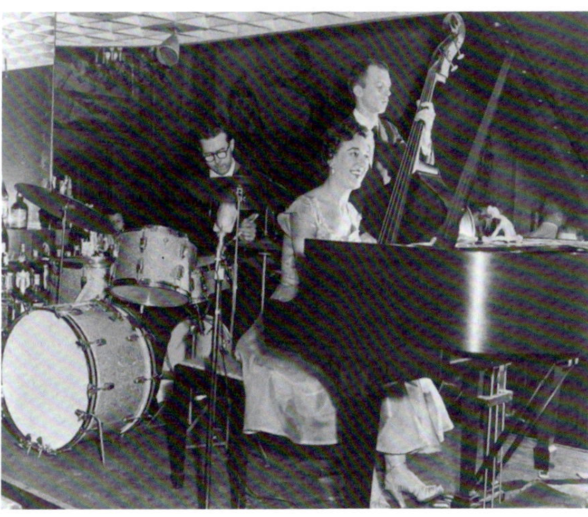

Marion McPartland Trio at the Hickory House in 1954
with Bill Crow on bass and Joe Morello on drums

OPPOSITE The Deryck Sampson Trio featuring vocalist Lynn Carver, guitarist Clair Dorward, and bassist Justin Arndt at the Famous Door in September 1947

Jazz pianist Marion McPartland enjoyed a twelve-year run with her trio at the Hickory House, which included bassist Bill Crow and drummer Joe Morello. Many jazz musicians would stop by the club for a meal and watch the trio, such as Duke Ellington, Billy Strayhorn, and Oscar Pettiford, sometimes even sitting in with the trio.

"Duke came in almost every night," McPartland says. "He always invited me over to his table. Billy Strayhorn was there, too, but he always sat alone at the bar and came up any time I asked him."

McPartland also remembers an encounter with Thelonious Monk. "I saw him on the street and asked if he would come and watch me play some of his tunes. Rather brash, I know," McPartland says. "He did come by. And he sat talking with a friend through the whole show. He left without ever speaking to me, and at the end of the evening I discovered he had left me with the bill! Joe and Bill thought that was hilarious."

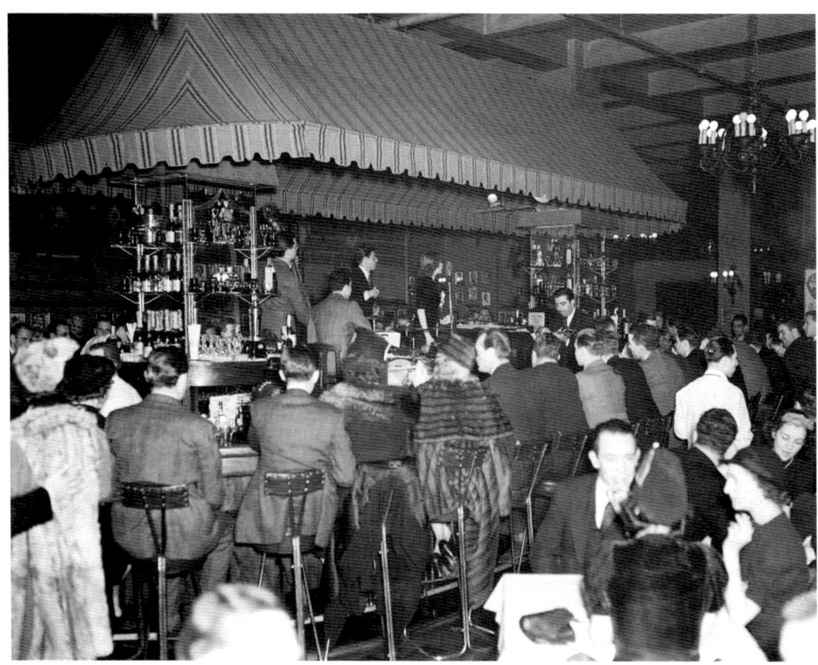

Joe Marsala and his band playing the Sunday afternoon jam session at the Hickory House in 1937: Joe Marsala (clarinet), Ray Biondi (guitar), Artie Shapiro (bass), and Danny Alvin (drums), with an unknown female vocalist. Starting in the spring of 1937, Marsala would play at the Hickory House for the best of ten years.

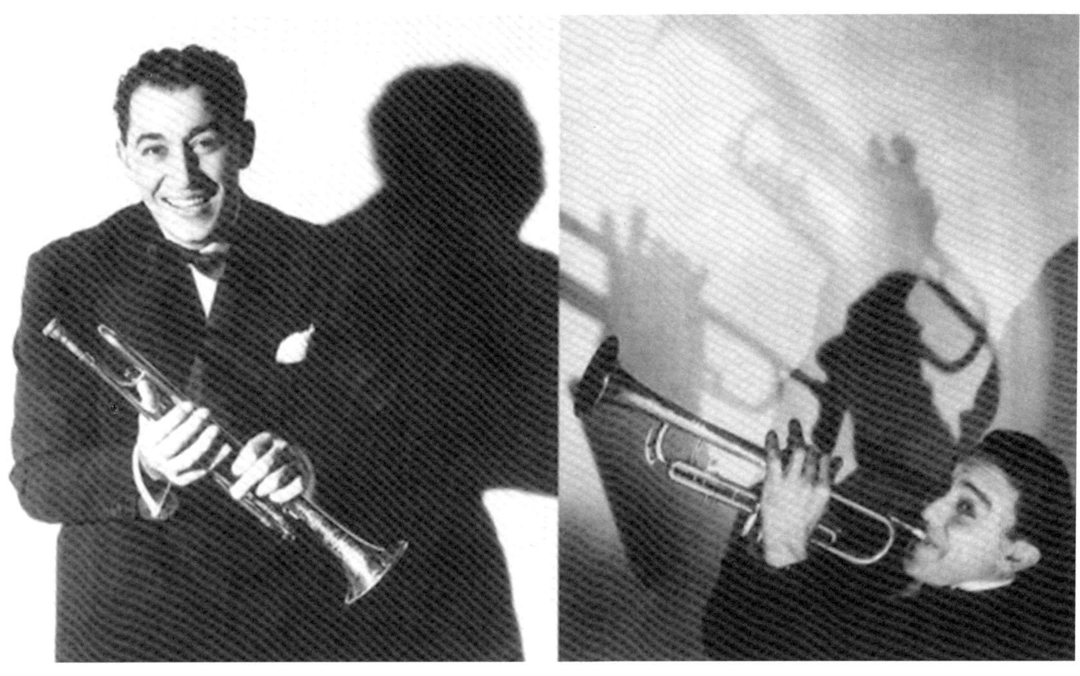

Jazz trumpeter Wingy Manone during the mid-1930s. Wingy and his orchestra starred at the Hickory House from 1935 to 1937. His Dixieland playing style and jivey vocals were reminiscent of his New Orleans compatriot Louis Prima.

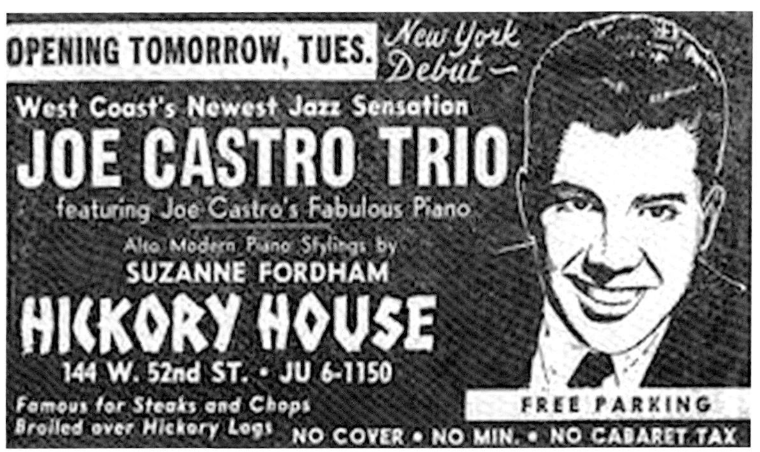

Hickory House advertisement for jazz pianist Joe Castro and his trio

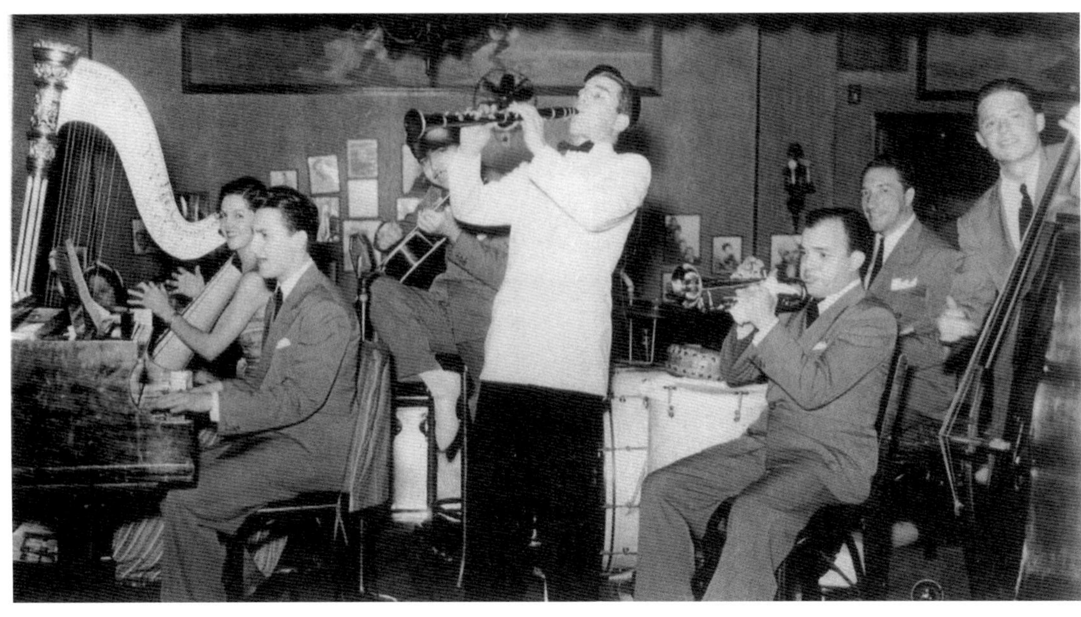

Joe Marsala and His Chicagoans at the Hickory House in 1937: Joe Marsala (clarinet), Adele Girard (harp), Marty Marsala (trumpet), Joe Bushkin (piano), Ray Biondi (guitar), Artie Shapiro (bass), and Danny Alvin (drums). Marsala would marry harpist Adele Girard that same year.

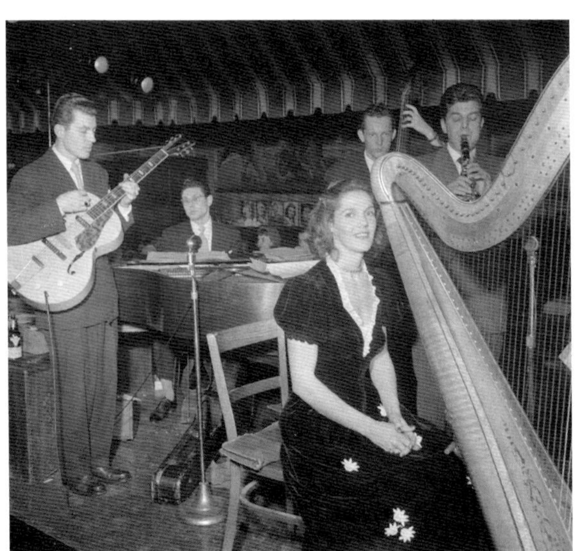

Joe Marsala group playing at the Hickory House in 1947: Chuck Wayne (guitar), Joe Bushkin (piano), Adele Girard (harp), Artie Shapiro (bass), and Joe Marsala (clarinet)

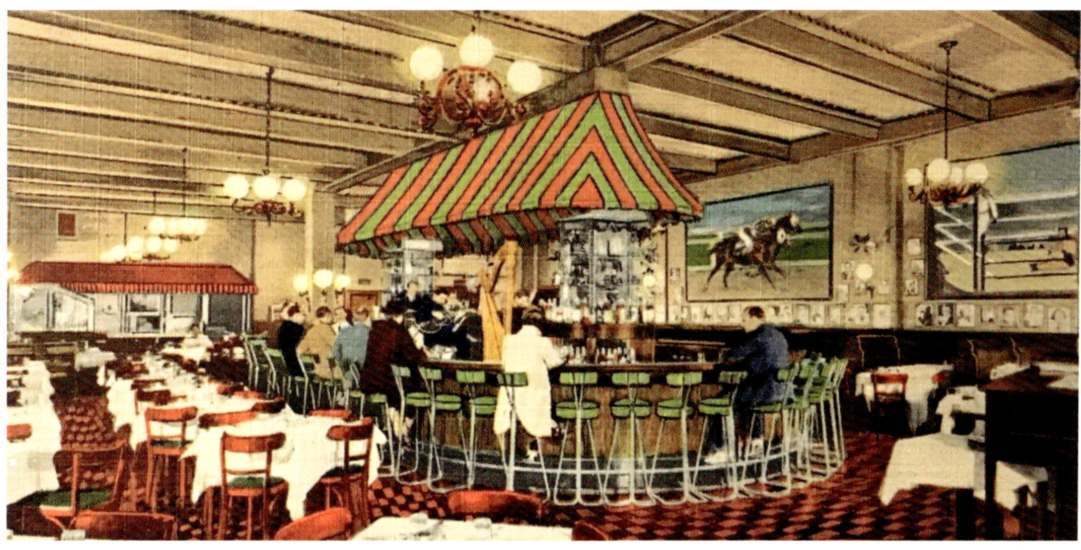

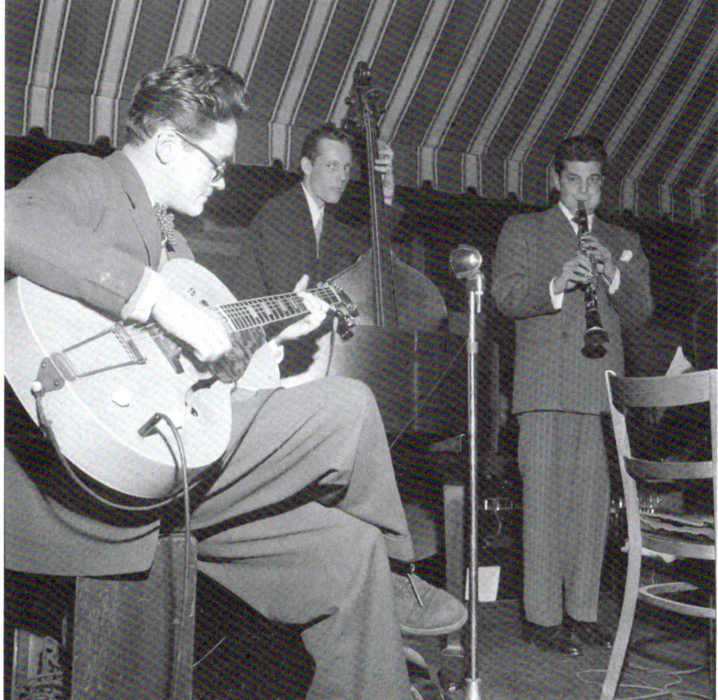

TOP Hickory House postcard

LEFT Toots Thielemans (guitar), Artie Shapiro (bass), and Joe Marsala (clarinet) at the Hickory House in 1947. Toots would later become famous for his mastery and artistic ability on the chromatic harmonica.

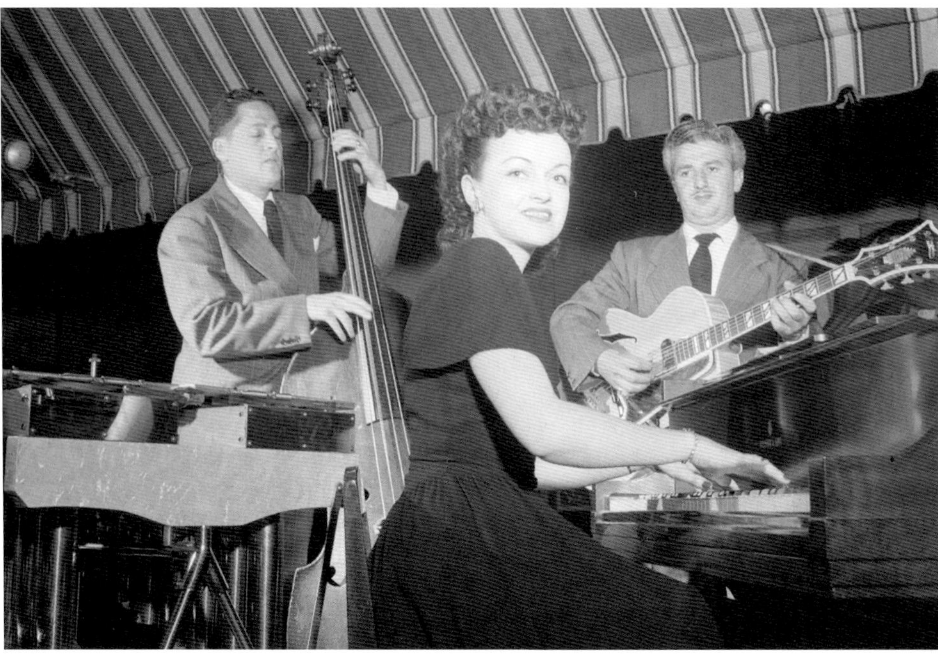

Dardanelle on piano at the Hickory House in July 1947, along with Joe Sinacore (bass) and Bert Nazer (guitar). Dardanelle (Marcia Marie Mullen) was a talented pianist, vibraphonist, and singer from Mississippi. She was known for performing with vibraphonist Lionel Hampton and guitarist Tal Farlow in her early years.

Abe Most on clarinet leading a band at the Hickory House in 1947, along with Pete Ponti (accordion), Sid Jacobs (bass), and Jimmy Norton (guitar)

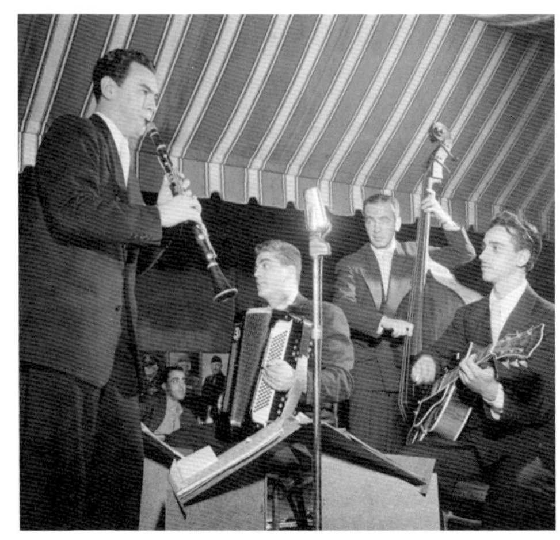

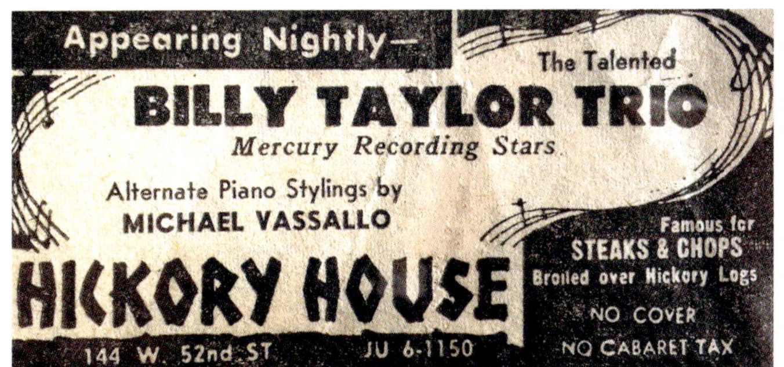

Hickory House advertisement for jazz pianist Billy Taylor and his trio

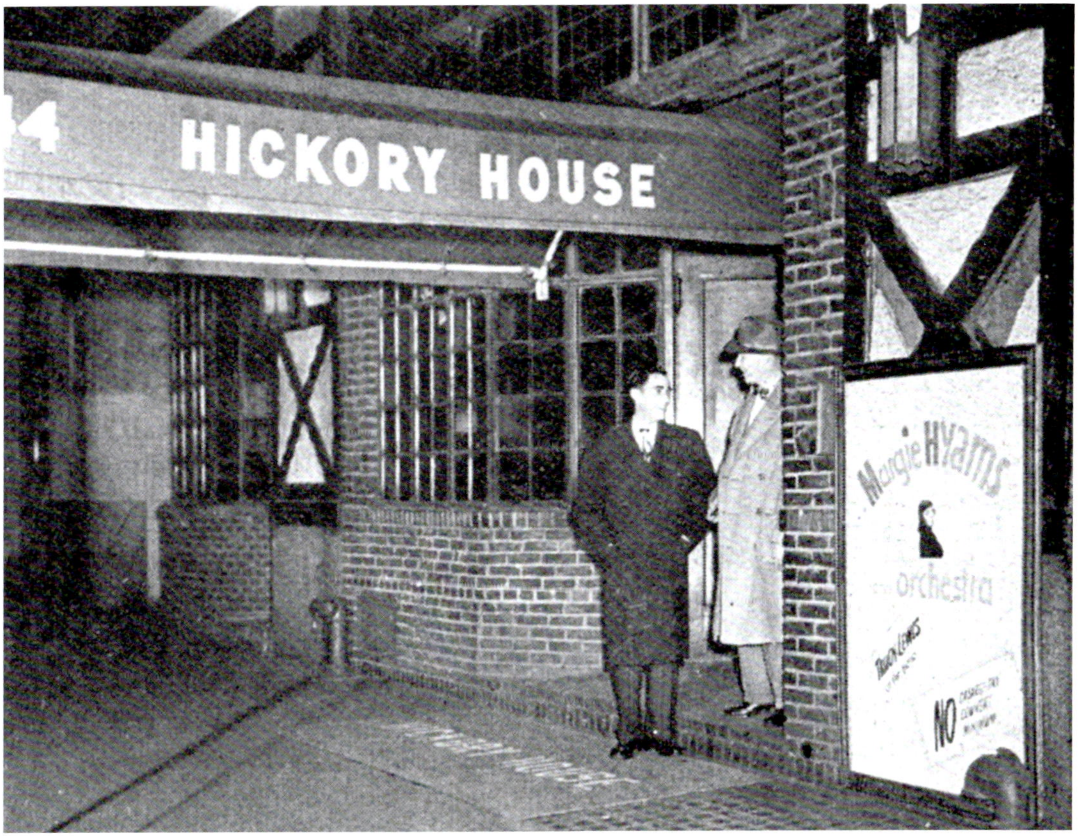

The Hickory House on 144 West 52nd Street in the mid-1940s. Margie Hyams and her orchestra were performing that evening.

JIMMY RYAN'S

Jimmy Ryan and brother-in-law Matty Walsh opened Jimmy Ryan's in September 1940 at 53 West 52nd Street. They purchased it from a friend, George McGough, who had been running it as the Troc club, which featured a fourteen-piece band led by cornetist Bobby Hackett.

Jimmy Ryan's opened with a strolling trio that included a violin, guitar, and accordion for two or three nights a week. Milt Gabler, who ran Commodore Music, suggested to Ryan that they might fare better if they put in a jazz group, since there were eight clubs on the block offering jazz at the time, so they decided to go with Dixieland bands seven nights a week, often keeping them for up to nine months at a time. Some of the musicians included trumpeters Red Allen and Max Kaminsky, trombonist J. C. Higginbotham, and soprano saxophonist Sidney Bechet. Starting in 1952, trombonist Wilbur De Paris and his brother, trumpeter Sidney De Paris, would remain at Ryan's for ten years until it closed in 1962. It would later relocate that year to 154 West 54th Street.

Milt Gabler was also instrumental in initiating a series of Sunday afternoon jam sessions at Ryan's in the early 1940s, attracting almost every notable jazz musician around. In 1949, the jams ended and the strippers replaced jazz musicians on 52nd Street, therefore moving the jam sessions to Central Plaza on Second Avenue.

Owner Matty Walsh attributes Ryan's longevity to giving value. "We have no cover, no minimum, and good entertainment. People know what to expect when they come in. They look forward to hearing and talking to the musicians, and afterwards, sitting down and having a drink with them."

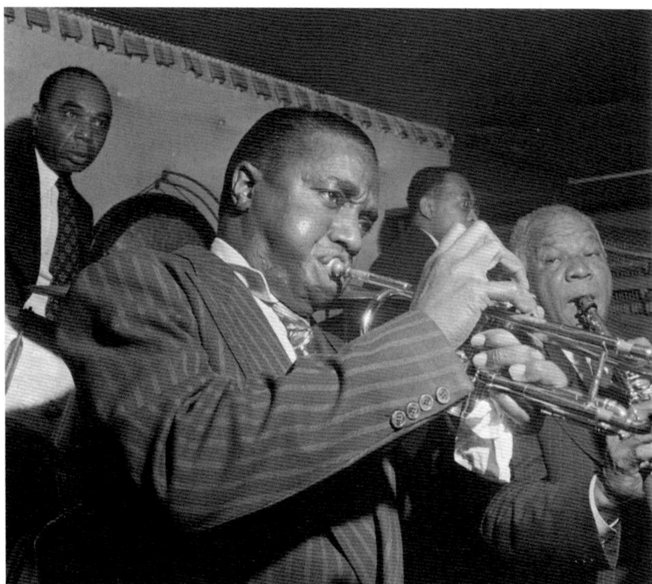

Hot Lips Page (trumpet), Sidney Bechet (soprano sax), Freddie Moore (drums), and Lloyd Phillips (piano) at Jimmy Ryan's in June 1947

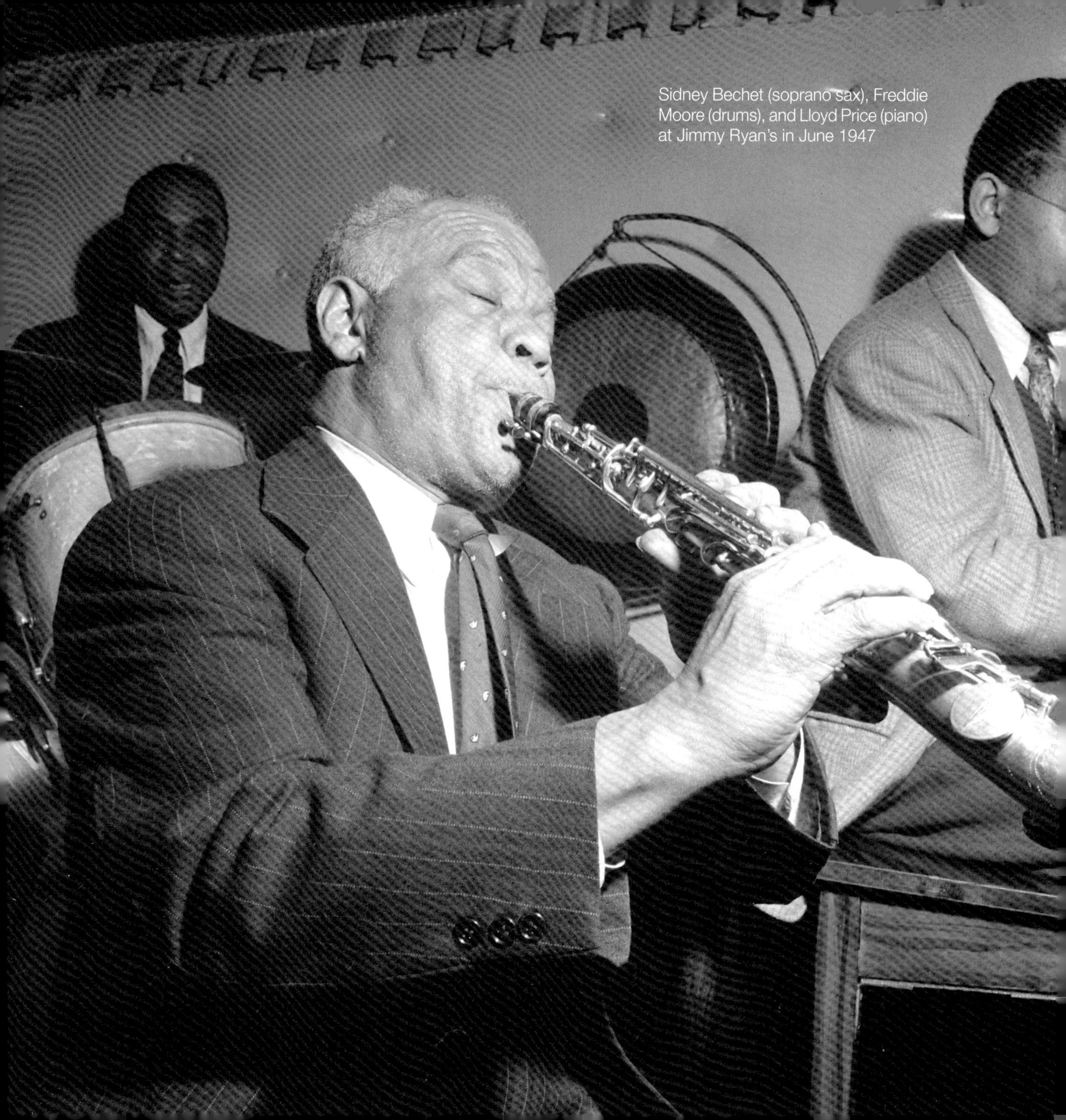
Sidney Bechet (soprano sax), Freddie Moore (drums), and Lloyd Price (piano) at Jimmy Ryan's in June 1947

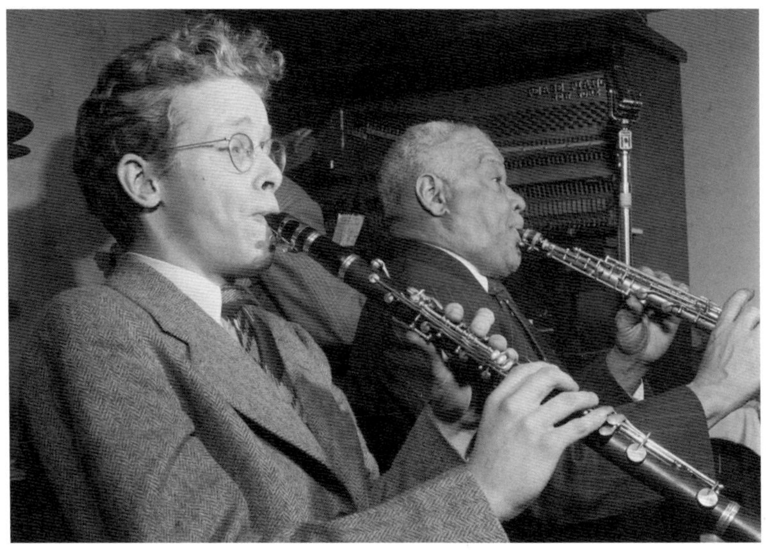

Bob Wilber (clarinet) and Sidney Bechet (soprano sax) at Jimmy Ryan's in June 1947

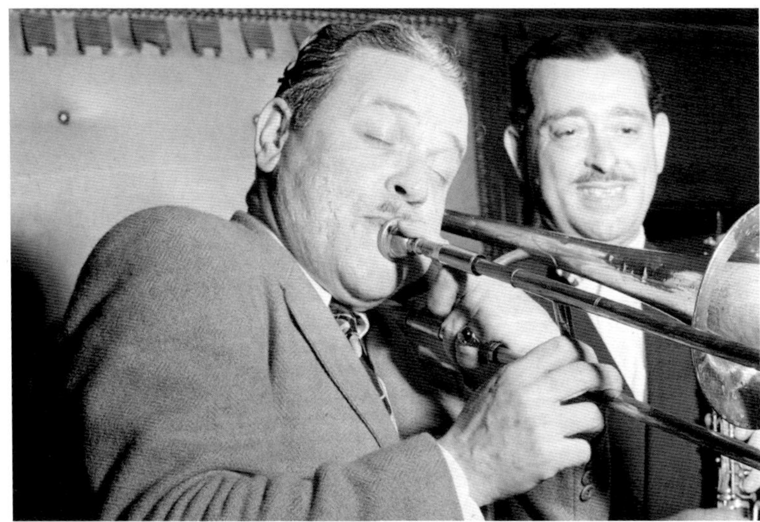

Georg Brunis (trombone) and Tony Parenti (clarinet) at Jimmy Ryan's in August 1946

OPPOSITE Wilbur De Paris (trombone), Sidney De Paris (trumpet), Eddie (Emmanuel) Barefield (clarinet), Jimmy Jones (piano), and Charlie Traeger (bass) at Jimmy Ryan's club in July 1947

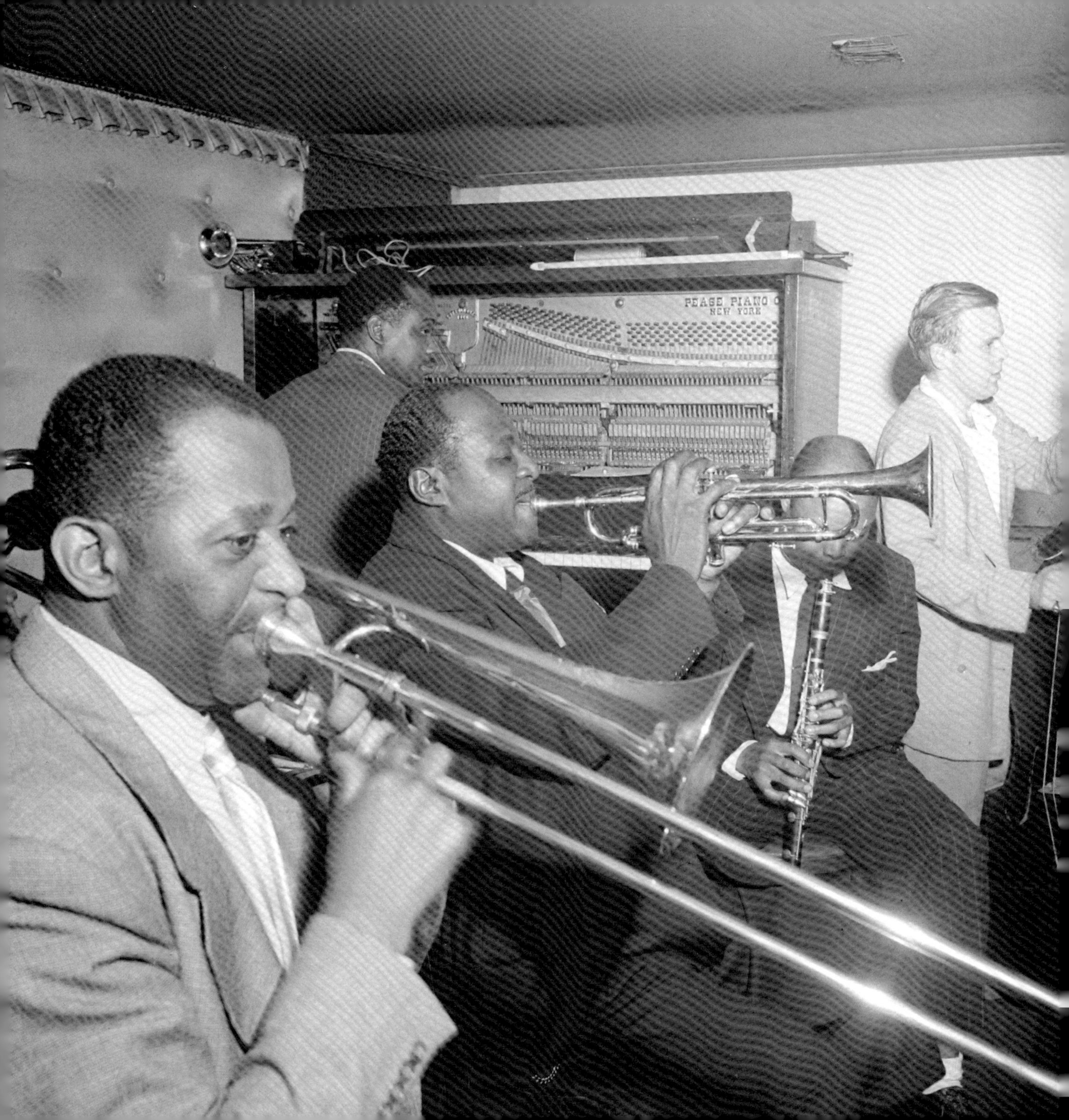
PEASE PIANO
NEW YORK

OUR ROSTER OF JAZZ IMMORTALS
They have appeared at previous sessions and should repeat their memorable performances this season. if available – Milt Gabler

GUITAR
Eddie Condon
Jack Bland
Teddy Bunn

PIANO
Joe Sullivan
Fats Waller
Earl Hines
Art Hodes
Albert Ammons
Pete Johnson
George Zack
Clyde Hart
Mel Powell
Dick Cary
Eddie Heywood
Kenneth Kersey
Joe Bushkin
Billy Kyle
Cliff Jackson
Sam Price
The Lion
The Beetle
James P. Johnson
Dave Bowman
Don Frye
Cow Cow Davenport
Jack Russin

DRUMS
Zutty Singleton
George Wettling
Kansas Fields
Big Sid Catlett
Eddie Dougherty
Ray McKinley
Danny Alvin
Joe Jones

BASS
Al Morgan
Elmer James
Israel Crosby
Sid Weiss
Earl Murphy
Pops Foster
John Simmons
Billy Taylor
Artie Shapiro
Gene Traxler
Bill King
Jack Kelleher
Pete Peterson

JIMMY RYAN'S presents the 3rd consecutive year!
Milt Gabler's
SUNDAY SWING CLUB
JAM SESSIONS
every Sunday from 5 to 8 pm
featuring as usual the most of the best Jazzmen.
COME EARLY! COUVERT $1.00

WE'RE READY TO BLOW!
starting SUNDAY-SEPT. 27th

TRUMPET
Sidney DeParis
Bobby Hackett
Max Kaminsky
Henry Red Allen
Roy Eldridge
Hot Lips Page
Marty Marsala
Wild Bill Davison
Emmett Berry
Muggsy Spanier
Jimmy McPartland
Charlie Shavers
Joe Thomas
Dizzy Gillespie
Frankie Newton

CLARINET
Pee Wee Russell
Rod Cless
Buster Bailey
Albert Nicholas
Joe Marsala
Edmund Hall
Doc Slovak

SAXOPHONE
Coleman Hawkins
Sidney Bechet
Scotty
Kenneth Hollon
Benny Carter
Joe Eldridge
Pete Brown
Cecil Scott
Happy Cauldwell
Don Bias

TROMBONE
George Brunis
J. C. Higginbotham
Brad Gowans
Frank Orchard
Benny Morton
Sandy Williams
Vic Dickerson
Claude Jones
Lou McGarity

SINGERS
Billie Holiday
Bea Booze
Ruby Smith
Hot Lips Page

FOR RESERVATIONS – PHONE EL5-9600
JIMMY RYAN'S 53 West 52nd ST., N.Y.

Milt Gabler advertising circular for Sunday, September 27, 1942, jam session

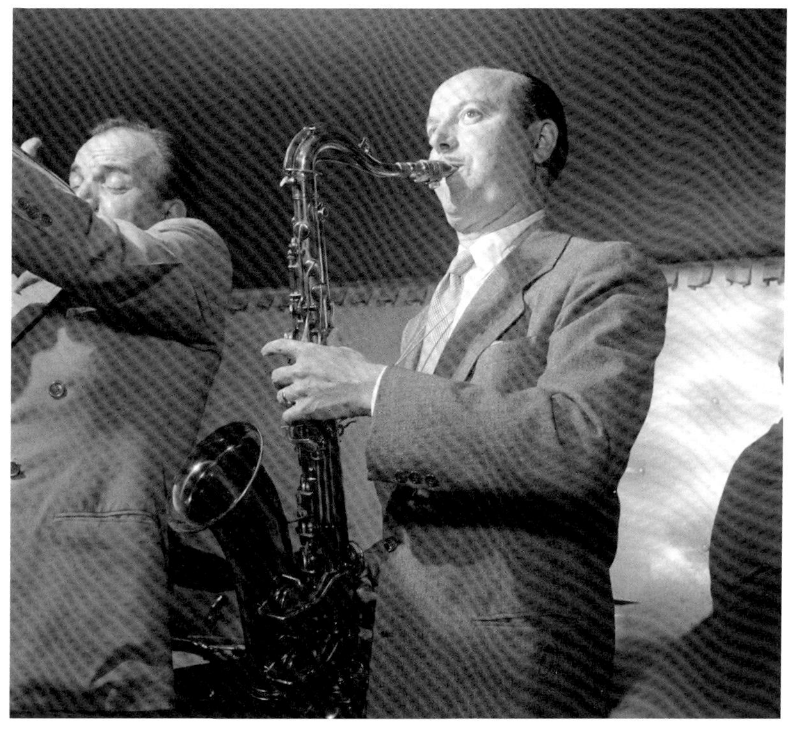

Marty Marsala on trumpet and Bud Freeman on tenor saxophone at Jimmy Ryan's in July 1947

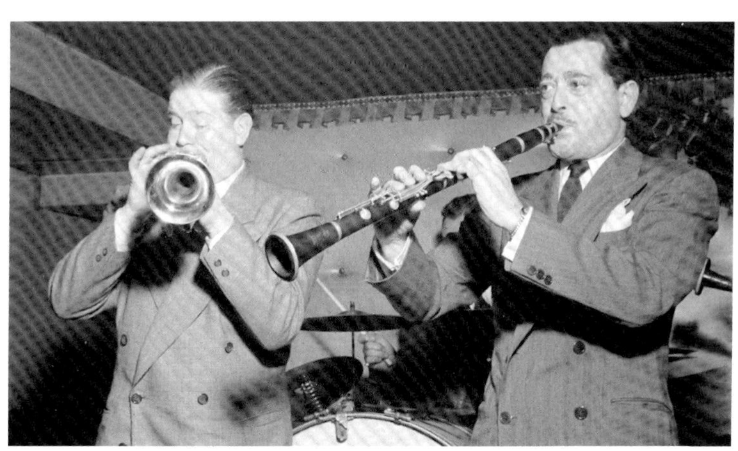

Wild Bill Davidson (trumpet) and Tony Parenti (clarinet) at Jimmy Ryan's in August 1946

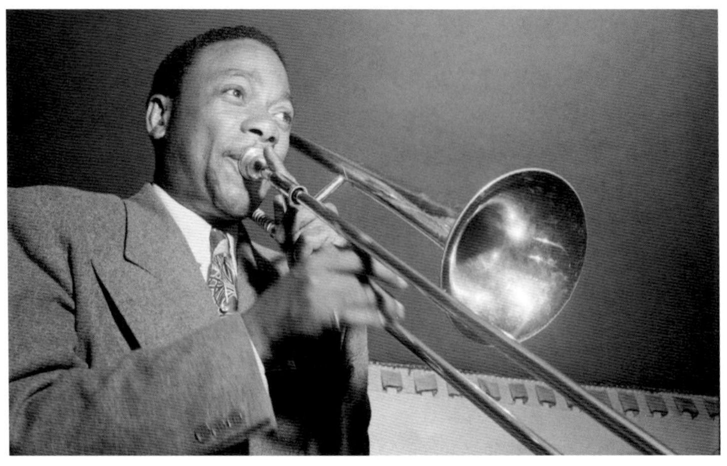

J. C. Higginbotham on trombone at Jimmy Ryan's in the late 1940s

JIMMY RYAN

presents

Milt Gabler's Jam Session

. . . featuring . . .

WILBUR De PARIS .... *Trombone*
SIDNEY De PARIS .... *Trumpet*
LEM JOHNSON .... *Saxophone*
PEE WEE RUSSELL .... *Clarinet*
BILLY TAYLOR .... *Bass*
EDDIE DOUGHERTY .... *Drums*
WILD BILL DAVISON .... *Trumpet*
BRAD GOWANS .... *Trombone*
POPS FOSTER .... *Bass*
CHARLIE SIMON .... *Drums*

and

MEL POWELL .... *Piano*

This Sunday, Nov. 7th, from 5 to 8 P.M.

at **JIMMY RYAN'S**

53 WEST 52nd ST., NEW YORK CITY

Jimmy Ryan's jam session handbill, Sunday, November 7, 1943

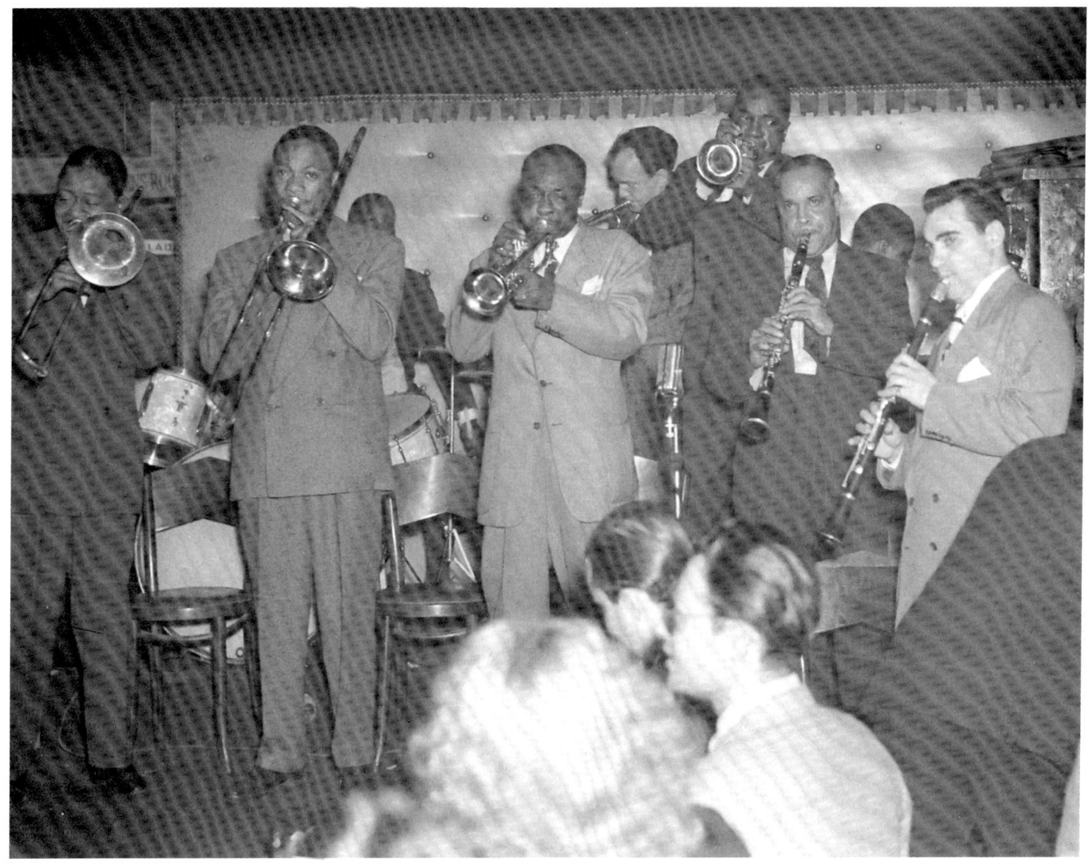

Sunday afternoon jam session at Jimmy Ryan's in the late 1940s, with Sandy William (trombone), J. C. Higginbotham (trombone), Freddie Moore (drums), Hot Lips Page (trumpet), Marty Marsala (trumpet), Emmett Berry (trumpet), Albert Nicholas (clarinet), Jimmy Jones (piano), and Sol Yaged (clarinet)

KELLY'S STABLE

Club owners Ralph Watkins and George Lynch would move from their original location at 141 West 51st Street to purchase the new Kelly's Stable at 137 West 52nd Street, opening it for business the first week of March 1940. The club would take on a bucolic atmosphere, with sawdust on the floor and carriage lamps on each side of a small stage. At the back of the stage was a large mural of a trotter on a racetrack.

Kelly's Stable was located opposite the Hickory House, and it wasn't long before Kelly's would begin running Sunday jam sessions, much the same as the Hickory House had been featuring years earlier under the direction of bandleader Joe Marsala.

After visiting the jam sessions on many an occasion, publicist and manager Monte Kay noted, "At Kelly's we worked with the musicians we liked, the music we liked, and in an atmosphere we liked. There was communication all around, interplay, and a feeling of excitement that I have seldom ever again experienced. We needed the little bread we made, but we ran the jams because they made us feel alive."

Unfortunately, the jams ended quite suddenly. Many say it was due to the churches nearby, and their parishioners complaining to the police.

In 1943, Kelly's would change its décor by painting the walls black and adorning them with collegiate pennants. That year the club would hire drummer Kenny Clarke's combo featuring tenor saxophonist Ike Quebec, and months later Dizzy Gillespie would share the bill with trumpeter Red Allen and Billie Holiday, with Clark Monroe's combo with Fats Navarro and Bud Powell rounding off the year. A year later Clark Monroe would become owner of the Spotlite Club on 52nd Street.

In 1939, Coleman Hawkins would perform the jazz standard "Body and Soul" at Kelly's. "Sometimes at night, after a couple quarts of scotch, I'd sit down and kill time and play about ten choruses on 'Body and Soul,' and then the boys would come in and play background until I finished up. That's all there was to it," remembered Hawkins.

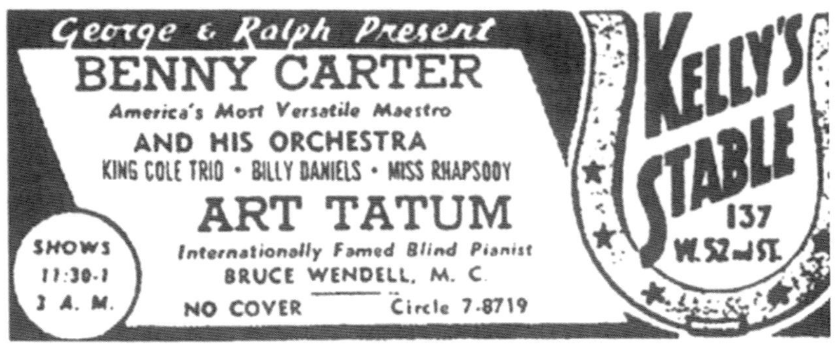

October 29, 1941

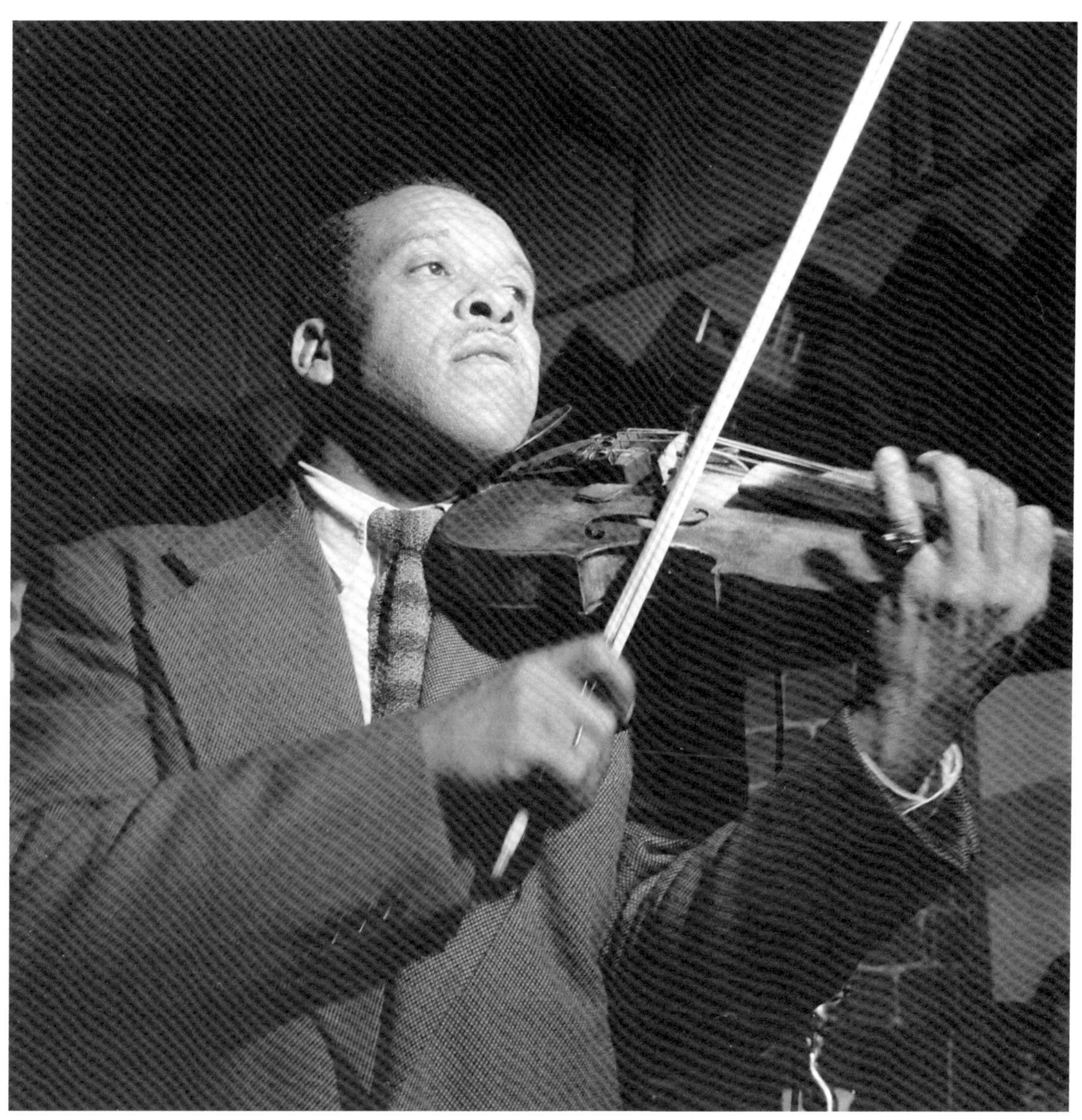

Jazz violinist Stuff Smith at Kelly's Stable in September 1946

Direct from European Triumphs

Coleman Hawkins

HIS SAXOPHONE

And His ORCHESTRA

Opening Thursday October 5 th

AT

Kelly's Stable

141 West 51st Street

Jazz saxophonist Coleman Hawkins and His Orchestra playing Kelly's Stable on October 5, 1939. Six days after this engagement, Hawkins would record his legendary tenor ballad "Body and Soul." Five months later, Kelly's Stable would move to 137 West 52nd Street from 141 West 51st Street. It would last for eight years, finally closing its doors on January 6, 1947.

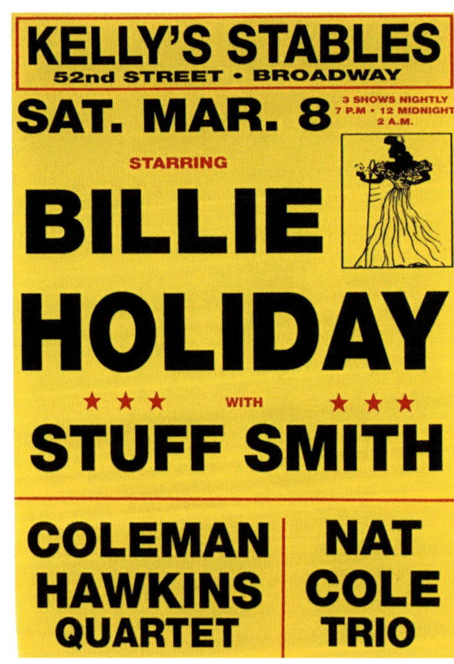

1941

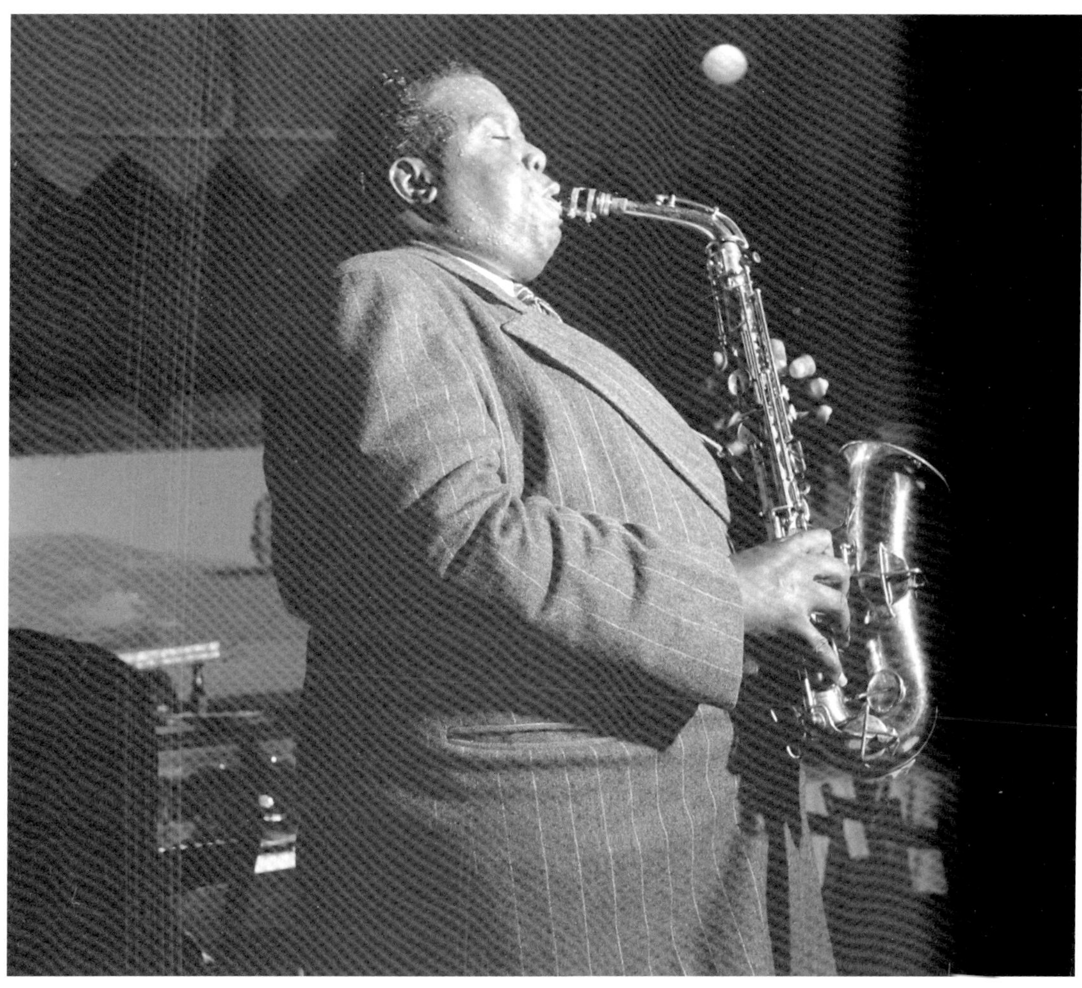

Jazz alto saxophonist Pete Brown at Kelly's Stable in the late 1930s. Brown would help establish the "jump" style that would eventually lead to rhythm & blues and rock & roll.

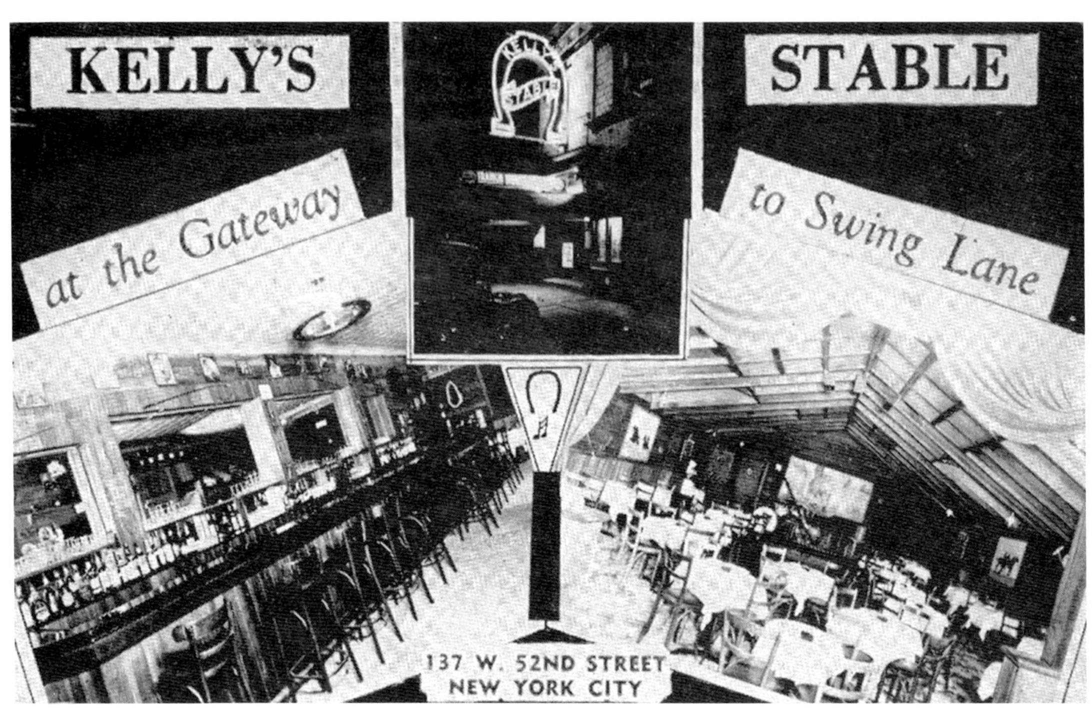

Kelly's Stable postcard

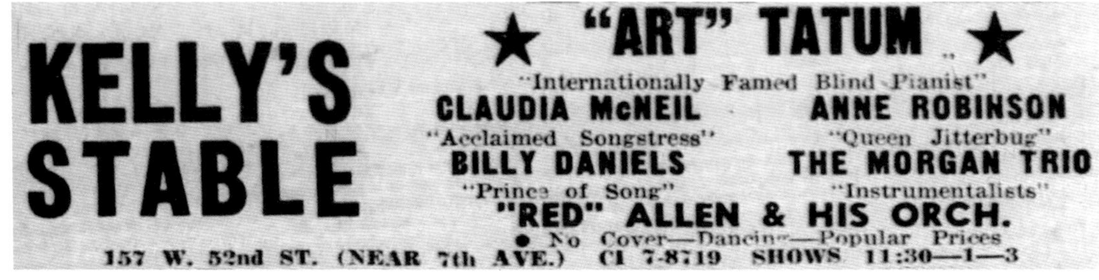

KELLY'S STABLE

★ "ART" TATUM ★
"Internationally Famed Blind Pianist"

CLAUDIA McNEIL
"Acclaimed Songstress"

ANNE ROBINSON
"Queen Jitterbug"

BILLY DANIELS
"Prince of Song"

THE MORGAN TRIO
"Instrumentalists"

"RED" ALLEN & HIS ORCH.

● No Cover—Dancing—Popular Prices

157 W. 52nd ST. (NEAR 7th AVE.) CI 7-8719 SHOWS 11:30—1—3

September 6, 1941

THE ONYX

The original Onyx was a speakeasy operated by Joe Helbock and located in a small apartment at the rear of a brownstone at 35 West 52nd Street in Manhattan. Opening in 1927, the Onyx speakeasy was accessed by going down some stone steps to an open basement door, walking down a short hall, climbing up a dark staircase, and finally arriving at a silver door, where you then had to provide a password through a hole in the door, commonly known as a Judas Hole. The entry password was often "802"—the number of the local musicians' union. When the door opened, you were in an absolute madhouse. The club was packed with musicians, talking, eating, and drinking, with a loud piano and phonograph playing in the background.

The speakeasy would later close in early 1934, when Joe Helbock responded to the end of Prohibition by closing his speakeasy and opening a legitimate Onyx club down the street at 72 West 52nd Street.

The Onyx's resident band was violinist Stuff Smith and his Onyx Club Boys. He would later leave for Hollywood and was replaced by bassist John Kirby and his group. In 1944 Dizzy Gillespie brought into the Onyx a group co-led with Oscar Pettiford that has been regarded as the first bop combo to appear in a club.

"We started with some pretty good talent at the Onyx, and the Onyx started some pretty big careers, with performers like Art Tatum, Maxine Sullivan, Louis Prima, Joe Sullivan, and Stuff Smith. I was the first to have Art Tatum. He played in the speakeasy for nothin'. I gave him all the beer he could drink. Almost a dozen quart bottles a night," said Joe Helbock.

The Onyx would close its doors to jazz in 1949 and became a strip joint, finally giving in to the changing times on Swing Street.

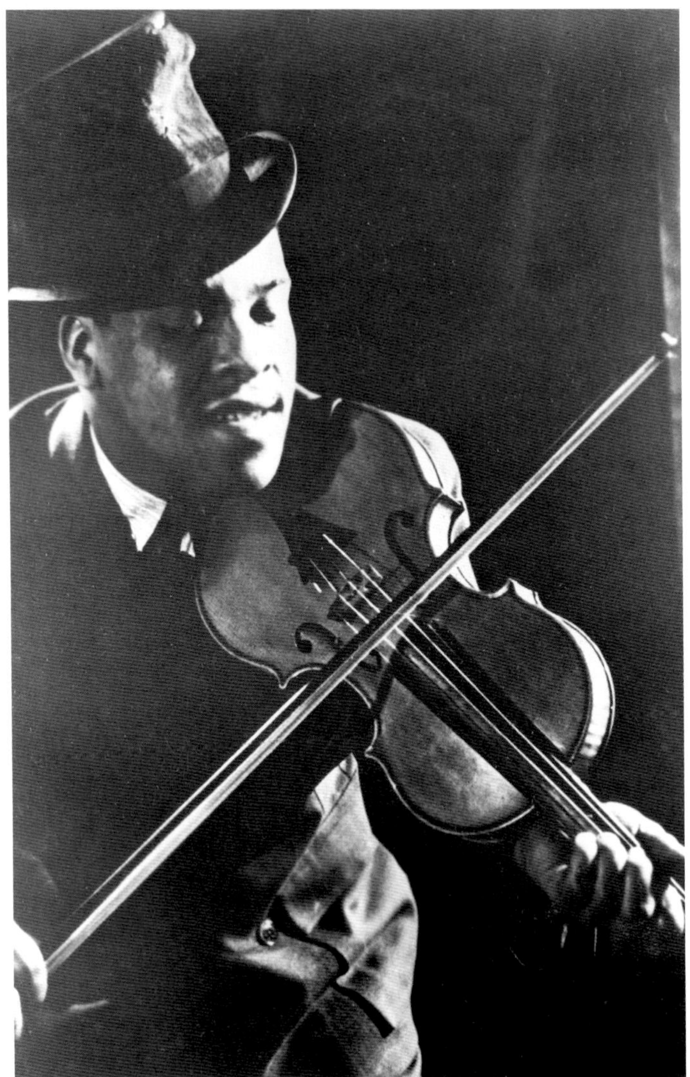

Stuff Smith at the Onyx Club in 1936 wearing his signature black stove top hat. In 1936, Stuff formed a sextet with his lifelong friend and trumpeter Jonah Jones, taking up residency at the Onyx and becoming an overnight sensation with their exciting, humorous, and driving rhythmic style of music, with included songs such as "You'se a Viper" and "Here Comes the Man with the Jive."

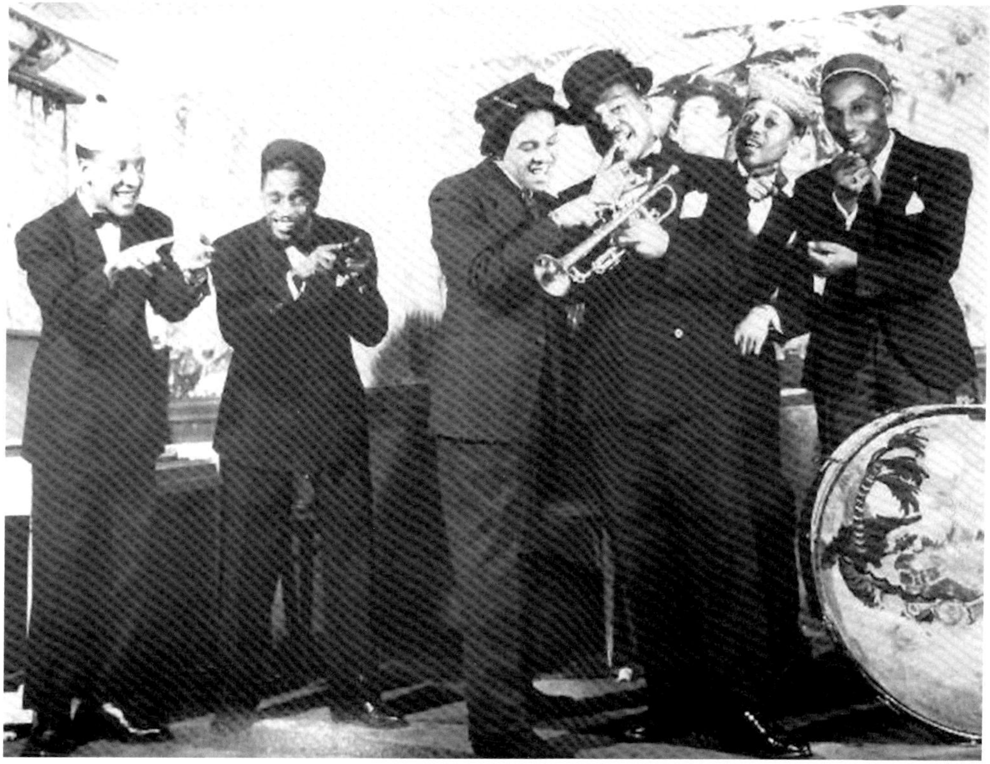

Stuff Smith (violin, vocals), Jonah Jones (trumpet), James Sherman (piano), Bobby Bennett (guitar), Mack Walker (bass), and Cozy Cole (drums) at the Onyx Club in 1936

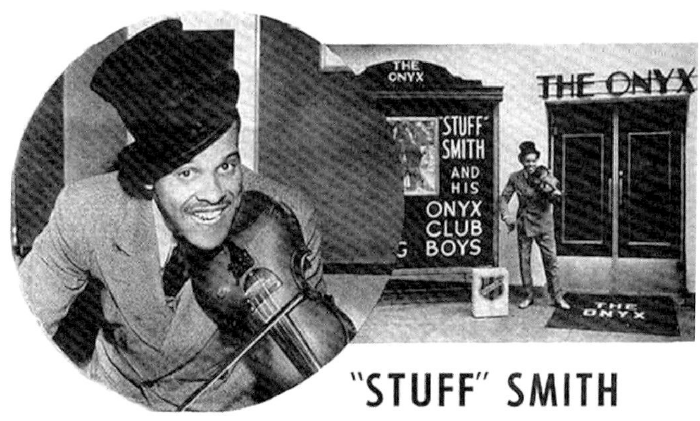

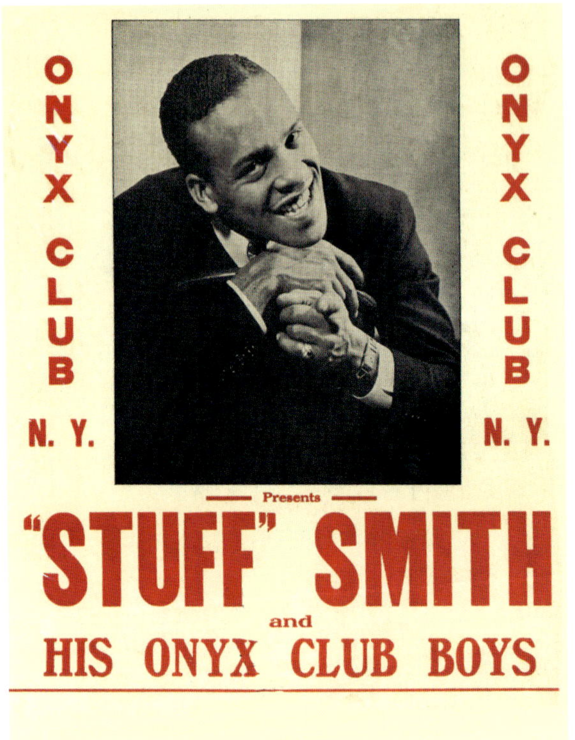

Stuff Smith and his Onyx Club Boys in 1936

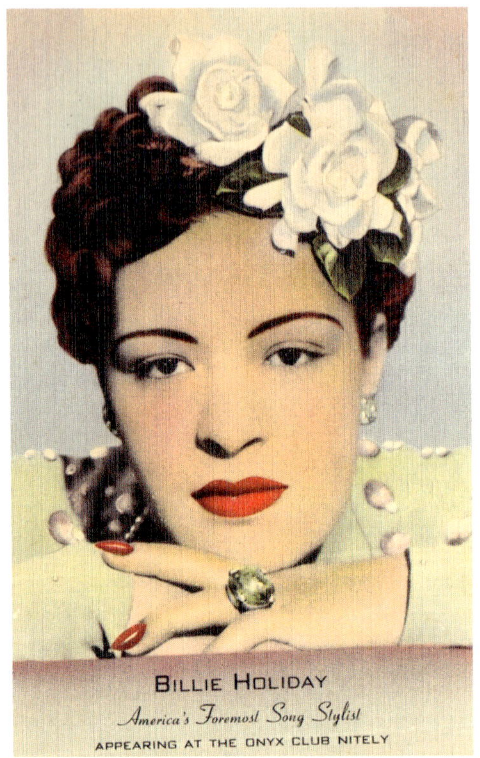

1943 Onyx Club postcard

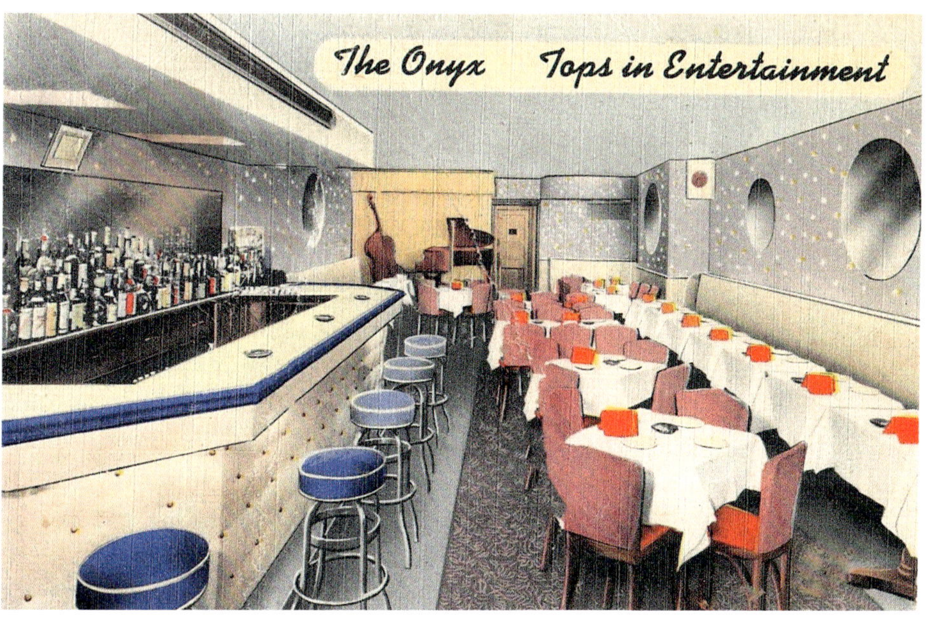

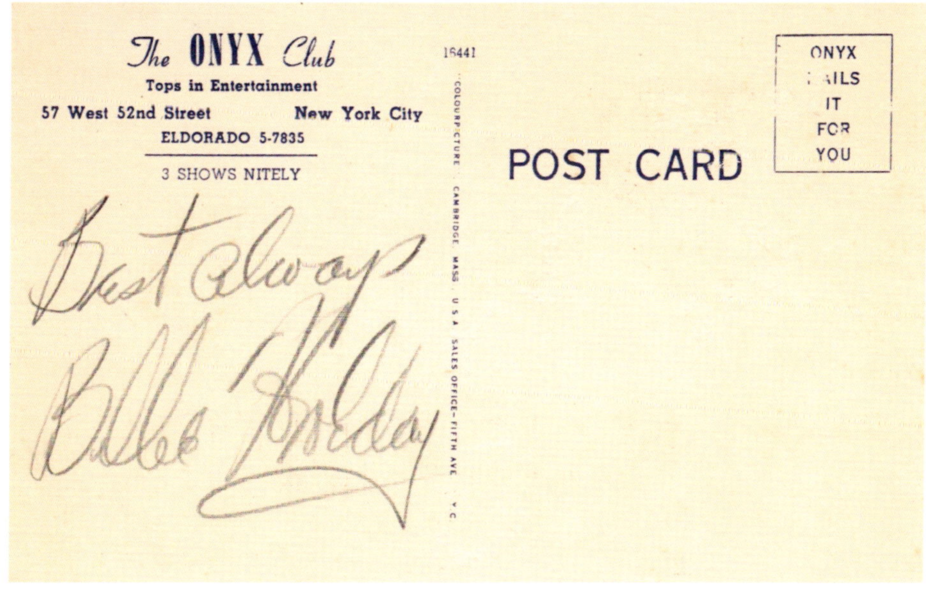

Billie Holiday autographed Onyx Club postcard

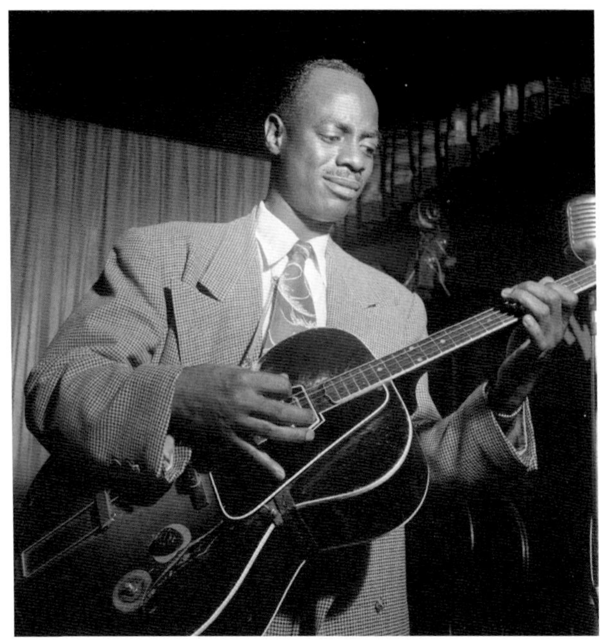

Jazz guitarist Tiny Grimes at the Onyx in the late 1940s. Tiny was part of the Art Tatum trio with Slam Stewart on bass from 1941 to 1944. Tiny was often known to slip in odd quotations in his improvisations while playing, to garner laughs from the audience. Playing a four-string electric guitar, Grimes was popular in the day as a backing musician on recording sessions, including a session with Charlie Parker.

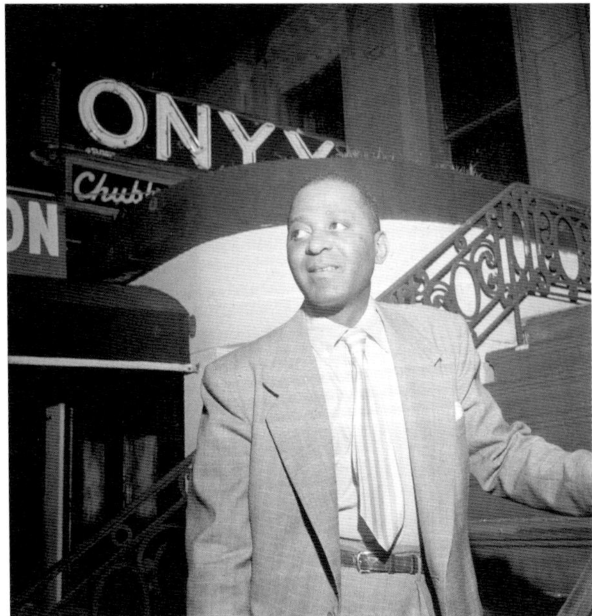

Dixieland jazz trombonist Wilbur De Paris, along with his brother Sidney on trumpet, reopened the Onyx at 57 West 52nd Street in July 1947. The Onyx would close a year later after almost twenty years on 52nd Street. The De Paris brothers would later move next door to Jimmy Ryan's, where they became the house band from 1952 to 1962.

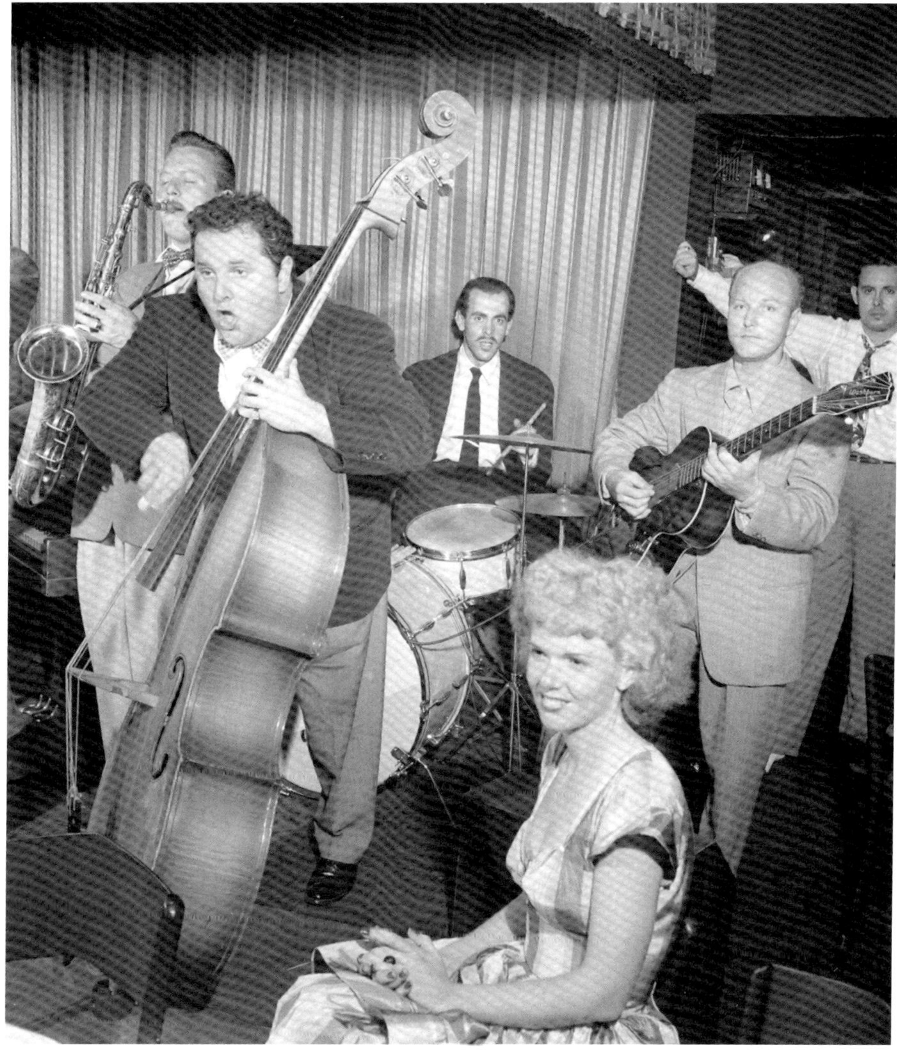

Chubby Jackson on bass with his group: Art Mardigan (drums), Dottie Reid (vocalist), and Billy Bauer (guitar), with unknown saxophonist at the Onyx in July 1947

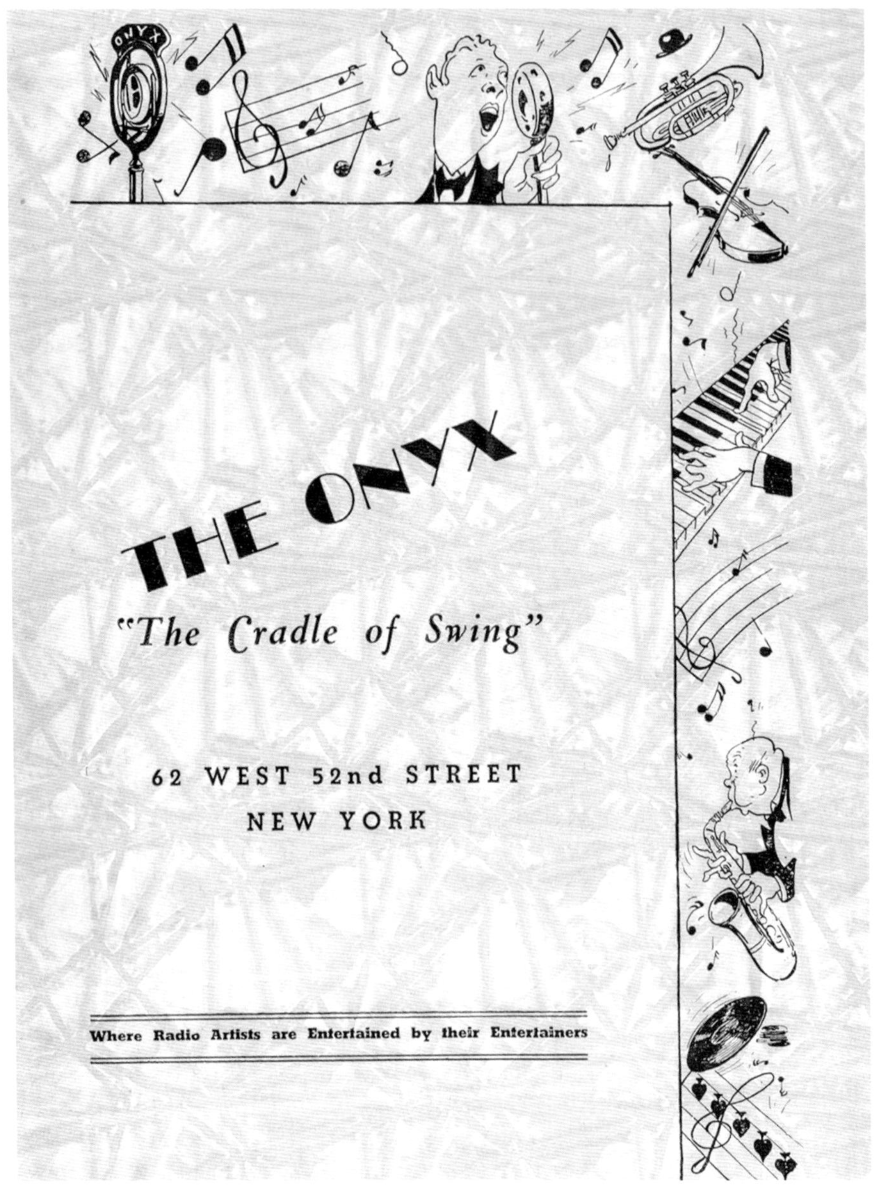

Onyx Club menu from 1937

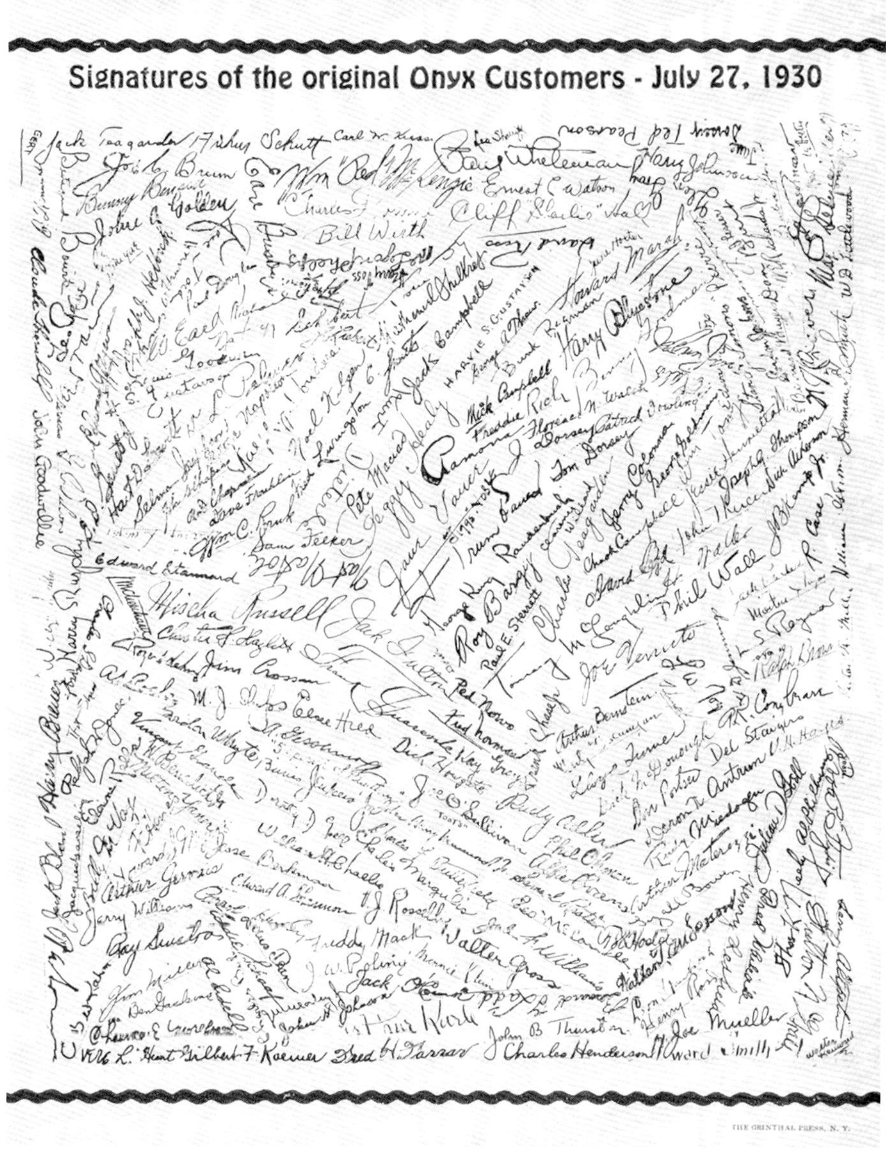

Back of menu with signatures from customers and musicians such as owner Joe Helbock, Jack and Charlie Teagarden, Benny Goodman, Joe Venuti, Arthur Bernstein, Jimmy and Tommy Dorsey, and Red Norvo

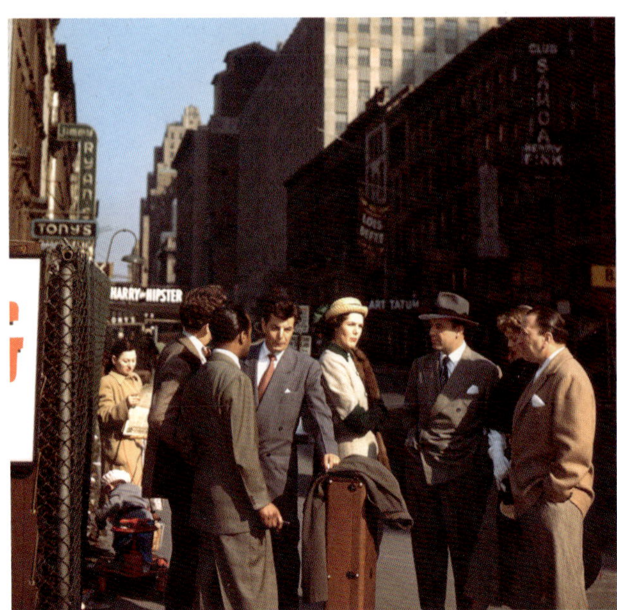

Left to right: Toots Thielemans, Joe Marsala (*red tie*), and Adele Girard standing on 52nd Street in 1948. On the north side of the street you can see Tony's restaurant, the Onyx (featuring Harry the Hipster), and Jimmy Ryan's, and on the opposite side, Club Samoa, and the Famous Door featuring Art Tatum.

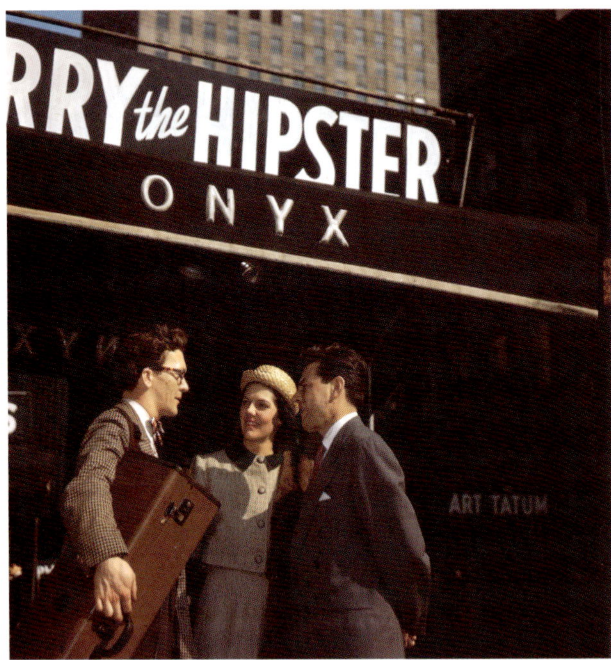

Left to right: Toots Thielemans, Adele Girard, and Joe Marsala standing outside the Onyx club in 1948. Harry "the Hipster" Gibson was the featured performer at the Onyx.

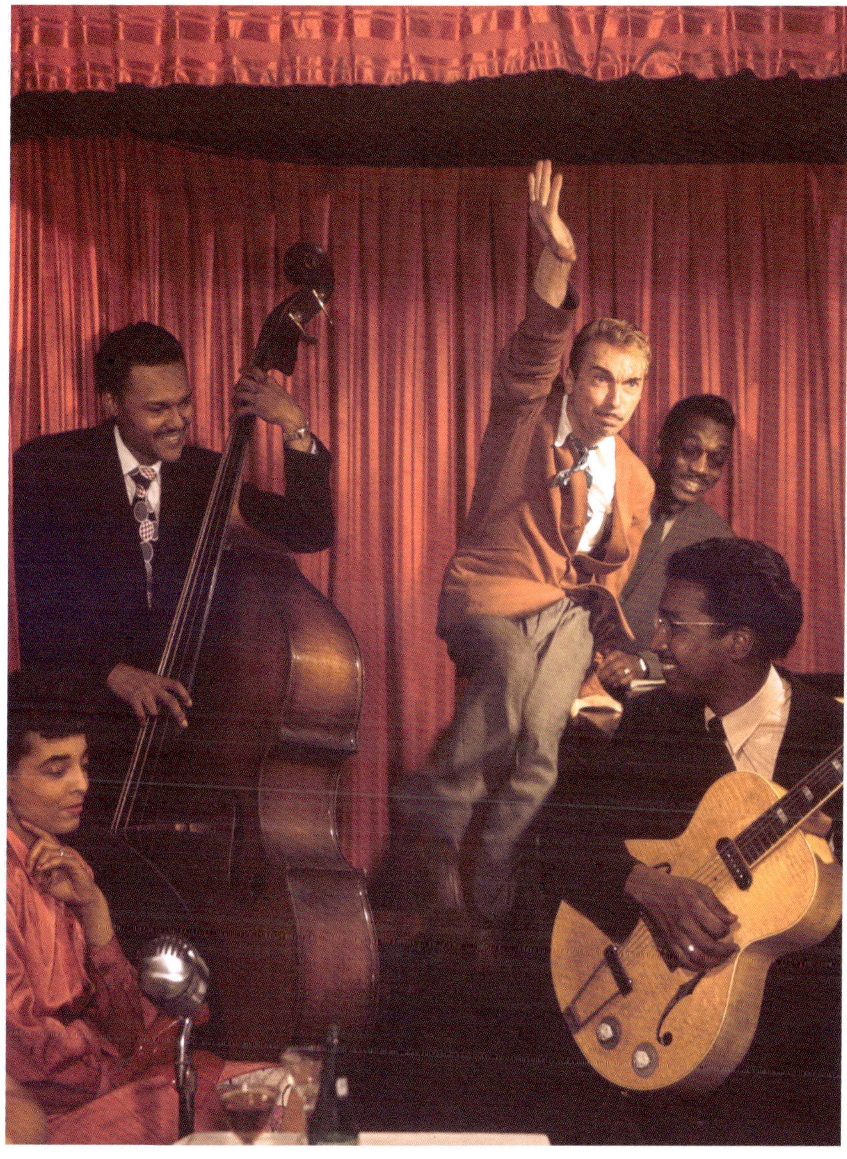

Stride and boogie-woogie pianist Harry "the Hipster" Gibson performing at the Onyx in July 1948. Harry enjoyed the notoriety as being the bop misleader of American youth, becoming famous for his popular number "Who Put the Benzedrine in Mrs. Murphy's Ovaltine?" and "Handsome Harry, the Hipster."

THE SPOTLITE

The Spotlite was opened in November 1944 at 56 West 52nd Street by Clark Monroe, a black club owner who also had a club in Harlem called Monroe's Uptown House. Monroe had briefly fronted a band at the Hickory House on 52nd Street in 1943.

Even though the Spotlite would last only for a brief two-year existence, it presented some of Swing Street's star attractions such as Billie Holiday, Coleman Hawkins, Ben Webster, Dizzy Gillespie, and Charlie Parker. Coleman Hawkins would occupy the bandstand at the Spotlite for much of 1946. The Spotlite would also become the scene of Charlie Parker's first gig as a leader in 1945.

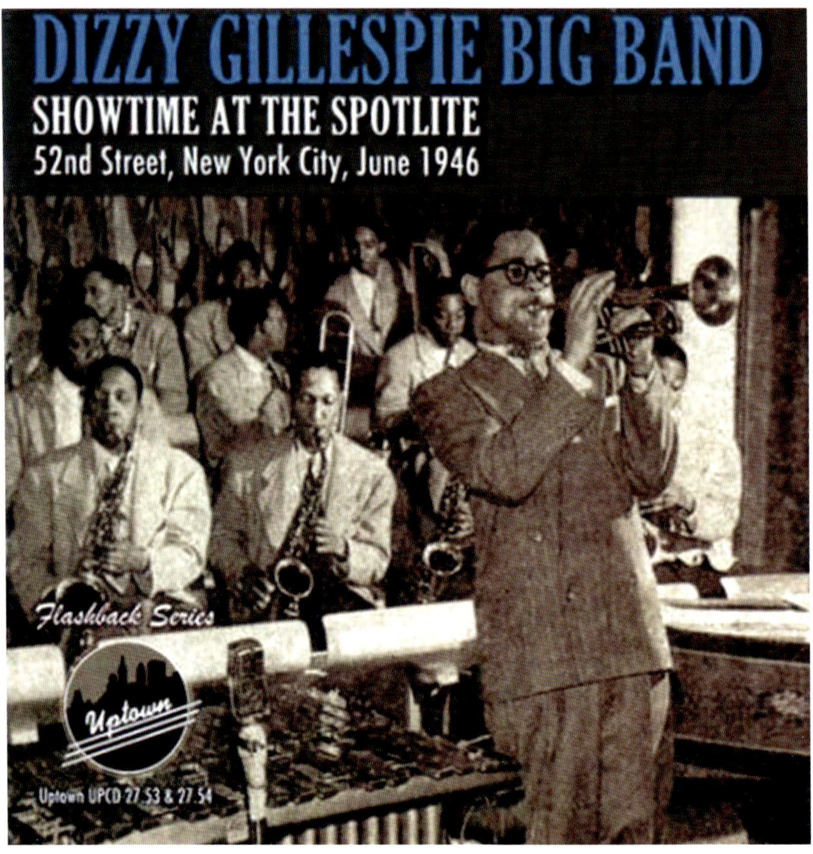

Dizzy Gillespie's big band live recording from the Spotlite Club in 1946

Journalist Leonard Feather's article on his impression of Dizzy Gillespie's big band at the Spotlite in 1946:

> Dizzy's second attempt to run a big band seems certain to be more successful than his first. Clark Monroe's Spotlite Club has squeezed the seventeen men into its limited space, giving them a good chance to whip the ensembles into shape.
>
> It's strange to hear numbers like Be Bop and others featured by the old quintet adapted for the big band. There are some moments of five-trumpet unison that are tremendously exciting. The brass section as a whole is powerful and sensitive in its concerted dynamics and boast a brilliant Diz disciple in trumpeter David Burns.
>
> Saxes are led by Sonny Stitt, who's a super Charles Parker, but during Sonny's illness a white boy, Johnny White, is leading. Howard Johnson, who toured Europe with Dizzy in 1937 in the old Teddy Hill band, does some nice Carter-ish alto work.
>
> Trombonist Slim Moore, tenors Ray Abramson and Warren Lucky contribute good solos. The fine rhythm section has Thelonious Monk, pianist and arranger of some of the best numbers; Ray Brown, featured solo bassist—great; and drummer Kenny Clarke. Vibraphonist Milt Jackson has improved vastly and provides some terrific kicks in solo numbers.
>
> All these and Dizzy too, topped by intriguing modern scores from Tadd Dameron, John Lewis, and Walter Fuller.

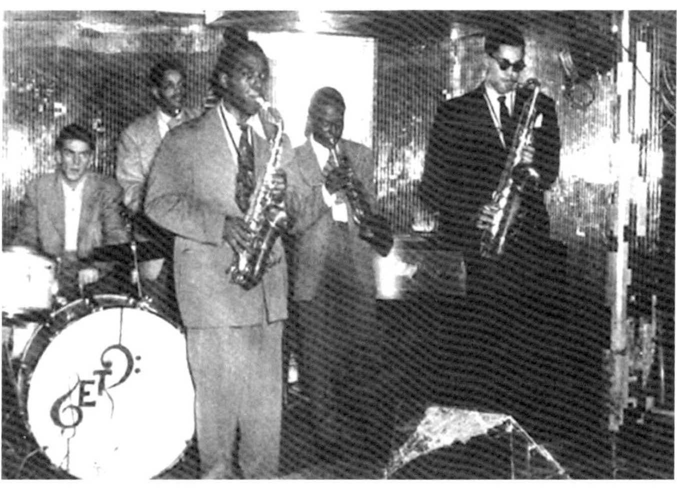

The Charlie Parker Sextet at the Spotlite in 1945 with Miles Davis (trumpet), Dexter Gordon (tenor sax), Leonard Gaskin (bass), and Stan Levy (drums). Pianist unknown.

MONTE KAY
presents a
MODERN JAZZ CONCERT
Starring 3 of America's Greatest Trumpeters

BUCK CLAYTON
Esquire's #1 Musician in the Armed Forces

DIZZY GILLESPIE
Esquire's New Trumpet King of 1945

HARRY EDISON
Dynamic Trumpeter with Count Basie
Featured in "Jammin' the Blues" at the Hollywood

DON BYAS
One of the Country's Finest Tenor Saxists

DEXTER GORDON
World's Weirdest Tenor Man - Out of Uniform

ERROL GARNER
Brilliant Young Pianist—A 1945 Jazz Discovery

SHELLEY MANNE
Driving Drummer formerly with Les Brown

SAMMY BENSKIN — Piano
LEONARD GASKIN — Bass

And Guests From Every Top Band In Town

SUNDAY AFTERNOON, FEB. 4, 4 to 8 P.M.

$1.50 Cover Charge—No Other Charge at Table
For Reservations: Call MAL BRAVEMAN
ELdorado 5-8148, Sunday after 2 P.M.

SPOTLITE CLUB 56 W. 52nd STREET
Bet. 5th and 6th Aves.

MONTE KAY presents a
MODERN JAZZ CONCERT
Starring

DIZZY GILLESPIE
Esquire's New Trumpet King of 1945

AL KILIAN
Skyrocket Trumpeter with Count Basie

HARRY EDISON
Driving Trumpeter of the Basie Band

DEXTER GORDON
Great Tenor Man — Ex Hampton and Eckstine

EDDIE DAVIS
Frantic New Tenor Saxist with Louis Armstrong

ERROL GARNER **KEN KERSEY**
Two Brilliant Young Pianists

SHELLY MANNE — Drums
LEONARD GASKIN — Bass

And Our Guests of Honor

BUDDY RICH
The World's Fastest Drummer

GEO. SCHWARTZ **HERB STEWART**
Terrific Trumpet and Tenor Men with Artie Shaw

SUNDAY AFTERNOON, FEB. 11, 4 to 8 P.M.

$1.50 Cover Charge—No Other Charge at Table
For Reservations: Call MAL BRAVEMAN
ELdorado 5-8148, Sunday after 2 P.M.

SPOTLITE CLUB 56 W. 52nd STREET
Bet. 5th and 6th Aves.

Spotlite Club handbills for Sunday afternoon jazz concerts on February 4 and 11, 1945

Mal Braveman and Milt Shaw

Present

FOUR SOLID HOURS OF

MAD MUSIC

☆

Featuring

Our Guest of Honor

DIZZY GILLESPIE
World's Most Outstanding Trumpeter

DON BYAS
New King of the Tenor Sax

CHARLIE PARKER
Alto Saxmania

AL KILLIAN
Great Basie—Barnet Trumpeter

MOREY FELD
Benny Goodman's Ace Drummer

AL HAIG
Piano

AL COHEN
Tenor

LEONARD GASKIN
Bass

FREDDIE RADCLIFFE
Drums

Plus Plenty of Name Guests from the
T. Dorsey - Barnet Bands

☆

SUNDAY AFTERNOON, Sept. 16th, 1945

4 to 8 P. M. **Admission $1.50**

SPOTLITE CLUB, 56 W. 52 St. New York

(Bet. 5th and 6th Aves.)

Call EL 5-8148, Sun. Aft. bet. 2-4 P.M. for Best Table Reservations

1945 Spotlite Club handbill with Charlie Parker and Dizzy Gillespie on the same bill

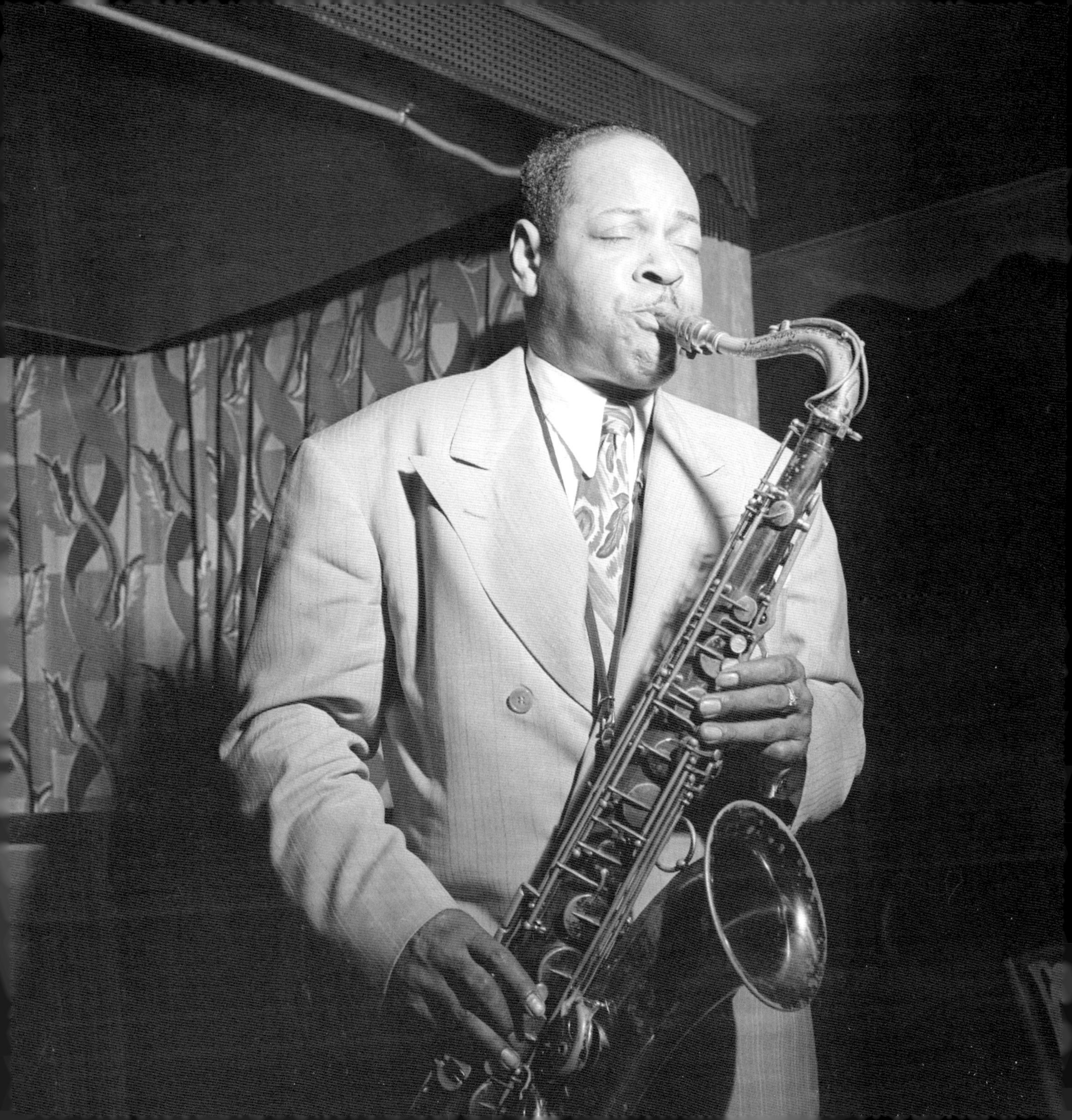

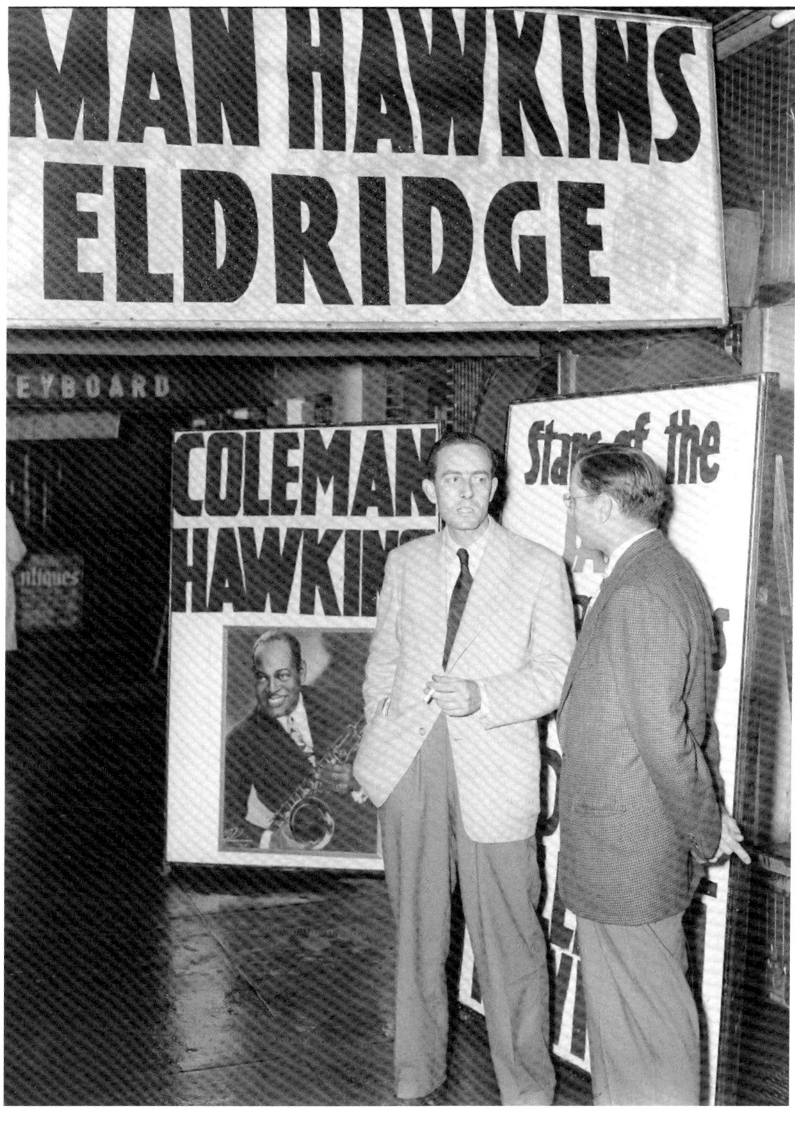

Jazz authors Charles Delaunay and Walter E. Schaap outside the Spotlite Club at 56 West 52nd Street in 1946. The Spotlite would later become the Famous Door in December of that year.

OPPOSITE Jazz tenor saxophonist Coleman Hawkins at the Spotlite in September 1946

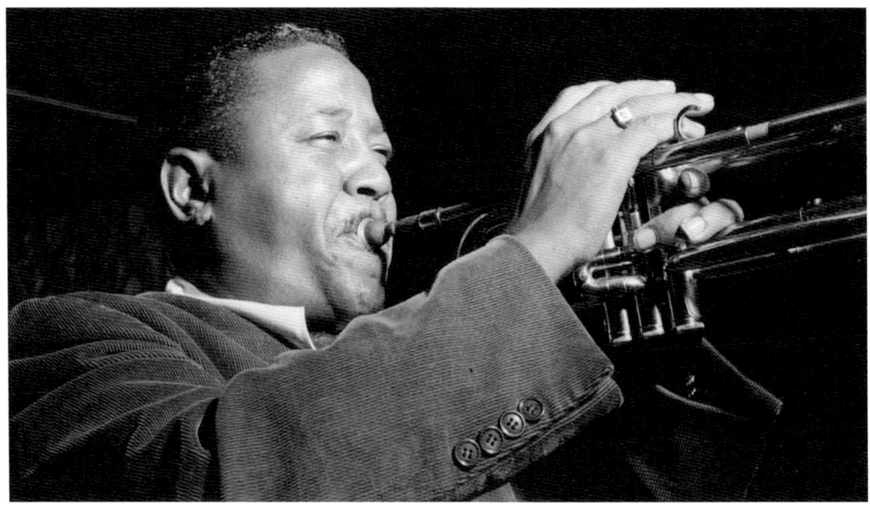

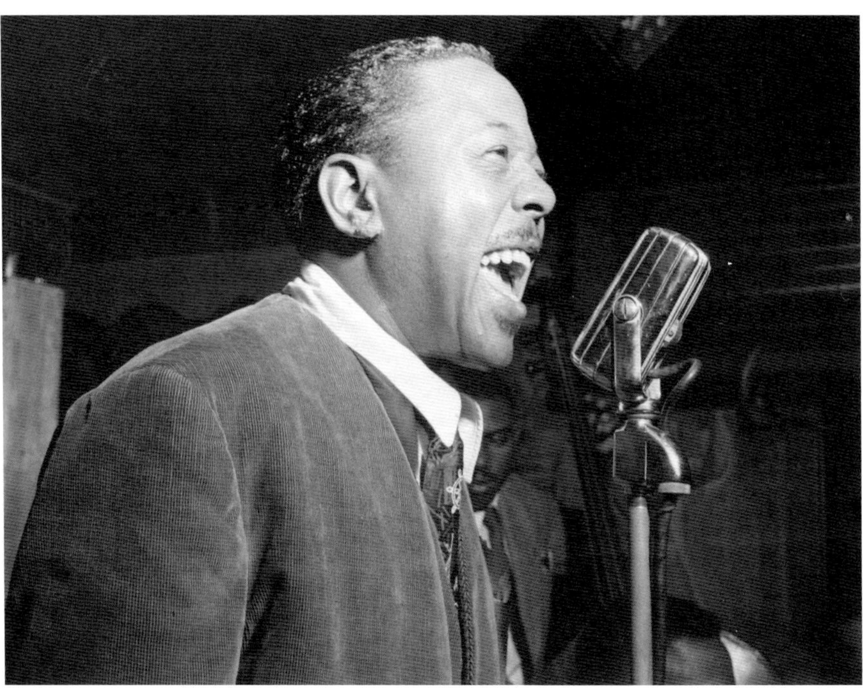

Roy Eldridge performing at the Spotlite in November 1946

THE THREE DEUCES

Charlie Parker frequently played the Three Deuces from 1947 to 1949 with his own band. His appearances were often eventful due to his tardiness, starting some clubs to pay Parker by the set because at times he wouldn't show up for the gig. Often his alto saxophone would be in hock, so the Three Deuces began to assign someone to go to the pawnshop every day and get Bird's horn out of hock and then return it after the gig.

Jazz guitarist Jimmy Raney remembers a humorous event: "One night Bird walked in and went right to the kitchen and started to make himself a few sandwiches. He was doing a magnificent job building them very big and garnishing them with all sorts of condiments. The managers of clubs had a very easygoing attitude with Bird, but this was a hectic evening, and the full bar was waiting for Charlie. The manager came into the kitchen and told Bird that he was on. Bird, his jaws chomping, kept on eating. The manager waited a bit and then said, 'Please, Bird, finish later; the crowd is getting restless.' No response for Bird. This went on until the manger was almost in tears, imploring him to go on, and Bird turned around and said, 'Man, why don't you try one of these sandwiches? They're crazy!'"

The Three Deuces would become the first time for Miles Davis to develop his improvisational skills in a small-combo setting after leaving the Billy Eckstine bebop big band.

In the summer of 1947, trumpeter Fats Navarro and Bud Powell sat in with Bird for one set, replacing Miles Davis and Duke Jordan. They opened up with Monk's "52nd Street Theme" at a fast tempo, with Bird and Navarro playing well. When it was Powell's turn to solo, he exploded into such a masterful improvisation over the next twenty-four choruses that he left the audience spellbound.

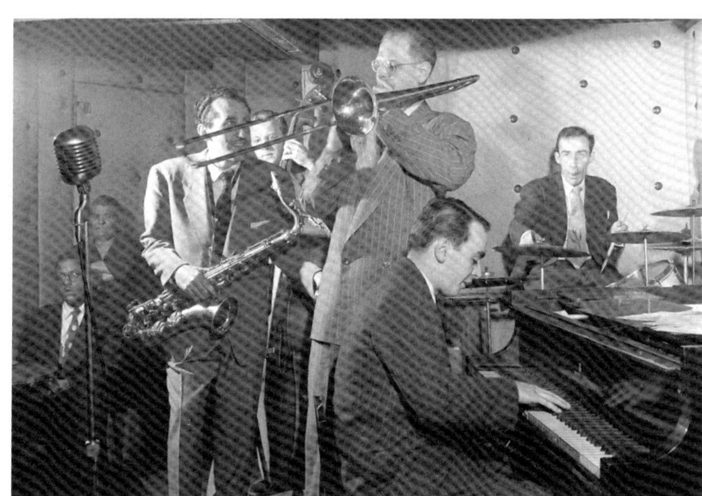

Charlie Ventura (tenor sax), Bill Harris (trombone), Ralph Burns (piano), and Dave Tough (drums) at Three Deuces in 1947

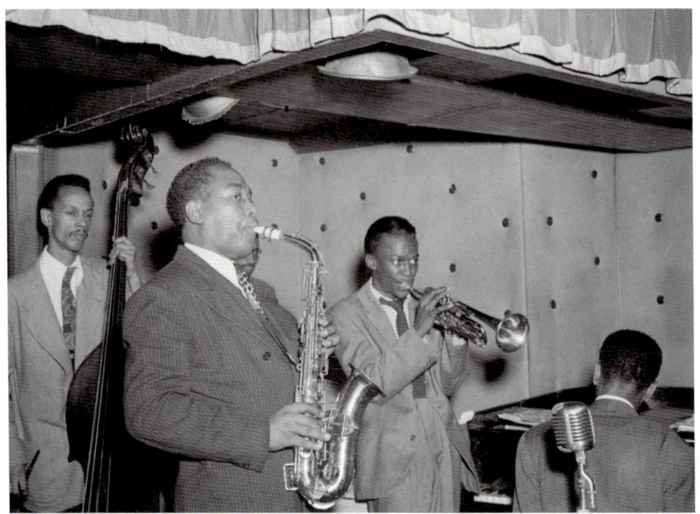

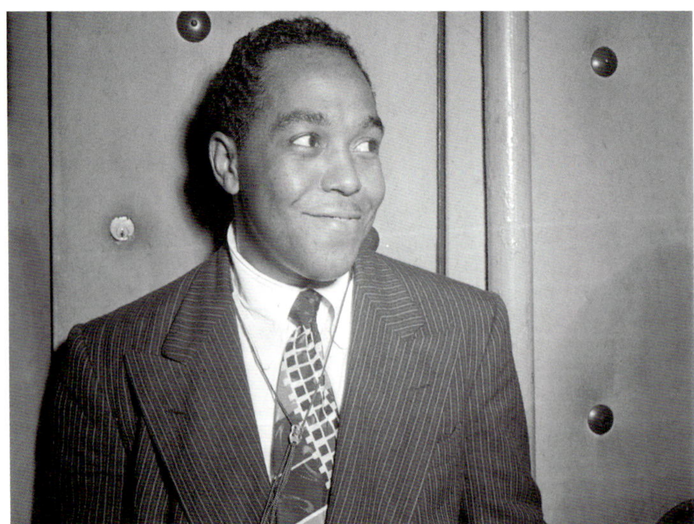

Charlie Parker Quintet at the Three Deuces in August 1947: Charlie Parker (alto sax), Miles Davis (trumpet), Duke Jordan (piano), Tommy Potter (bass), and Max Roach (drums)

OPPOSITE Jazz drummer Max Roach playing with the Charlie Parker Quintet at the Three Deuces in August 1947

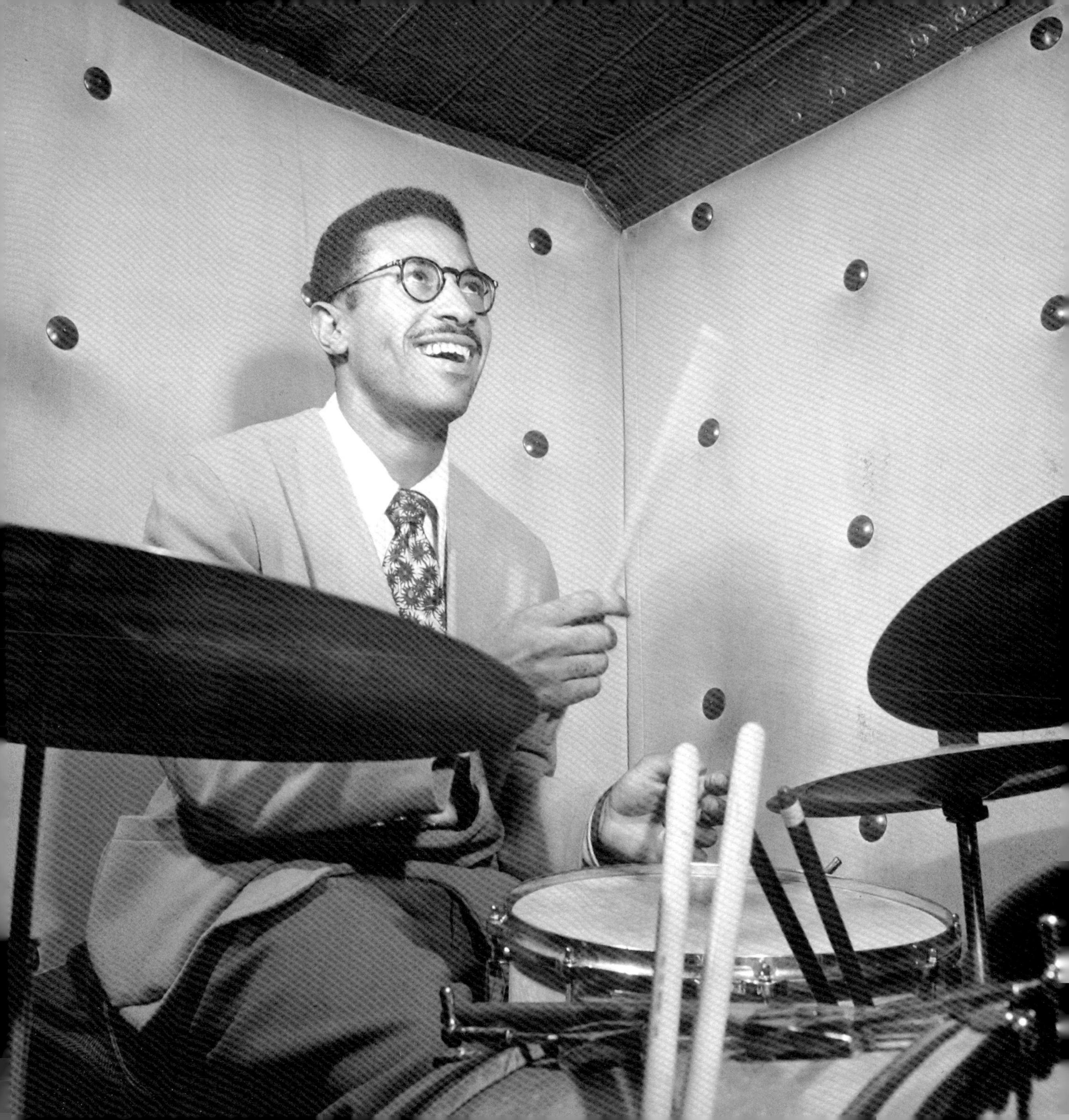

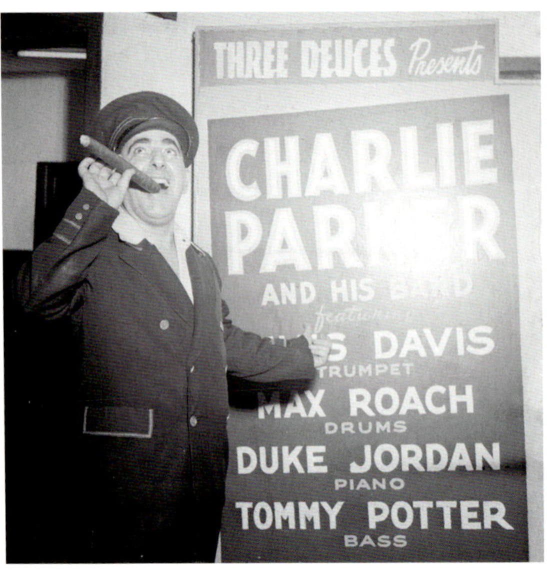

Gilbert G. Pincus in front of the Three Deuces in August 1947. The proclaimed "Mayor of 52nd Street" has been a doorman on Swing Street since the early 1930s. A little man with a big cigar, oversized hat, and long coat, he worked at practically every club on the Street, always donning a smile and a twinkle in his eye.

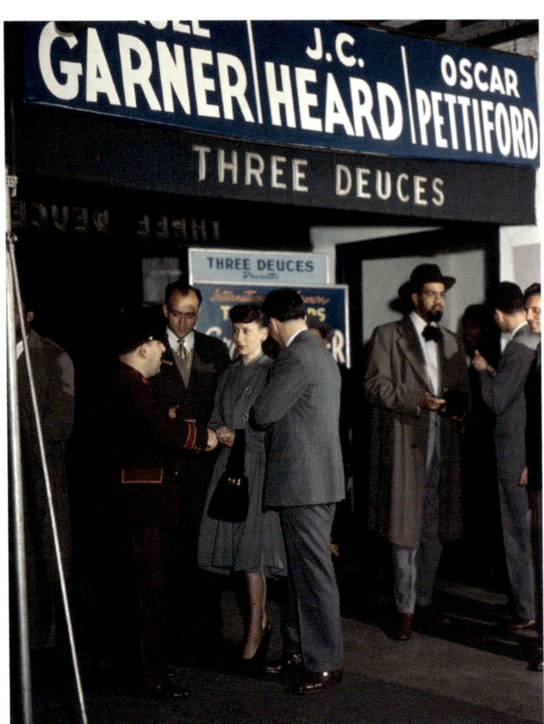

Gilbert G. Pincus greeting folks in front of the Three Deuces in July 1948. The gentleman to the right, wearing the black hat and bow tie, is jazz bassist Al McKibbon.

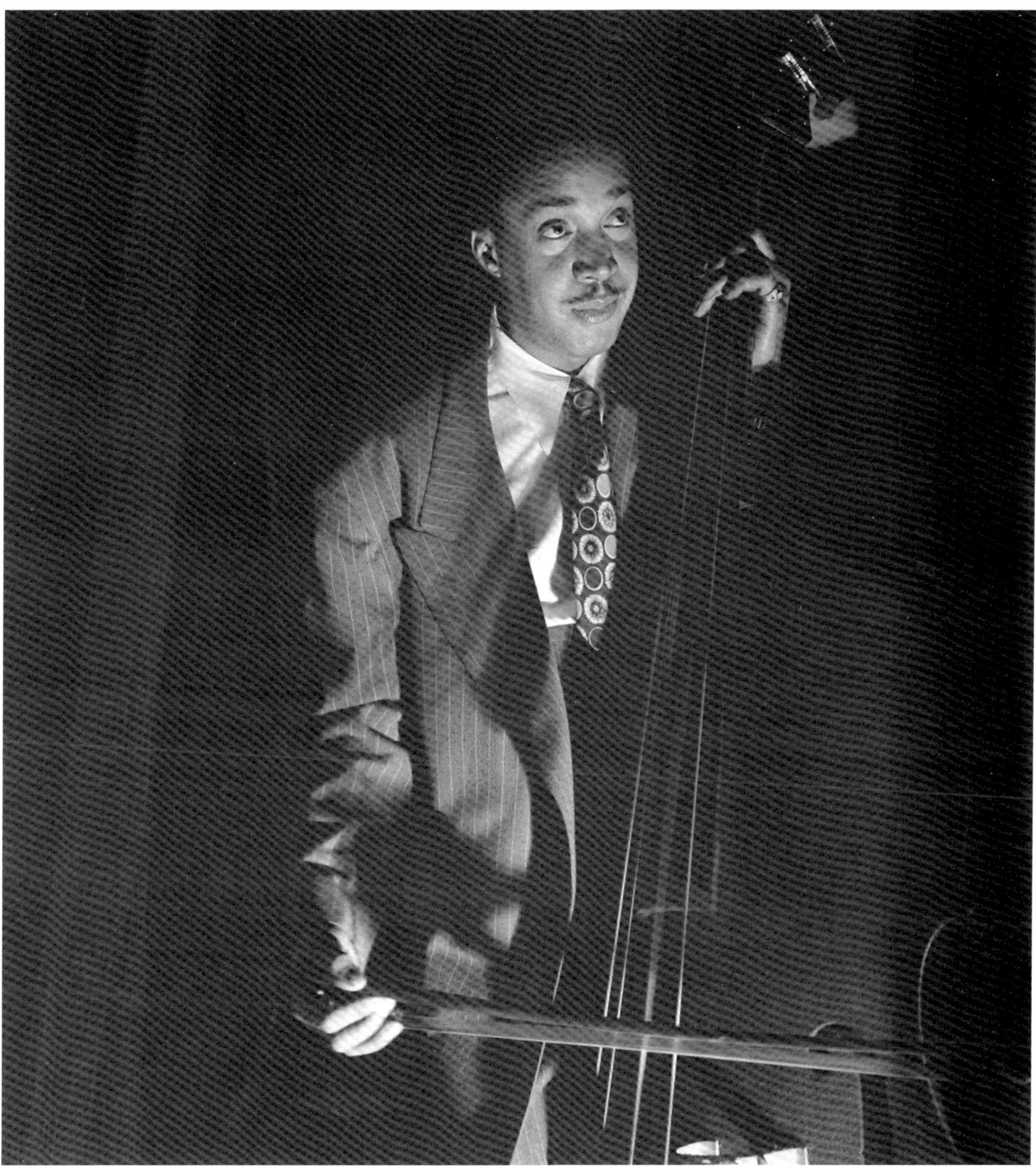

Jazz bassist extraordinaire Slam Stewart at the Three Deuces in September 1946. Slam had the unique ability to bow the bass and hum and sing an octave higher.

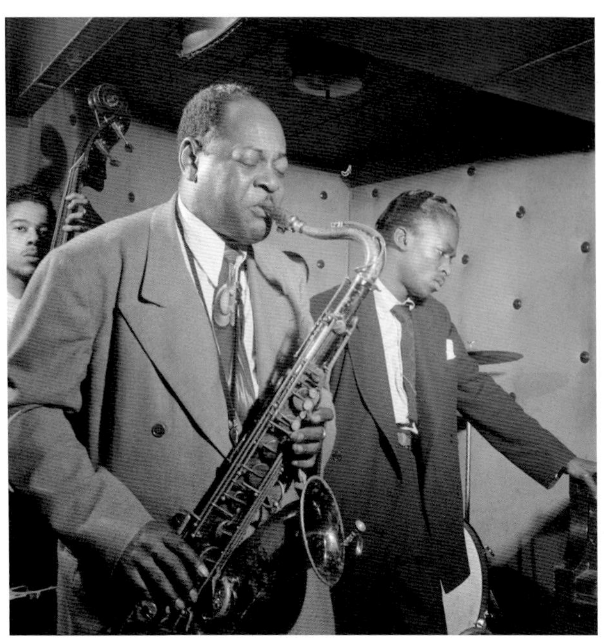

Jazz tenor saxophonist Coleman Hawkins with trumpeter Miles Davis at the Three Deuces in July 1947. Bean or Hawk, as musicians called him, recorded the famous jazz classic "Body and Soul" on October 11, 1939.

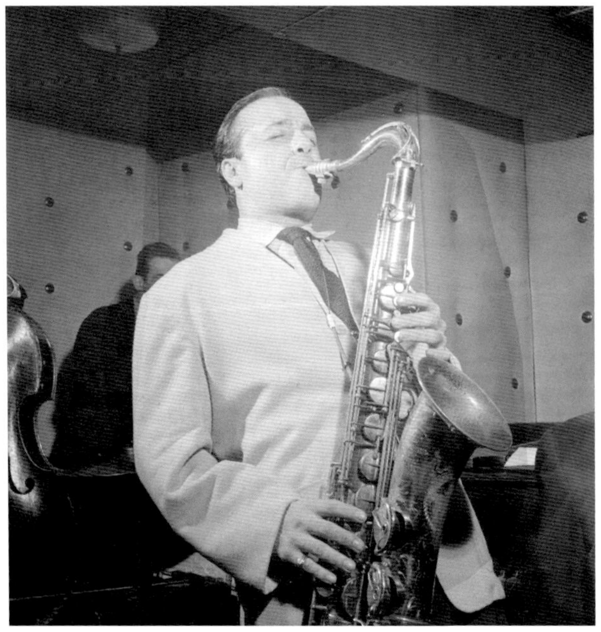

Jazz tenor saxophonist Flip Phillips at the Three Deuces in June 1947, starring with the Bill Harris combo. Known on Swing Street as Joe Flip, Phillips first drew excited attention in 1943, playing at the Hickory House. He later moved on to work with jazz vibraphonist Red Norvo. His sweet and mellow tone often had jazz fans comparing him to Hawkins.

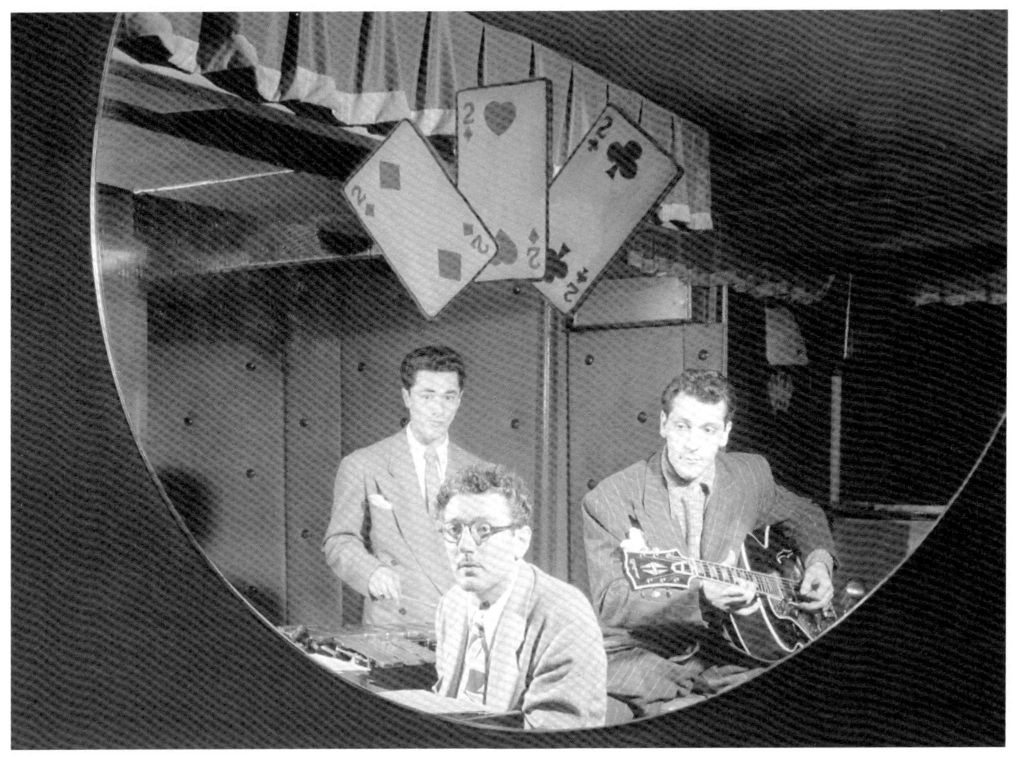

Terry Gibbs (vibraphone), Harry Bliss (piano), and Bill De Arango (guitar) at the Three Deuces in June 1947

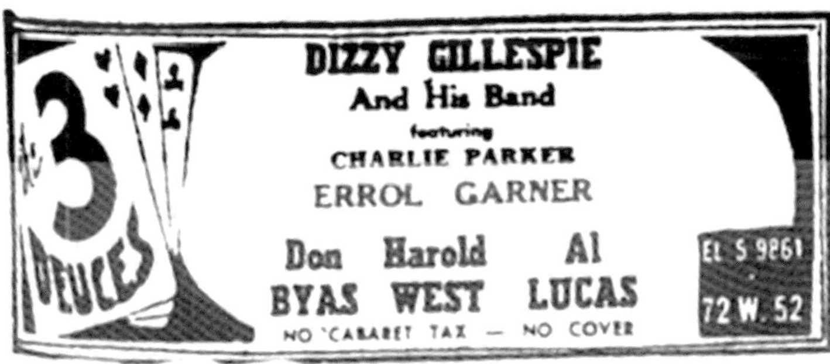

April 26, 1945

Jazz violinist Sam Hall with Frenchy Cauette (bass), Chuck Wayne (guitar), and Deryck Sampson (piano) at the Three Deuces in June 1947

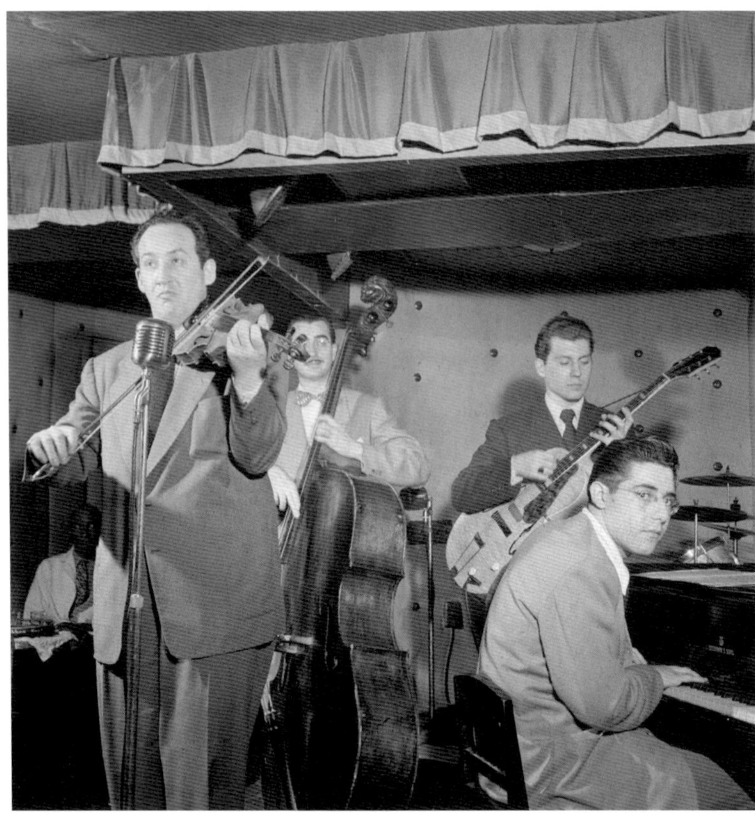

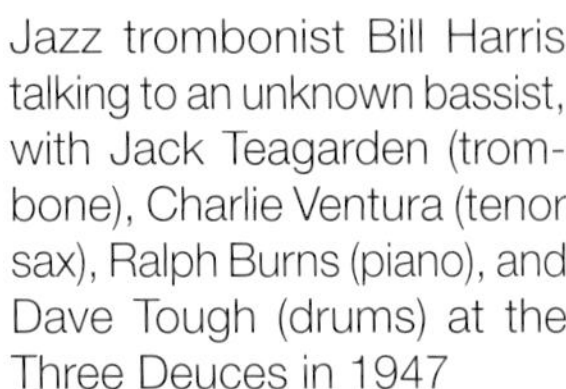

Jazz trombonist Bill Harris talking to an unknown bassist, with Jack Teagarden (trombone), Charlie Ventura (tenor sax), Ralph Burns (piano), and Dave Tough (drums) at the Three Deuces in 1947

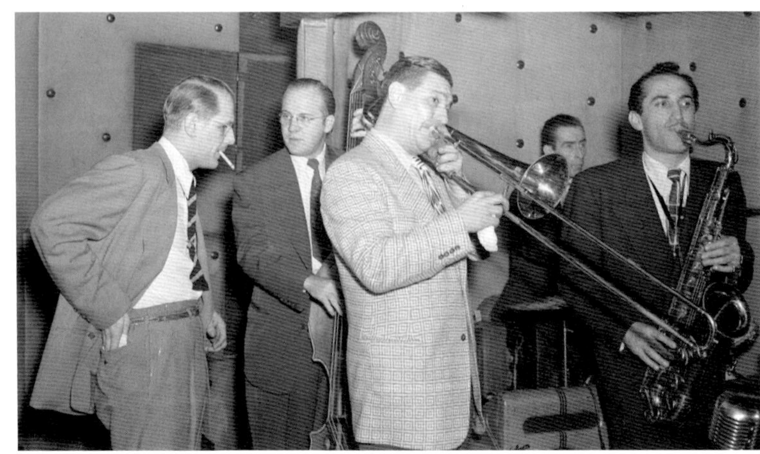

CHAPTER THREE

SWING STREET

OTHER NEIGHBORHOOD CLUBS

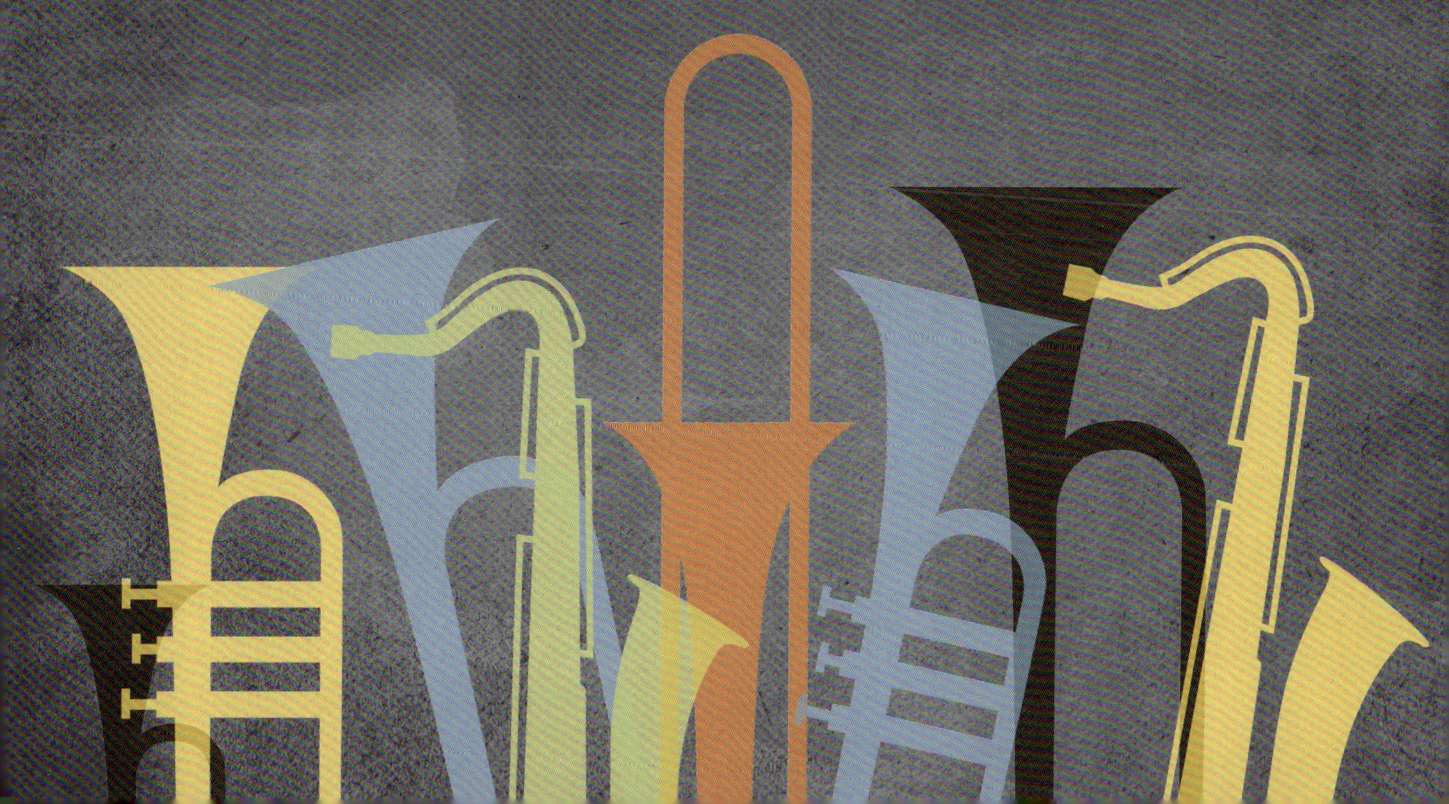

THE AQUARIUM

The Aquarium made its official move to 52nd Street from 48th Street on January 1, 1929, after being raided by the police. It took over the Onyx Club on the ground floor of a brownstone at 35 West 52nd Street while the Onyx moved up to the second floor. The Aquarium was known for its tank of fish behind the bar.

The Aquarium would later move to 38 West 52nd Street, where it would survive for a while until moving to its final resting spot at 701 7th Avenue, on the corner of 7th Avenue and West 47th Street.

In October 1946, Duke Ellington and his orchestra would play the Aquarium from October 2 to 30, for $5,000 a week. The owner, Ben Harriman, had doubts about whether his street-front spot would be the type of club to handle such a top-name band as Duke Ellington's. Even booking agent Joe Glaser, who put name bands into the Aquarium, had many other bookers and location owners questioning their decision to spend the big bucks hiring Ellington's orchestra, but much to their surprise the four-week engagement was a big success.

It was extra special being able to have the world-famous Django Reinhardt join the orchestra at the end of the month and travel around the United States and Canada for the next sixty days. Duke's drummer, Sonny Greer, was enthralled getting to play with Django: "Man that cat could take a guitar and make it talk. Nobody played like him. Once me and Django were sitting backstage, playing one of the things he used to play in France with his Hot Five group. I had some brushes and a newspaper when Duke walked in and said, 'I like that.' So we played it as a surprise encore that night, and it went over gangbusters with the audience."

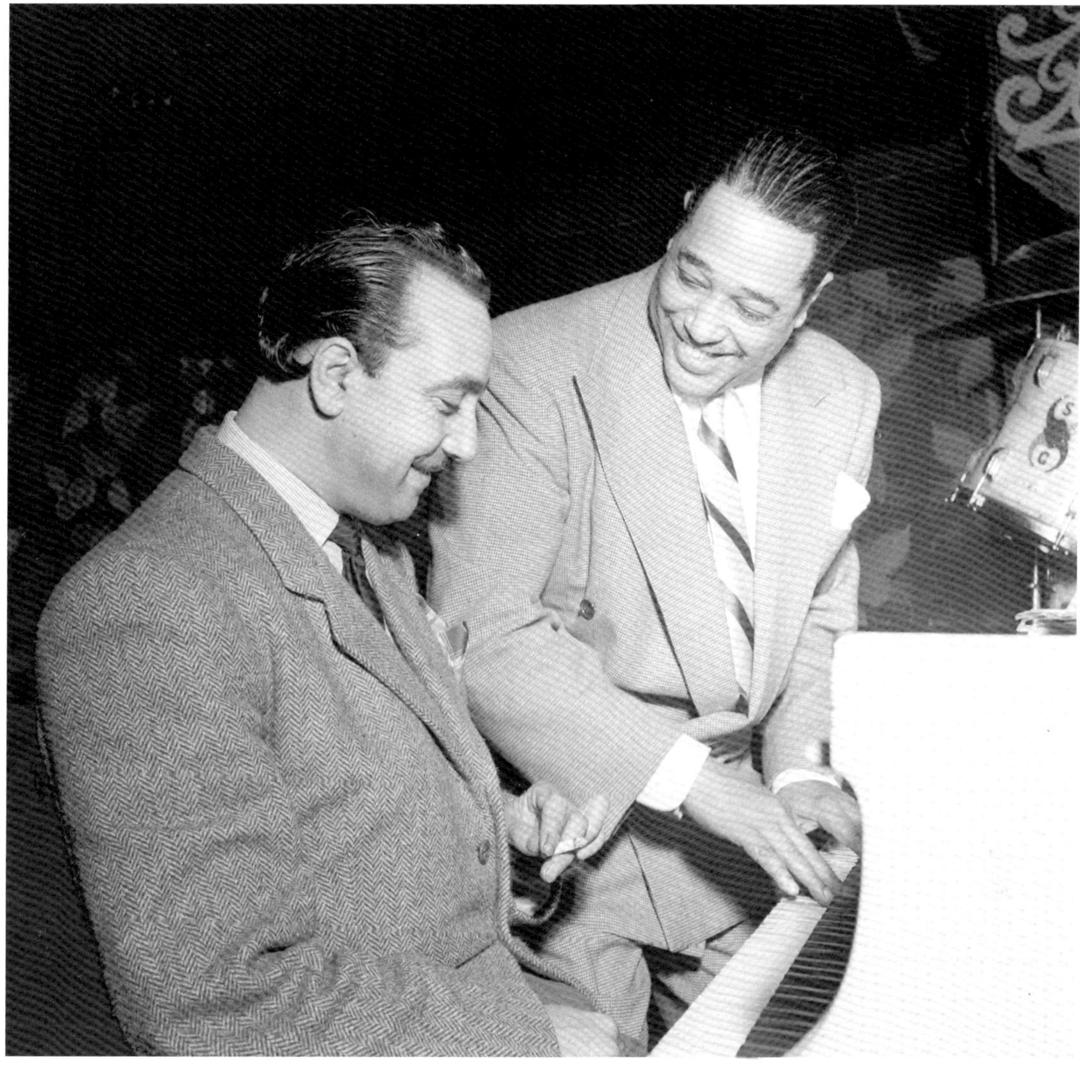

Jazz pianist and bandleader Duke Ellington humoring jazz guitarist Django Reinhardt on the piano at the Aquarium on October 30, 1946. Django arrived in New York City from France to become part of Ellington's Concert Troupe and was thrown a welcoming party by Duke and the Morris Agency. Django would return to France on December 21, 1946, after a successful tour with the Duke Ellington Orchestra.

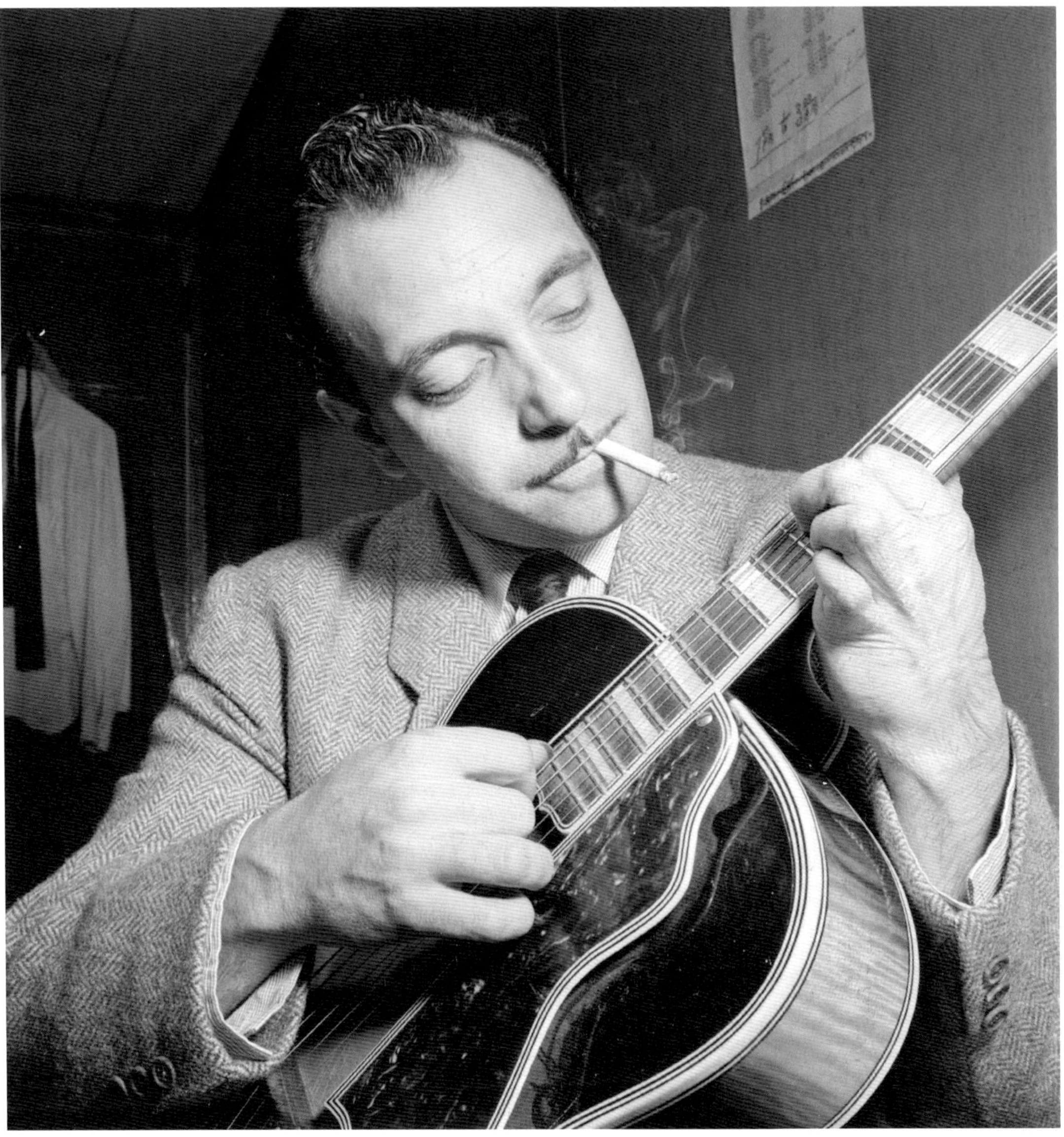

Jazz guitarist Django Reinhardt trying out Ellington guitarist Fred Guy's guitar in the dressing room at the Aquarium on October 30, 1946. Django came to New York on a sixty-day visa without his guitar and had to borrow an electric Gibson ES-300 guitar to be heard in the large US concert halls. Ellington stated, "Django is all artist. One of those musicians who is unable to play a note that's not pretty or in good taste."

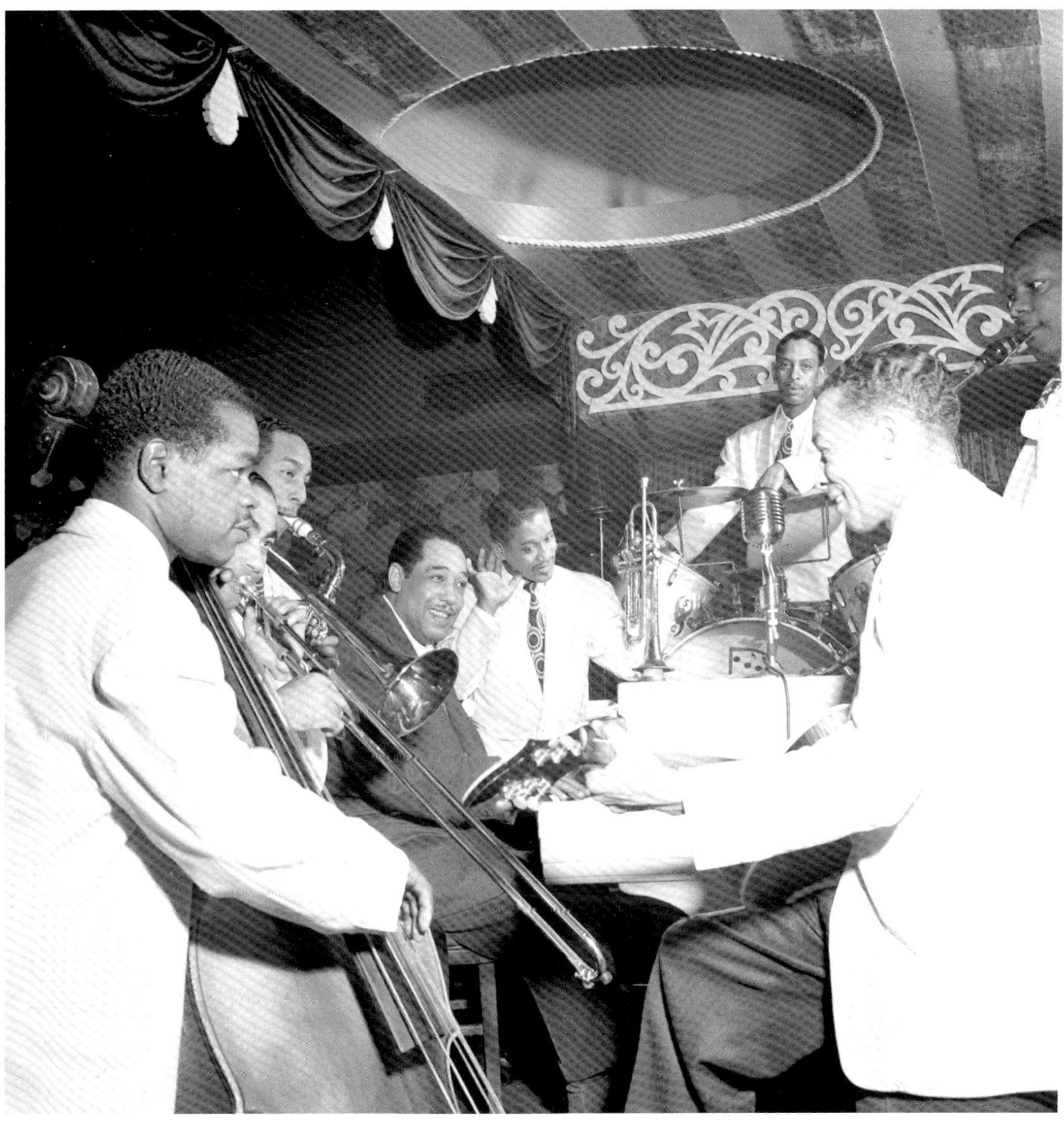

Duke Ellington seated at the piano with a group of his sidemen posing for a candid shot in October 1946. Junior Raglin (bass), Lawrence Brown (trombone), Johnny Hodges (alto sax), Ray Nance (trumpet), Sonny Greer (drums), Fred Guy (guitar), and Harry Carney (baritone sax).

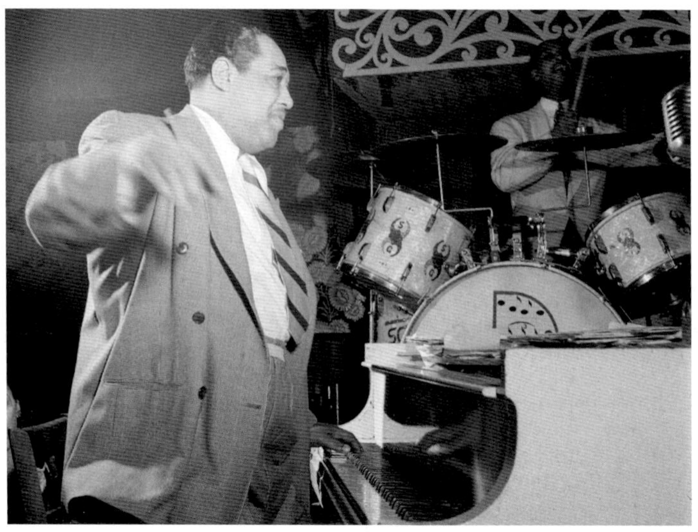

Duke Ellington conducting his orchestra with drummer Sonny Greer in the background at the Aquarium in October 1947

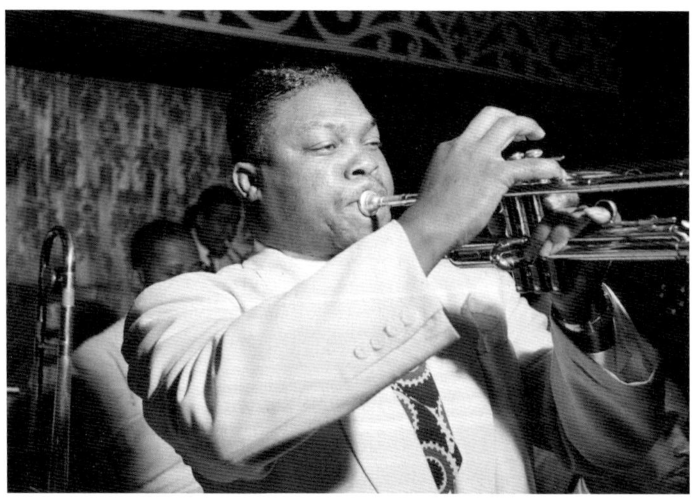

Jazz trumpeter Cat Anderson with the Duke Ellington Orchestra at the Aquarium in October 1947. Cat was known for his high-note playing, being able to play in the extreme high register of the trumpet with great power—up to a triple C.

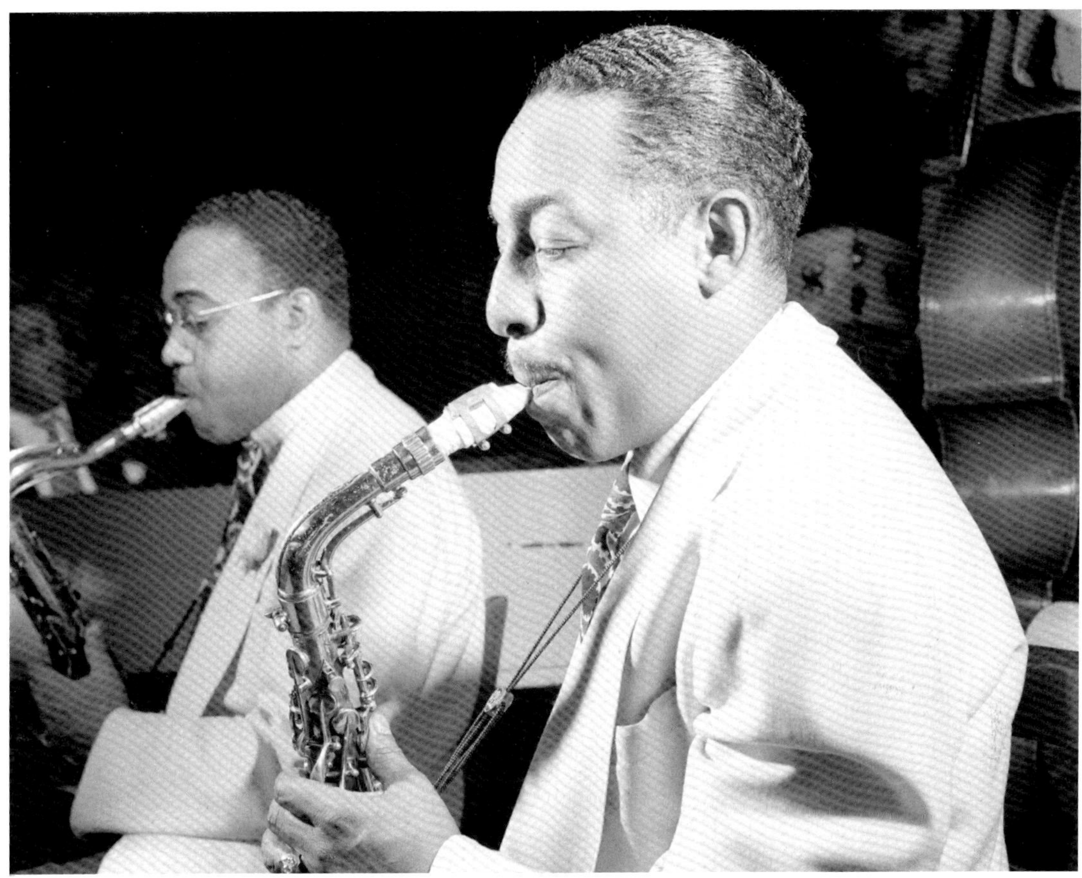

Al Sears (tenor sax) and Johnny Hodges (alto sax) with Ellington at the Aquarium in October 1947. Ellington often stated that Hodges's tone was so beautiful, it sometimes brought tears to his eyes. Both Sears and Hodges would leave Ellington in 1949.

Lunch Dinner Supper

The Aquarium

B. B. INN, INC.

RESTAURANT

GROUND FLOOR

OPEN FROM 10 A. M. TO 2.30 A. M.

38 WEST 52ND ST.
NEW YORK

TELEPHONES
MURRAY HILL 2-8328 · 9725

LUNCH DINNER SUPPER

The New Aquarium

38 WEST 52ND STREET, NEW YORK CITY

BASEMENT

YOU HAVE BEEN DULY ELECTED KEEPER
OF THE FISH

OPENING DAY JUNE 17TH, 1932

Two business cards from the early years of the Aquarium

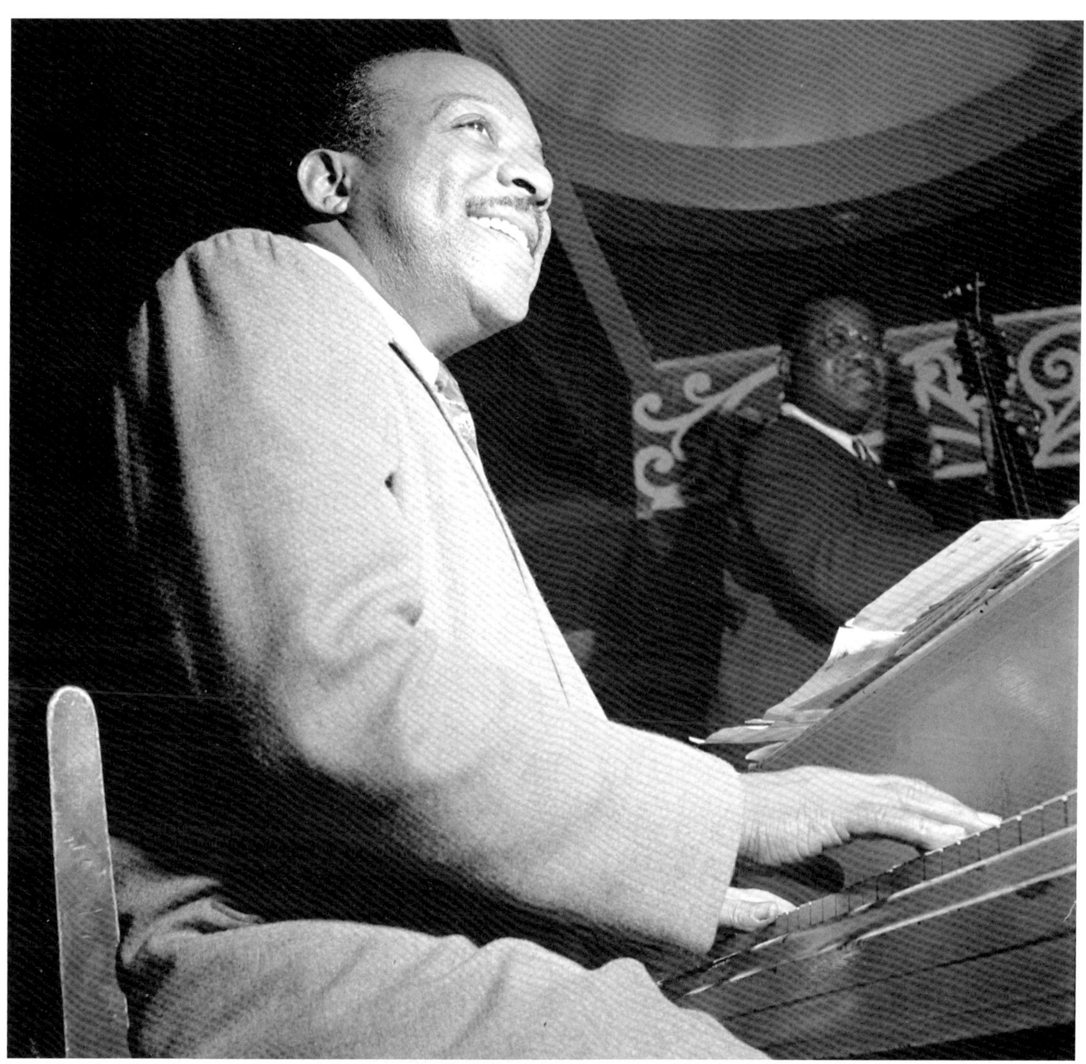

Jazz pianist and bandleader Count Basie at the Aquarium in 1946

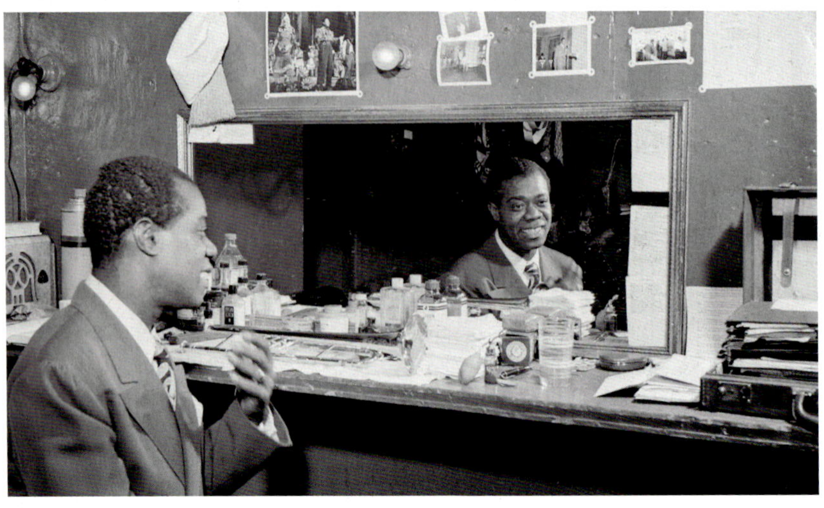

Jazz trumpeter Louis Armstrong in the dressing room at the Aquarium in July 1946

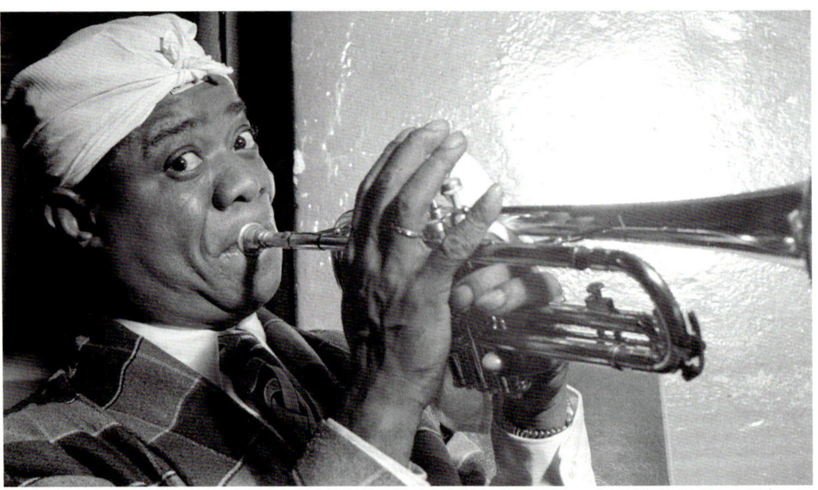

Louis Armstrong warming up in his robe and hair tonic cap backstage between shows at the Aquarium in July 1946

OPPOSITE Blues, swing, and balladeer singer Jimmy Rushing singing with the Count Basie Orchestra at the Aquarium in 1946. Rushing was the featured vocalist with the Basie Orchestra from 1935 to 1948.

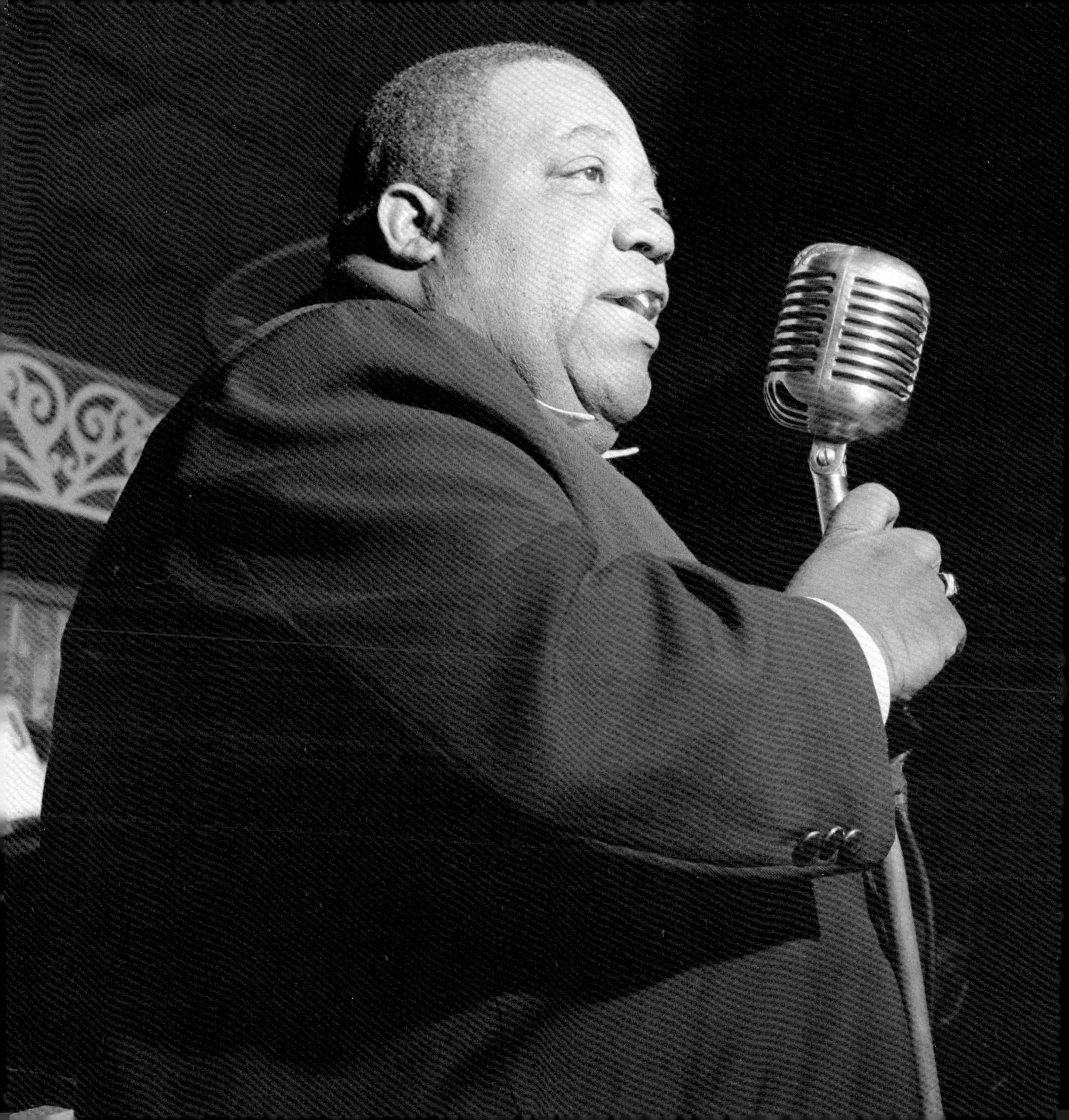

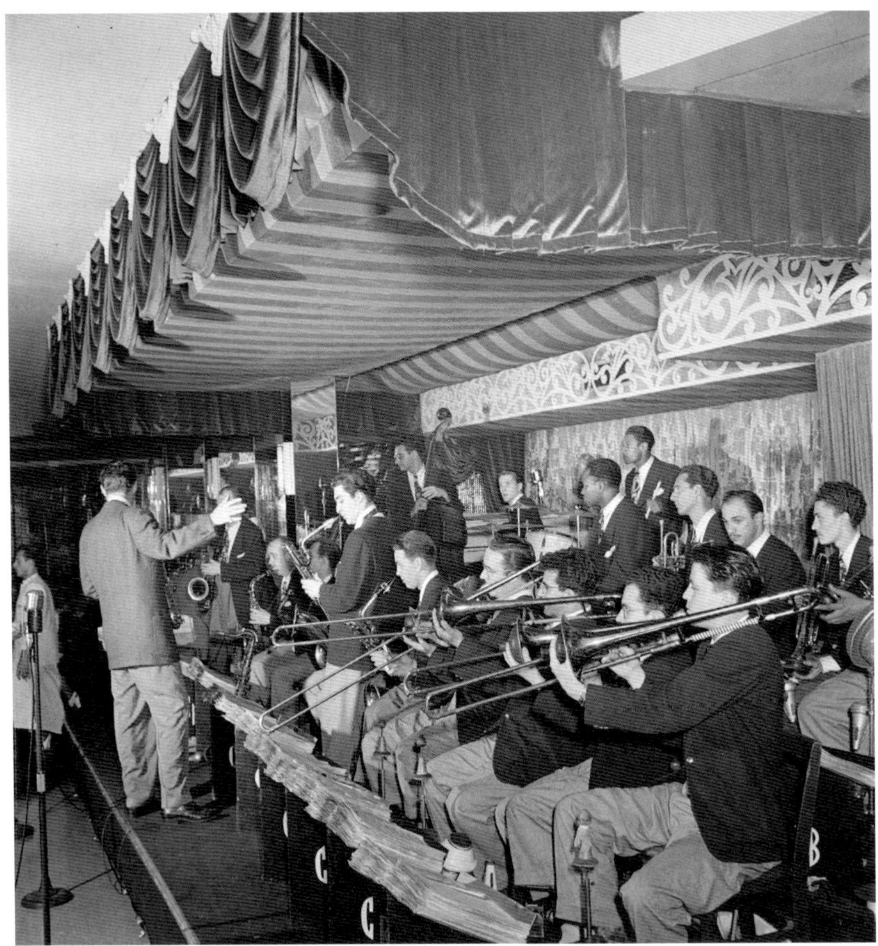

Charlie Barnet Orchestra at the Aquarium in August 1946. That evening the orchestra was broadcasting live on WOR radio in New York City. Trumpets: Jimmy Pupa, Everett McDonald, Al Killian, Guy Chiaverini, Paul Webster, and Art Robey; trombones: Sam Nestro, Porky Martin, Edward Fromm, and Frank Bradley; saxes: Rae De Goer, Gene Kinsey, Kurt Bloom, Dave Matthews, Danny Bank, and Johnny McAfee; rhythm: Bill Miller (piano), Irv Lang (bass), and George Jenkins (drums). Charlie Barnet was on tenor, with vocalist Fran Warren.

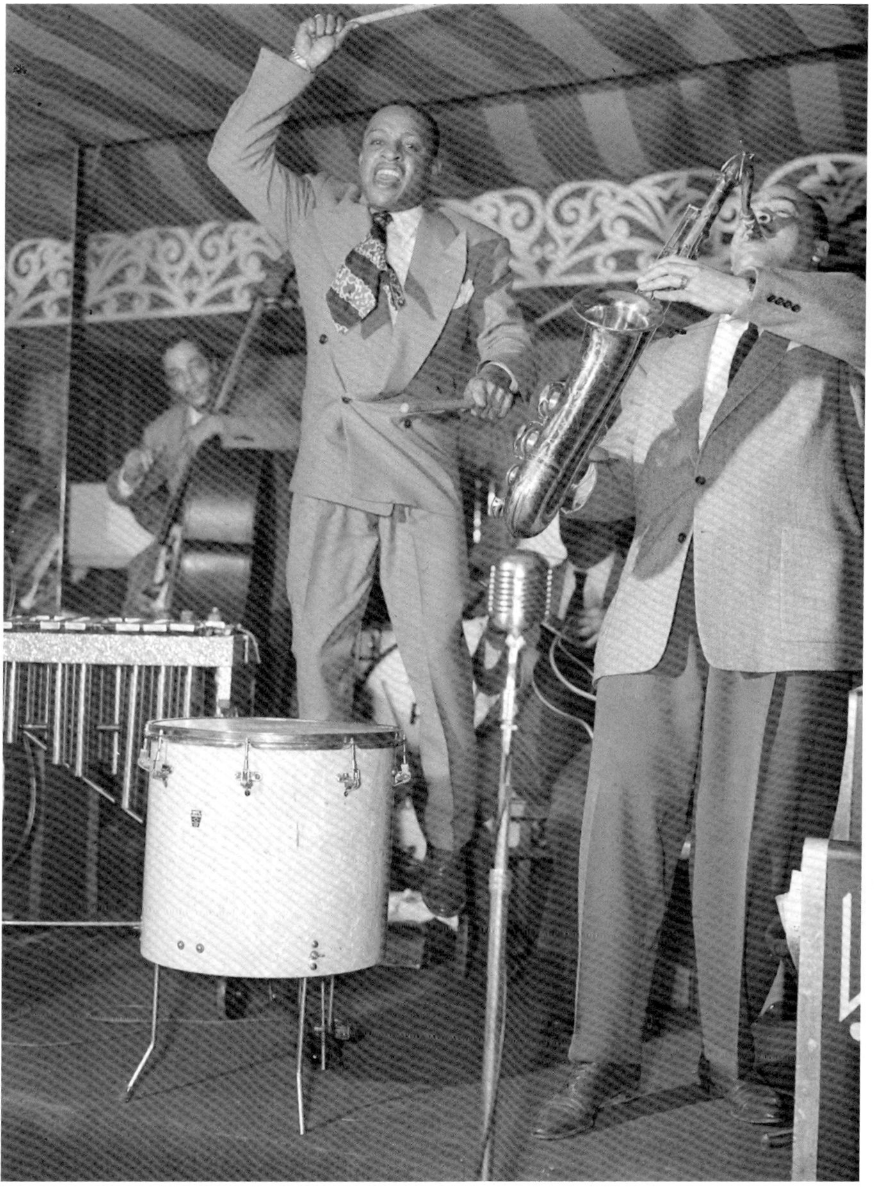

Jazz vibraphonist, percussionist, and bandleader Lionel Hampton with Texas tenor sax sensation Arnett Cobb at the Aquarium in June 1946

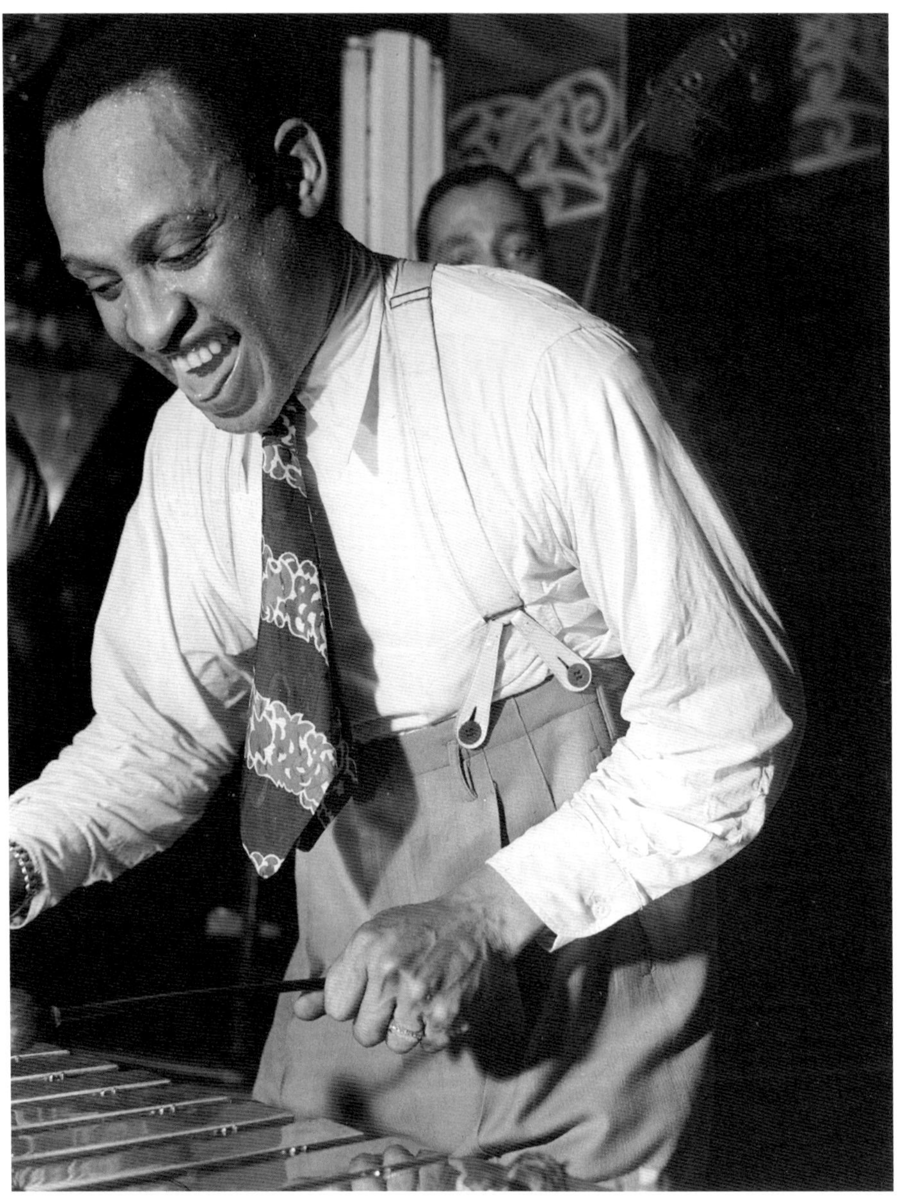

Lionel Hampton soloing on the vibes at the Aquarium in June 1946

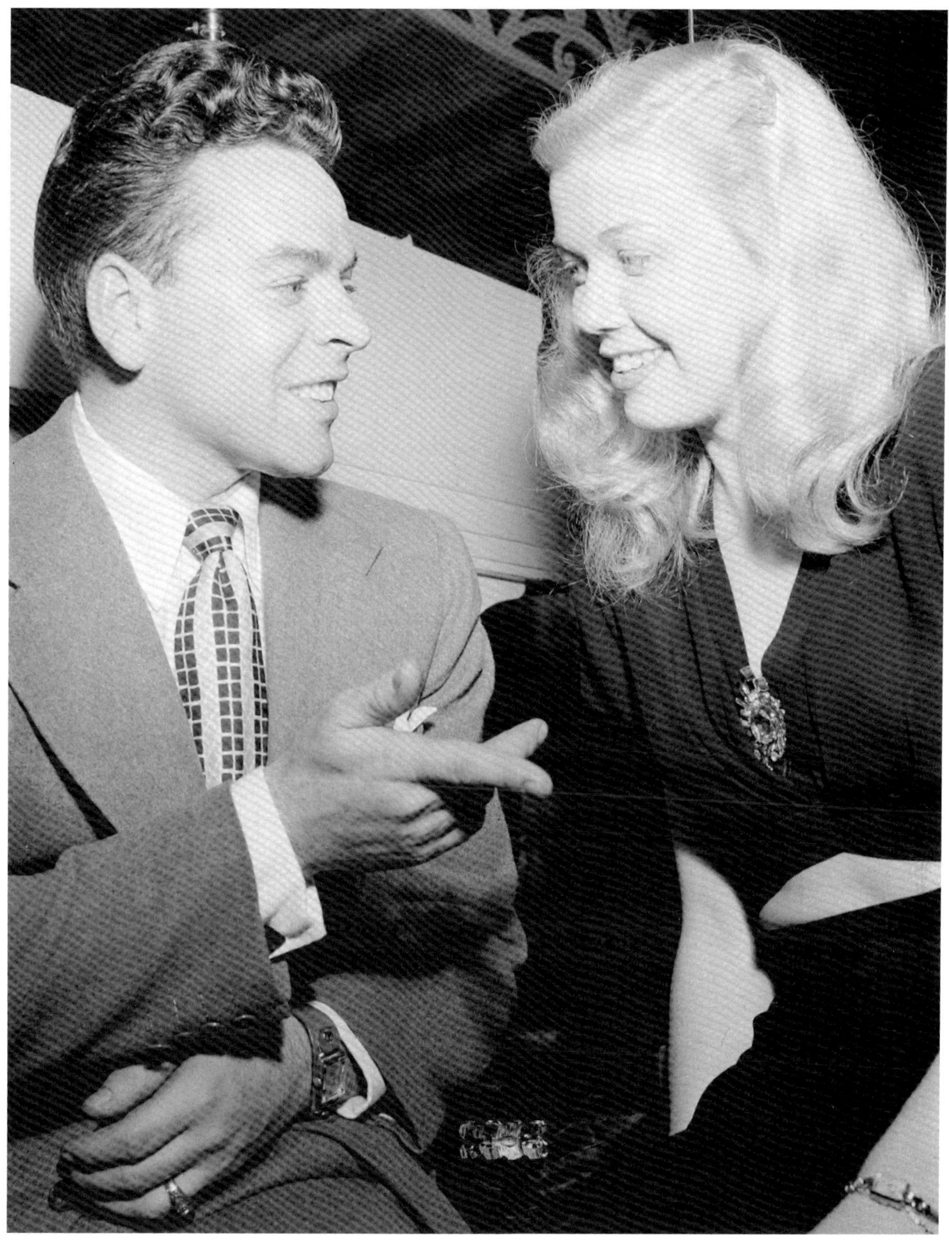

Bandleader Les Brown and singer/actress Doris Day at the Aquarium in July 1946

THE 21 CLUB

The 21 Club at 21 West 52nd Street (an exclusive and expensive restaurant) came into existence when cousins Jack Kriendler and Charlie Berns threw a black-tie party on New Year's Eve in 1929 at their location on 49th Street. When the guests arrived, they were given a bottle of champagne and a pickax and were told to tear everything down. After midnight the club owners announced that they would be relocating the club to 21 West 52nd Street, so the guests proceeded to pick up the iron gate surrounding the 49th Street bar and march it three blocks north, putting it out in front of its current location today.

Before the end of Prohibition in 1933, the 21 Club had safeguards installed in case a federal agent would appear at the club. If an agent were to appear, the doorman would press a button that sounded an alarm at the bar upstairs, notifying the waiters to gather all the bottles and put them on the bar, then pressing an additional button that would slide the bar into a hidden compartment in the wall. The bottles were then tipped into a chute that sent them falling into a specially constructed sandpit that absorbed the alcoholic evidence. The button would also cut off any operating trick doors in the cellar, where bootleg liquor was stored.

Although the 21 Club never had entertainment or live music, it still stands as the longest-lived club on 52nd Street and remains an iconic location for dining by the rich and famous.

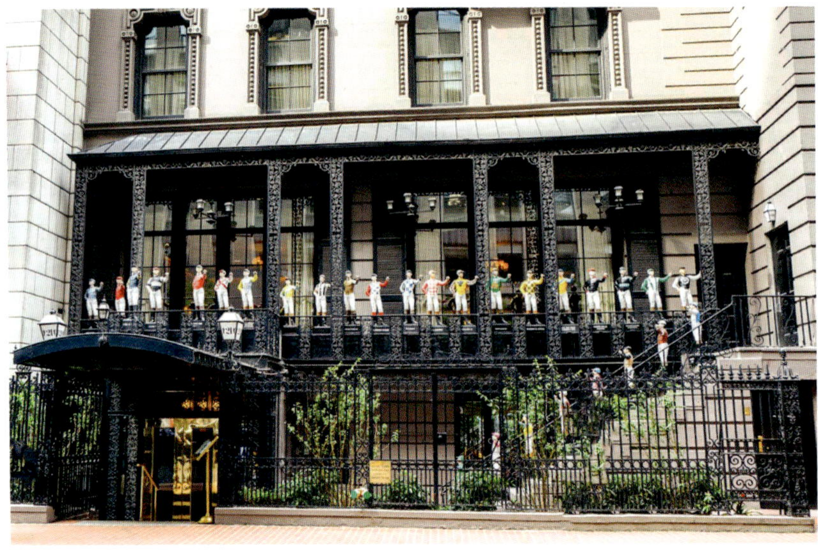

The 21 Club today is still as popular and exclusive as it was in the 1930s. The 21 Club is the sole surviving club existing on 52nd Street.

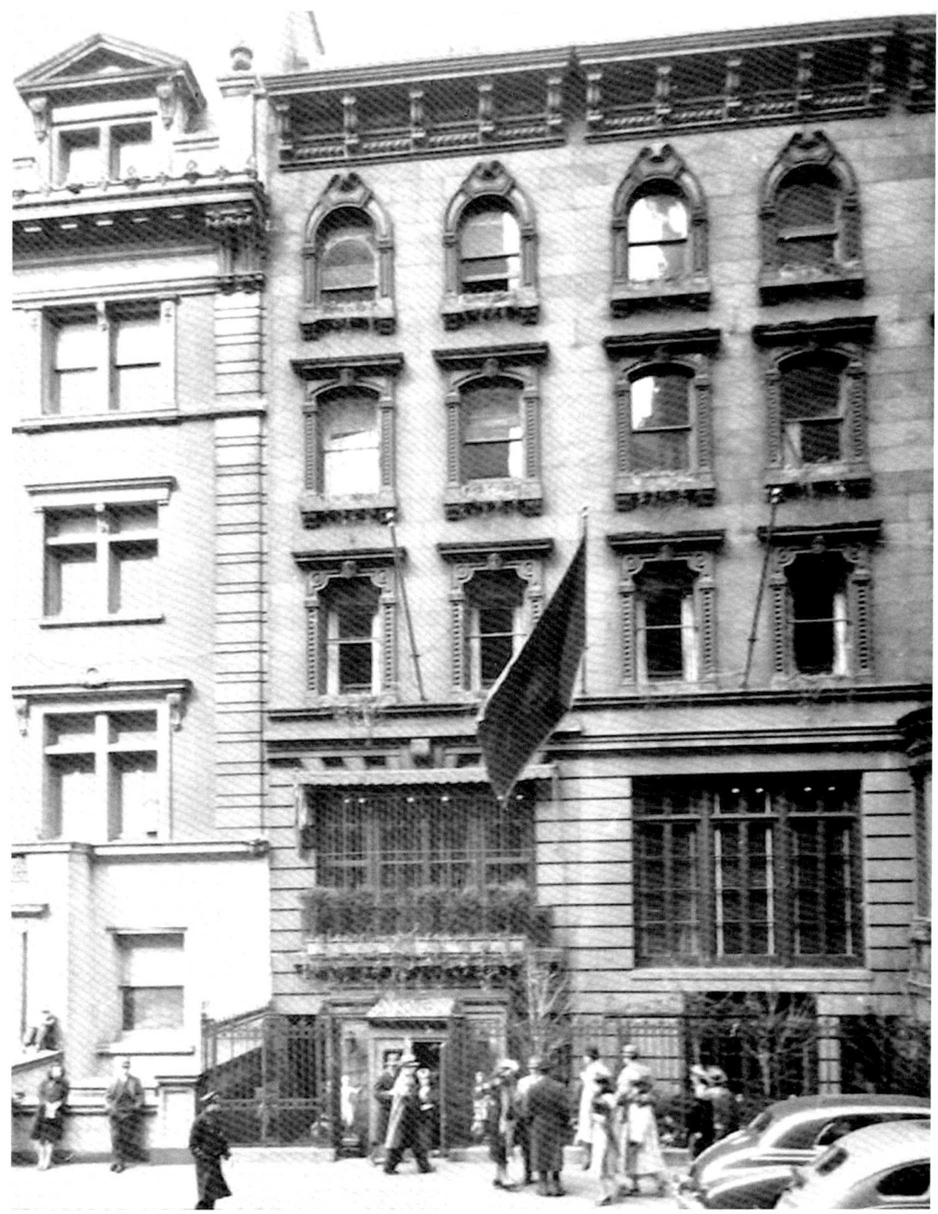

Patrons entering the 21 Club on 52nd Street on a busy afternoon in 1940. The 21 Club was named after its address on 52nd Street.

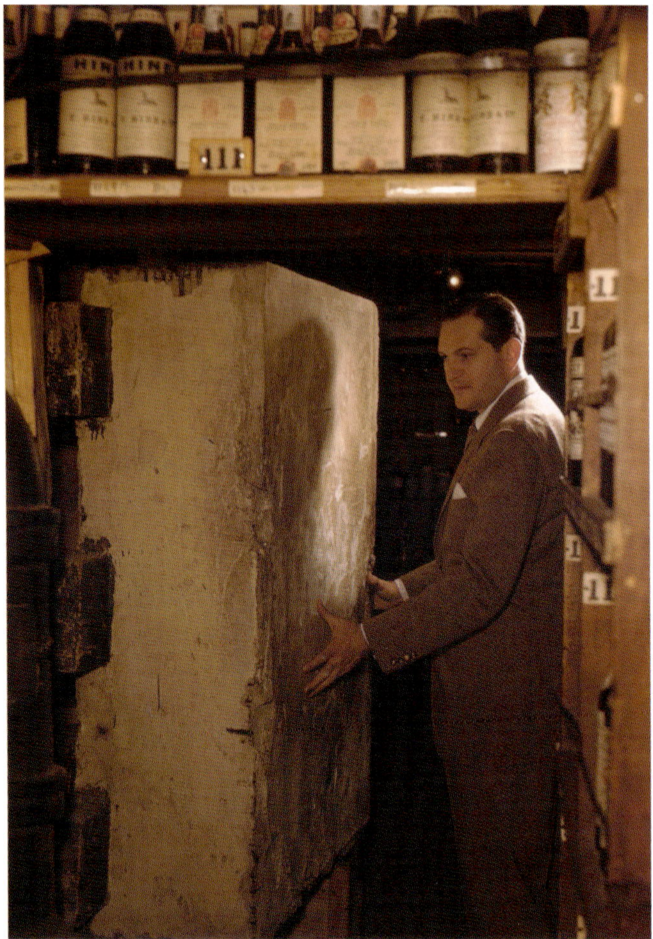

The 21 Club secret wine cellar, used during Prohibition to conceal the wine stock. The "secret" wine cellar was actually located at 19 West 52nd Street, which helped confuse investigators during Prohibition-era liquor raids. The restaurant workers were able to truthfully tell inspectors that there wasn't any booze on the premises.

The "secret" cellar vault door was made to look like an old brick wall in the basement, concealed by a pantry of canned goods and hanging meats. The 2½-ton cement door could be opened only by using a meat skewer placed into one of the cracks in the cement.

LEON & EDDIE'S

Leon & Eddie's was an entertainment cabaret on New York's Swing Street, just west of 5th Avenue. It was situated between the Swing Club and the 21 Club. It was mostly a dinner and show club and not a jazz nightspot.

With an investment of $1,900, singer and emcee Eddie Davis would open a speakeasy in 1928 at 18 West 52nd Street with his partner Leon Enken, naming it Leon & Eddie's. The Prohibition-era speakeasy seated only thirty patrons, but when Prohibition ended in 1933 they moved next to the 21 Club at 33 West 52nd Street, to a location that could seat over 470 customers.

In the beginning the going was hard, and the two partners drew only $10 each as salary every Saturday night. Leon Enken remembers, "I tell you the truth; I was scared to death. I was scared I would fail. I couldn't sleep nights. Then Eddie sang a song one night, a kind of naughty song, and from then on, like magic, we made money."

Most of Leon & Eddie's customers were from out of town, folks who were attracted by the club's risqué entertainment and who wanted to let loose in the big city.

On Sunday nights, however, the customers were more likely to be New Yorkers, especially people in show business. Leon & Eddie's soon developed the reputation of being a place where talented but relatively unknown entertainers could get a chance to strut their stuff. The club's Sunday night celebrity parties would attract a large clientele of show business celebrities, such as Bob Hope, Red Skelton, Milton Berle, Jackie Gleason, and Frank Sinatra, to name just a few.

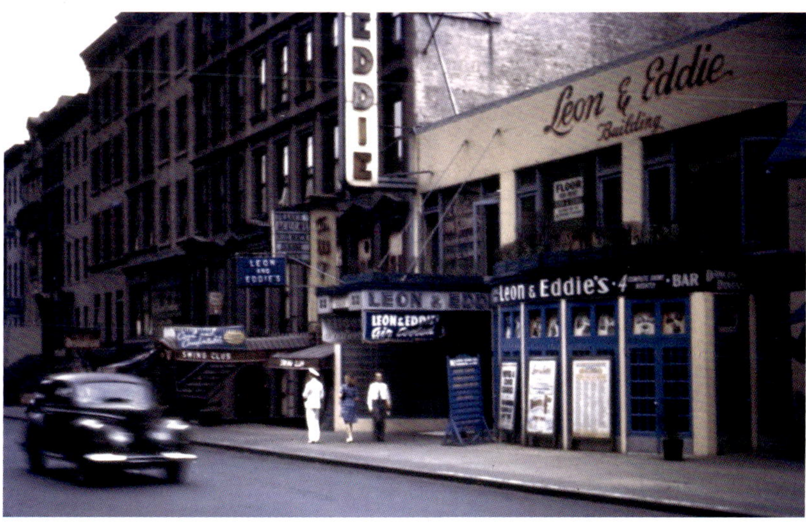

Leon & Eddie's entertainment nightspot at 33 W 52nd Street in the summer of 1943

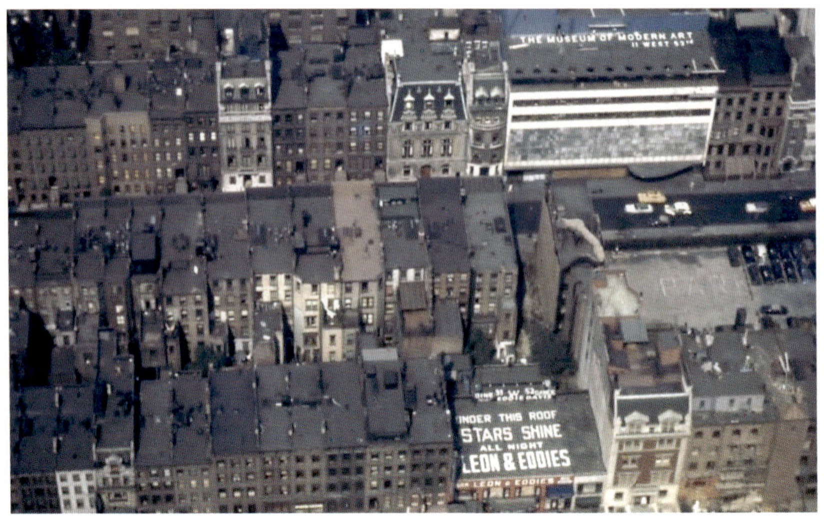

Aerial photo taken from the thirtieth floor of the Rockefeller Center, showing Leon & Eddie's rooftop advertising in the early 1940s. The 21 Club is next door on the right.

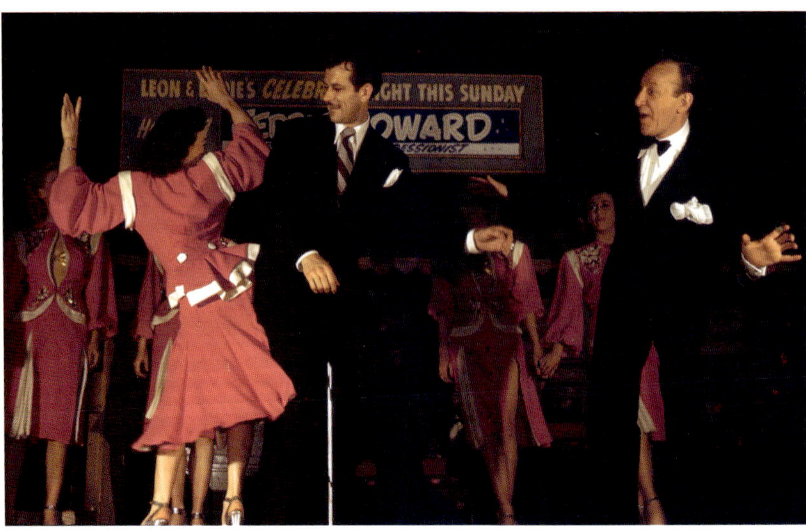

Eddie Davis (*far right*) hosting a dance contest in July 1948

CLUB 18 / DIXON'S / CLUB TROUBADOUR

One of the shortest-lived clubs on 52nd Street had to be Dixon's. During its less-than-a-year run, it briefly revived memories of Swing Street in its days of musical glory. Dixon's was the old Club 18, managed by Freddy Lamb, who refurbished the club with thick rugs and orchid-colored lights. The band it presented was the Joe Mooney Quartet, which brought a steady stream of customers who kept the joint jumping during the fall of 1946.

Once the Mooney Quartet departed, Dixon's failed to maintain its flow of customers. By the fall of 1947, the sign at 131 West 52nd Street read Club Troubadour. Saxophonist Georgie Auld would lead a swinging band at Club Troubadour, bringing in outstanding jazz performers such as Mary Lou Williams, Anita O'Day, and Mildred Bailey. But the existence of the Troubadour was even briefer than that of Dixon's. In a last-ditch effort, they brought in Louis Jordan and His Tympany Five, which proved to be a disaster. And before long the premises were occupied by the Ben Yee Chinese restaurant. By then, many of the clubs east of Sixth Avenue featured striptease dancers, while the clubs west of Sixth Avenue housed so many Chinese eateries that the area became known as Chow Mein Lane. When Ben Yee took over the Club Troubadour address, a columnist wrote: "52nd Street is being strangled by a G-string dipped in soya sauce."

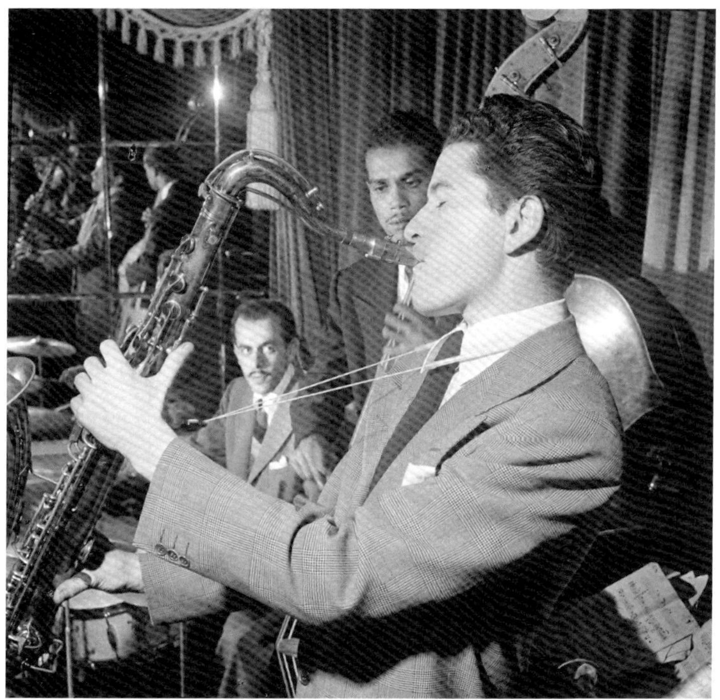

One of the last official bands at Club 18 was Allan Eager and the Be Bop Boys, which included bandleader Allan Eager (tenor sax), Curly Russell (bass), Art Mardigan (drums), and Duke Jordan on piano (not in photo). Club 18 has completed a full circle. After closing as Club 18, it became Dixon's, which upon closing became Club Troubadour, which later became Club 18, finally closing its door permanently. Sadly, this became business as usual on 52nd Street.

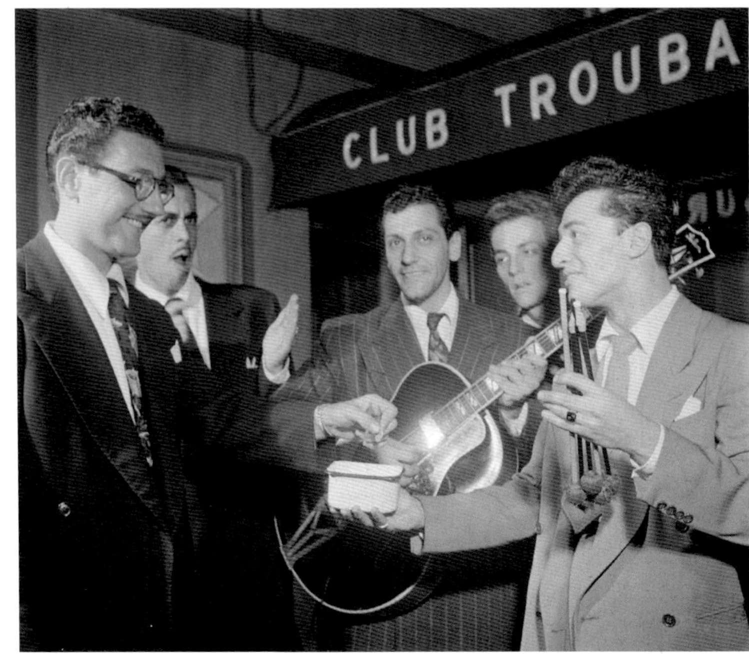

Pianist Bill Bliss, guitarist Bill De Arango, and vibraphonist Terry Gibbs hanging out in front of Club Troubadour in June 1947 for a candid shot. They were playing alongside the Georgie Auld band that evening.

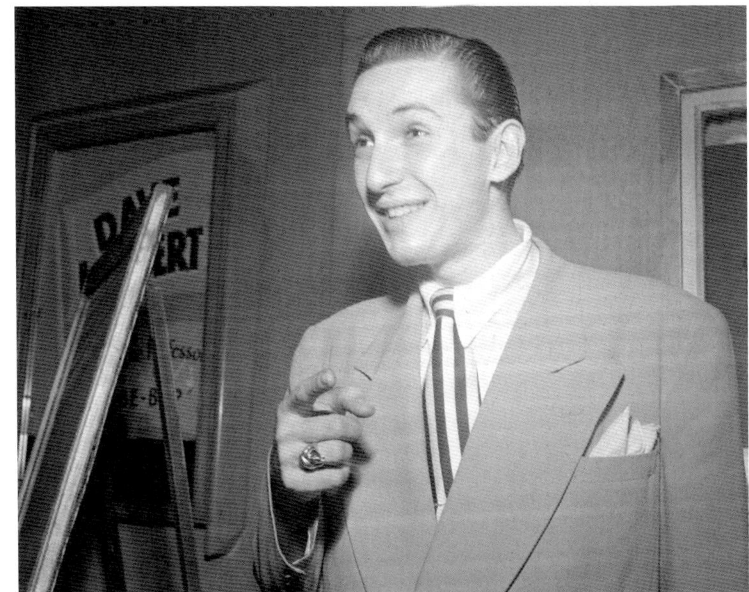

Baritone saxophonist Serge Chaloff taking ten outside Club Troubadour in June 1947. He was playing with the Georgie Auld Orchestra that night. Also working the club that night was jazz vocalist Dave Lambert, who would later become famous as part of the jazz-singing trio Lambert, Hendricks, and Ross.

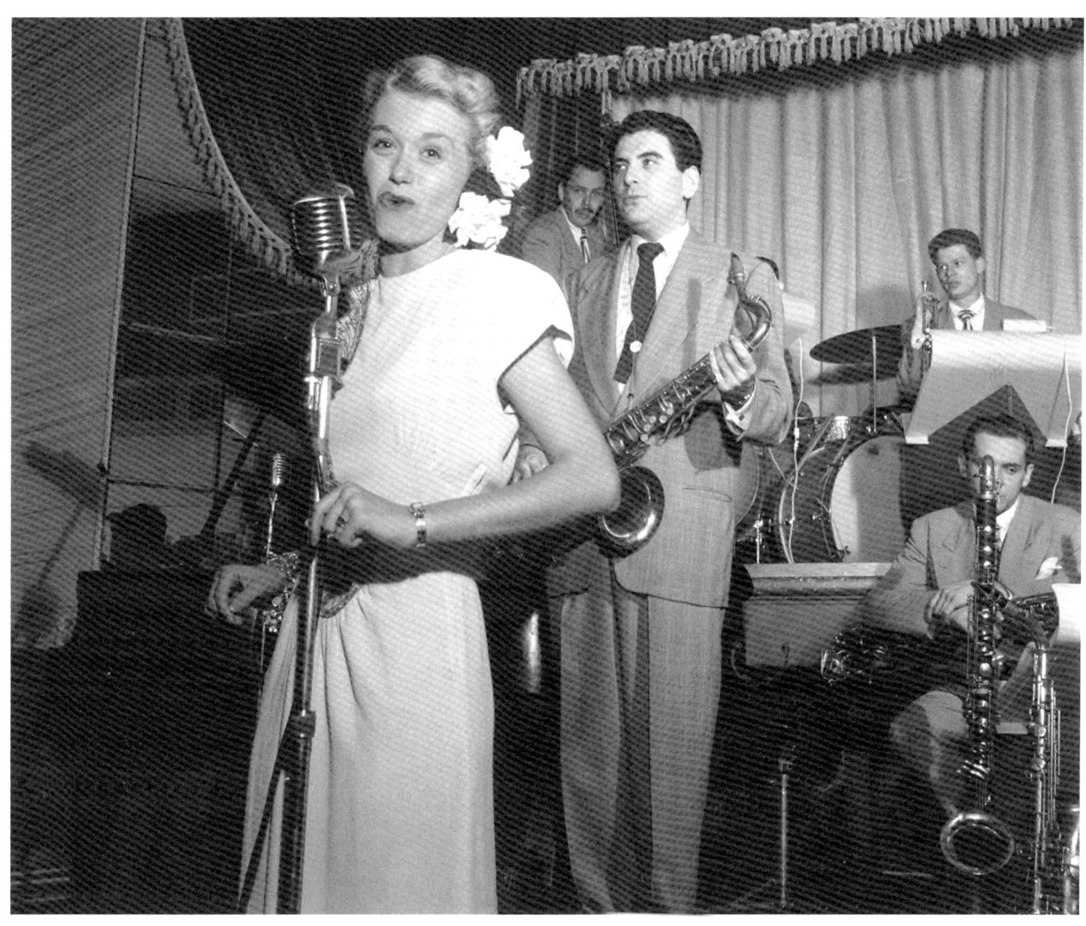

Georgie Auld Orchestra featuring vocalist June Christy at Club Troubadour in September 1947, with Red Rodney on trumpet

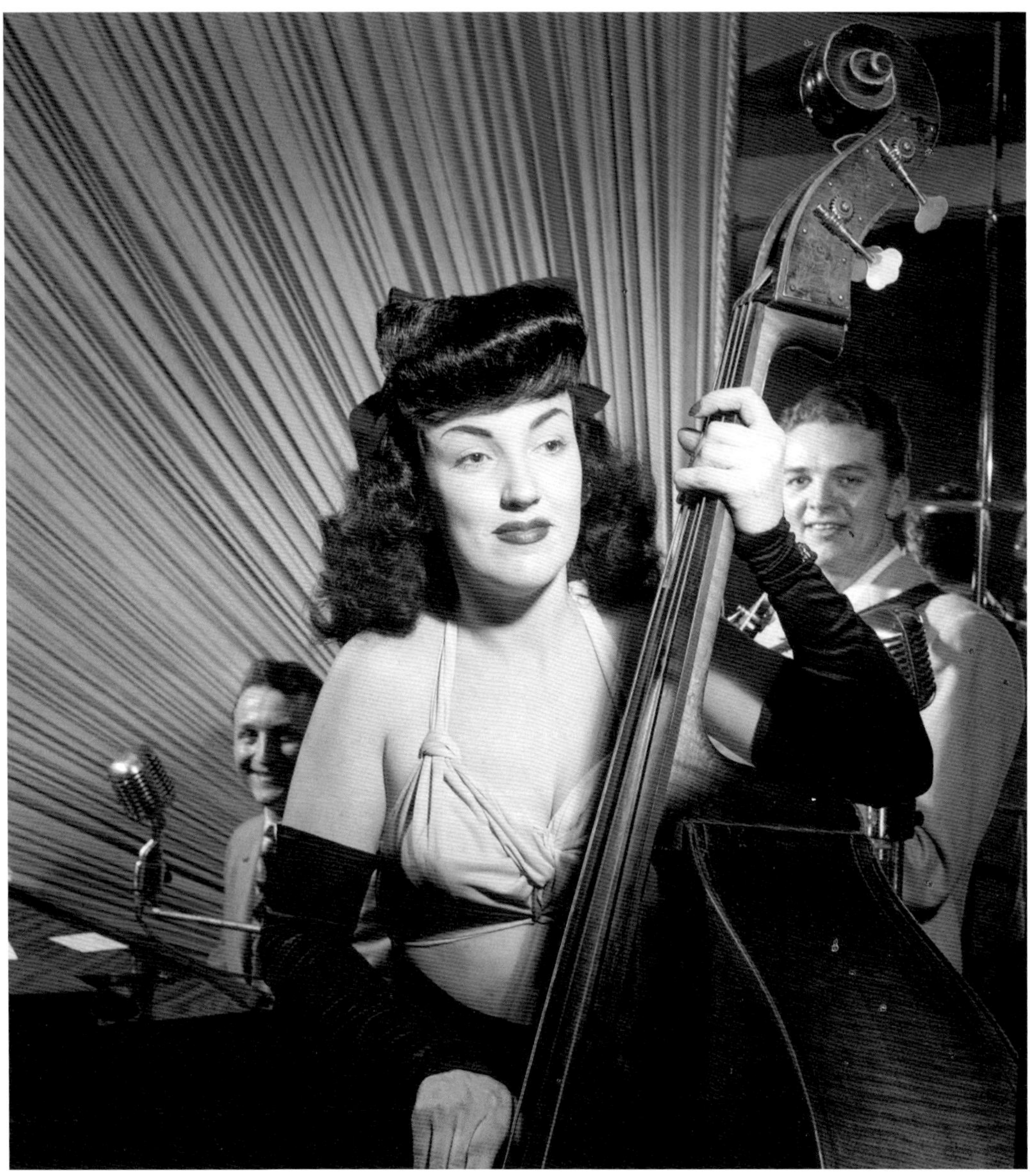

The Vivien Garry Trio at Dixon's in May 1947: Vivien Garry (bass), Teddy Kaye (piano), and Vivien's husband, Arv Garrison (guitar). Vivien was the only female bassist to ever play on 52nd Street. In 1946, Vivien would form Vivien Garry and Her All-Girl Band, recording and filming "A Woman's Place Is in the Groove."

CHAPTER FOUR

BIOGRAPHIES OF SELECT 52ND STREET MUSICIANS

Charlie Barnet (1913–1991). New York City, New York. Tenor saxophonist and bandleader Charlie Barnet was known for his unique sound and hard-swinging style on the saxophone. In the mid-1930s, Charlie was one of the first bandleaders to integrate his band. His band would record hit versions of "Cherokee" and "Skyliner."

Count Basie (1904–1984). Red Bank, New Jersey. A legendary big-band leader, pianist, and composer, forming his first band in 1935 and successfully leading them for over fifty years. Basie was a huge draw on 52nd Street, starting off at the Famous Door in 1938; he would perform such standards as "One O'Clock Jump," "Shiny Stockings," and "Lil' Darlin'."

Sidney Bechet (1897–1959). New Orleans, Louisiana. Known for his soprano saxophone work, Bechet never achieved worldwide acclaim until the late 1940s. He moved to France in 1950, where he found well-paid work and a surge in his popularity. He would compose and record the international hit "Petite Fleur" in 1952.

Louie Bellson (1924–2009). Rock Falls, Illinois. Drummer, composer, and bandleader Louis Bellson worked with most of the big bands during the 1940s and 1950s. Duke Ellington once called him "the world's greatest drummer." A prolific composer, Bellson wrote more than 1,000 compositions and arrangements during his lifetime.

Pete Brown (1906–1963). Baltimore, Maryland. Jazz alto saxophonist Pete Brown began working on 52nd Street both as a sideman and a bandleader. A swinging balladeer and restless improviser, Brown would establish the "jump" style that led to R&B and later rock & roll.

Barbara Carroll (1925–2017). Worcester, Massachusetts. Jazz pianist and vocalist Carroll worked steady on 52nd Street during the 1940s with her trio. Being dubbed "the first lady of bebop," she would later in life receive the coveted Mary Lou Williams / Women in Jazz Lifetime Achievement Award.

Benny Carter (1907–2003). Harlem, New York City, New York. Multi-instrumentalist, composer/arranger, and bandleader, Carter was known for defining the sound of the alto saxophone, and for his eighty-year career in jazz. Playing 52nd Street during the early 1940s, Carter would go on to achieve numerous awards, including the National Medal of Arts in 2000.

Arnett Cobb (1918–1989). Houston, Texas. Originator of the "Southern Preacher" style of playing with that bar-walking tenor saxophone sound, earning him the nickname "Wild Man of the Tenor Sax." Cobb would captivate audiences worldwide with his uninhibited playing style.

Nat "King" Cole (1919–1965). Montgomery, Alabama. Jazz pianist, vocalist, and TV host, Nat would become the first African American to host his own variety program. In the early years, Cole would lead his own trio for over a decade, playing 52nd Street in the early 1940s and becoming a successful recording artist from the late 1940s to the mid-1960s.

Eddie Condon (1905–1973). Goodland, Indiana. Bandleader, jazz rhythm guitarist, and leading figure in Chicago jazz, Condon was known for his wisecracking, fast-talking style. Condon worked with many of the acts on 52nd Street during the 1930s and 1940s, eventually opening his own club, "Eddie Condon's," in New York City.

Tadd Dameron (1917–1965). Cleveland, Ohio. Jazz pianist, composer, and arranger, Dameron was the most influential arranger of the bebop era, composing several bop and swing standards, including "Hot House" and "If You Could See Me Now." Tadd played at many of the 52nd Street clubs with his sextet during the 1940s.

Miles Davis (1926–1991). Alton, Illinois. Jazz trumpeter and one of the most recognized and influential jazz artists, having been involved with almost every important innovation and stylistic development in music. Miles's trumpet sound was instantly recognizable, and many of his original compositions became classics, such as "All Blues," "Nardis," and "Milestones." Miles was a regular on 52nd Street with Charlie Parker.

Billy Eckstine (1914–1993). Pittsburgh, Pennsylvania. Legendary singer of ballads and bandleader of the swing era, Eckstine was known for his smooth baritone voice and distinctive vibrato. The Billy Eckstine Orchestra was the first bop big band of its time on 52nd Street during the 1940s, employing many up-and-coming jazz artists.

Harry "Sweets" Edison (1915–1999). Columbus, Ohio. Jazz trumpeter, bandleader, and member of the Count Basie Orchestra at the Famous Door on 52nd Street in 1938, Edison was one of the hardest-swinging, bluesiest jazz trumpeters of the twentieth century.

Roy Eldridge (1911–1989). Pittsburgh, Pennsylvania. Nicknamed "Little Jazz," Eldridge was an exciting trumpeter with a competitive spirit and chance-taking soloing style, always pushing himself to the limit. Roy was regarded as the key trumpet stylist of the 1930s, as Louis Armstrong was of the 1920s.

Duke Ellington (1899–1974). Washington, DC. Pianist, composer, and originator of big-band jazz, Duke would lead the Duke Ellington Orchestra from 1923 until his passing in 1974. Duke composed thousands of scores during his fifty-year career, including the swing hits "Satin Doll" and "It Don't Mean a Thing If It Ain't Got That Swing."

Ella Fitzgerald (1917–1996). Newport News, Virginia. The "First Lady of Song"; Ella's beautiful voice and wide range could outswing anyone. A brilliant scat singer who always sounded and looked happy to be singing. During her lengthy career, Ella won thirteen Grammys and would become a dominant figure and drawing card on 52nd Street.

Slim Gaillard (1916–1991). Detroit, Michigan. Jazz singer and multi-instrumentalist who was noted for his comedic "vocalese" singing (scat singing using improvised nonsense syllables) such as "Bee Bop Da Bwee Dee." Gaillard worked at many of the 52nd Street clubs during their heydays.

Erroll Garner (1923–1977). Pittsburgh, Pennsylvania. A brilliant jazz pianist and composer with one of the most distinctive sounds of all time. Garner played with such enthusiasm, having the ability to play stunning runs while displaying pure joy. His ballad composition "Misty" has become a jazz standard.

Harry "the Hipster" Gibson (1915–1991). New York City, New York. Jazz pianist, singer, and songwriter; Harry's playing style was stride and boogie-woogie, while singing in a wild, eccentric, unrestrained style. He became a hit on 52nd Street playing and singing his original songs such as "Who Put the Benzedrine in Mrs. Murphy's Ovaltine."

Dizzy Gillespie (1917–1993). Cheraw, South Carolina. Jazz trumpeter, bandleader, and composer whose combination of musicianship and showmanship made him a leading figure in jazz. Along with Parker in the 1940s, Dizzy was a dominant force in the creation of bebop and modern jazz, with standards such as "Groovin' High" and "A Night in Tunisia." Gillespie played on 52nd Street during the 1930s and 1940s.

Benny Goodman (1909–1986). Chicago, Illinois. Bandleader and jazz clarinetist known as the "King of Swing," Benny was one of the most popular figures of the swing era, having a distinctive sound for big band and combos alike. Benny worked on 52nd Street during the early 1930s and would continue to perform to sold-out audiences for over fifty years.

Lionel Hampton (1908–2002). Louisville, Kentucky. Bandleader, drummer, and vibraphonist, Lionel was the first jazz vibraphonist, working with Armstrong and Goodman before forming his own big band in 1940, rising to prominence with such hits as "Flying Home," "Hamp's Boogie Woogie," and "Hey! Ba-Ba-Re-Bop."

Coleman Hawkins (1904–1969). Saint Joseph, Missouri. Pioneer of the tenor saxophone and influential to many up-and-coming jazz musicians, Coleman was always at the top of his game and will forever be remembered for his performance on the ballad "Body and Soul."

Woody Herman (1913–1987). Milwaukee, Wisconsin. Starting off in vaudeville as "the Boy Wonder of the Clarinet," Herman led one of the most varied and successful big bands (Thundering Herd) in the history of jazz. His famous showstoppers were "Woodchopper's Ball," "Four Brothers," and "Caldonia."

Billie Holiday (1915–1959). Philadelphia, Pennsylvania. One of the most influential singers in the history of jazz. Her poignant renditions of songs and incredible depth of emotion added a new dimension to jazz singing. Billie would become the brightest star on 52nd Street during the 1930s and 1940s, going on to become a jazz legend.

John Kirby (1908–1952). Winchester, Virginia. Jazz bassist and bandleader Kirby would successfully take over and lead the "Onyx Club Boys" from 1937 to the early 1940s on 52nd Street, later known as "the Biggest Little Band in the Land." They would record trumpeter Charlie Shavers's composition and arrangement of "Undecided."

Wingy Manone (1900–1982). New Orleans, Louisiana. Dixieland trumpeter whose jivey vocal singing style was reminiscent of his contemporary Louis Prima. The nickname Wingy was due to the loss of his right arm at ten from a streetcar accident. Wingy and his orchestra starred at the Hickory House on 52nd Street from 1935 to 1937.

Joe Marsala (1907–1978). Chicago, Illinois. Jazz clarinetist and composer Marsala was a talented swing clarinetist, leading his own group at the Hickory House from 1937 to 1947. He later retired from full-time playing in 1948 to work in music publishing. He would marry harpist Adele Girard in 1937, who was then a member of his group.

Marian McPartland (1918–2013). Slough, United Kingdom. Jazz pianist, writer, and composer, McPartland was harmonically and rhythmically complex, as well as an inventive improviser. Marian led her own trio at the Hickory House on 52nd Street from 1952 to 1960, which included drummer Joe Morello and bassist Bill Crow.

Thelonious Monk (1917–1982). Rocky Mount, North Carolina. Pianist, composer, and one of the first creators of modern jazz, Monk had a playful improvisational style that featured dissonances, with a percussive piano approach. Many of his compositions have become jazz standards, including "Well, You Needn't," "Blue Monk," and "'Round Midnight."

Fats Navarro (1923–1950). Key West, Florida. Jazz trumpet virtuoso and one of the founders of bebop, Navarro was a leading trumpeter in the 1940s, working with Tadd Dameron, Allan Eager, and Kenny Clarke on Swing Street, often sitting in with bands such as Charlie Parker at the Three Deuces.

Red Norvo (1908–1999). Beardstown, Illinois. Jazz vibraphonist and marimba player Norvo and his wife, singer Mildred Bailey, were known as "Mr. and Mrs. Swing." Red worked with such names as Paul Whiteman, Benny Goodman, and Woody Herman, later putting together a trio with guitarist Tal Farlow and bassist Charles Mingus in the 1950s.

Oran "Hot Lips" Page (1908–1954). Dallas, Texas. Jazz trumpeter, singer, and bandleader Page was a scorching soloist and powerful vocalist, becoming a popular and successful performer on 52nd Street from the late 1930s to the 1950s. He was known as "Mr. After Hours" because of his ability to take on challengers in late-night jam sessions.

Charlie Parker (1920–1955). Kansas City, Kansas. Jazz alto saxophonist Charlie Parker is arguably one of the greatest jazz saxophonists of all time, as well as a one of the founders of bebop. A master soloist with incredible technique, Charlie Parker would popularize bebop playing on 52nd Street in the 1940s.

Oscar Pettiford (1922–1960). Okmulgee, Oklahoma. Jazz bassist and composer Oscar Pettiford was one of the top bass players of his time, a bop pioneer. He would colead one of the first bebop groups at the Onyx Club on 52nd Street with Dizzy Gillespie, which included Lester Young, George Wallington, and Max Roach.

Bud Powell (1924–1966). Harlem, New York. A giant of the jazz piano, and the most important pianist in the bebop style, Powell was influenced at an early age by Art Tatum and was later tutored by Thelonious Monk. Bud's immeasurable contribution and influence on other musicians were astounding.

Louis Prima (1910–1978). New Orleans, Louisiana. Singer, songwriter, actor, bandleader, and trumpeter; Prima's distinctive sound encompassed New Orleans–style jazz, boogie-woogie, and jump blues. He and his band, "the New Orleans Gang," would officially open the Famous Door on 52nd Street to rave revues and sold-out audiences, adopting their signature hit song, "Way Down Yonder in New Orleans."

Buddy Rich (1917–1987). Brooklyn, New York. One of the best jazz drummers and big-band leaders in the history of jazz, recognized for his amazing technique, speed, power, and precision. His impressive career spanned over sixty years, from working as a child star in vaudeville to leading his own world-famous big band for decades.

Max Roach (1924–2007). Newland, North Carolina. Drummer, percussionist, composer, and a pioneer of bebop, Roach is considered one of the most important and influential jazz drummers in history. Having worked with the who's who of the jazz world, Max was awarded many musical achievement awards and honorary doctorate degrees.

George Shearing (1919–2011). London, England. Pianist with a unique quintet sound, which featured piano, vibraphone, electric guitar, bass, and drums. Shearing composed over 300 musical compositions, which included the jazz standard "Lullaby of Birdland," composed in 1952 while he was working at Birdland.

Stuff Smith (1909–1967). Portsmouth, Ohio. Jazz violinist Stuff Smith was undoubtedly one of the three greatest swing and prebop violinists of the early twentieth century. A virtuosic and technically adventurous player, getting his major break forming his sextet and taking residency at the Onyx on 52nd Street in 1936 with his "Onyx Club Boys."

Slam Stewart (1914–1987). Englewood, New Jersey. Jazz double bassist Slam Stewart was a swing bassist who had the unique ability to bow the bass and hum the solo lines an octave apart. During the late 1930s, Slam would team up with guitarist Slim Gaillard, forming the group "Slim and Slam," working at the Hickory House on 52nd Street.

Maxine Sullivan (1911–1987). Homestead, Pennsylvania. Jazz vocalist Maxine Sullivan was known for her cool, soothing style of singing. During the late 1930s, Maxine performed as the main act at the Onyx Club on 52nd Street alongside the John Kirby band, later recording her signature piece, a swing version of "Loch Lomond."

Art Tatum (1909–1956). Toledo, Ohio. One of the greatest and most influential jazz pianists of all time. Tatum's virtuosic technique set the new standard for all jazz pianists. His speed, precision, and creative imagination kept him in a league of his own. Art's performances of "Tiger Rag" and "Tea for Two" showcase his mastery of stride piano.

Billy Taylor (1921–2010). Greenville, North Carolina. Jazz pianist, composer, and educator Taylor was flexible playing many styles of jazz, moving to New York City in 1942 to work on 52nd Street with such major jazz musicians as Stuff Smith, Ben Webster, and Slam Stewart, among others. Later in the 1950s he would form his own trio.

Jack Teagarden (1905–1964). Vernon, Texas. Jazz trombonist and singer Jack Teagarden was an exceptional prebop trombonist, vocalist, and daring soloist. Nicknamed "Big T" because of his large Texan stature, Jack would play 52nd Street with his bands and was known to often sit in with many other bands on Swing Street in a single evening.

Lennie Tristano (1919–1978). Chicago, Illinois. Pianist, composer, arranger, and educator, Lennie moved to New York City in the late 1940s, performing with Charlie Parker and Dizzy Gillespie. His complex harmonic and rhythmic approach to jazz improvisation was ahead of its time and was often misunderstood by critics and listeners alike.

Sarah Vaughan (1924–1990). Newark, New Jersey. Jazz singer with a four-octave vocal range, from soprano to baritone, and a variety of vocal textures, including a remarkable scat-singing ability. "The Divine One" or "Sassy," as she was affectionately named, starred on 52nd Street on many an occasion.

Dinah Washington (1924–1963). Tuscaloosa, Alabama. Jazz singer with the title of "Queen of the Blues" was one of the most popular vocalists and recording artists of the 1950s. Her gritty, high-pitched voice, clarity of diction, and bluesy phrasing packed clubs and concert halls from New York to Vegas.

Ben Webster (1909–1973). Kansas City, Missouri. One of the three most important swing tenor saxophonists, along with Lester Young and Coleman Hawkins; was affectionately known as "the Brute." Webster's sound on tenor could be warm and tender on ballads, and large and raspy on stomps. Known for his work with Fletcher Henderson and Duke Ellington.

Mary Lou Williams (1910–1981). Atlanta, Georgia. Jazz pianist, arranger, and composer, Williams was one of greatest female jazz musicians, with a long and productive career of over fifty years, always evolving musically but never forgetting her roots in the older styles. She wrote and arranged music for many of famous jazz artists of the day.

Teddy Wilson (1912–1986). Austin, Texas. Jazz pianist Teddy Wilson was a solid and impeccable swing pianist, working on 52nd Street with Billie Holiday and later with the Benny Goodman trio. Wilson played and was featured on records with many of the biggest names in jazz over his long and illustrious career.

Lester Young (1909–1959). Woodville, Mississippi. Lester Young was one of the finest tenor saxophonists of his era, coming to prominence with Count Basie's orchestra. Young had a cool, relaxed tone with a free-floating style. Often known as "Prez," a nickname given to him by Billie Holiday; Lester's playing style influenced many tenor players of the day, such as Stan Getz and Zoot Sims.

PHOTO CREDITS

Courtesy of Library of Congress
William P. Gottlieb Collection

Front Cover: LC-GLB04-0280 DLC
Back Cover: LC-GLB13-0275 DLC
Title Page: LC-GLB23-0425 DLC

Chapter One
Page 8: LC-GLB13-0275 DLC
Page 10: LC-GLB13-0278 DLC
Page 12: LC-GLB13-0198 DLC
Page 15: LC-GLB23-0311 DLC
Page 16: LC-GLB13-1123 DLC
Page 17: LC-GLB13-0163 DLC

Chapter Two

Club Downbeat
Page 22a: LC-GLB23-0425 DLC
Page 22b: LC-GLB13-0422 DLC
Page 26a: LC-GLB13-0831 DLC
Page 26b: LC-GLB23-0315 DLC
Page 27b: LC-GLB23-1186 DLC
Pag3 28a: LC-GLB23-0323 DLC
Page 28b: LC-GLB23-0324 DLC
Page 29a: LC-GLB23-0035 DLC
Page 29b: LC-GLB23-0285 DLC
Page 30b: LC-GLB23-0686 DLC
Page 32: LC-GLB13-0833DLC
Page 33a: LC-GLB23-0144 DLC
Page 33b: LC-GLB13-0871 DLC
Page 34a: LC-GLB23-0281 DLC
Page 34b: LC-GLB23-1122 DLC
Page 36b: LC-GLB23-0116 DLC
Page 37: LC-GLB23-0410 DLC
Page 38a: LC-GLB23-0112 DLC
Page 38b: LC-GLB13-1252 DLC

Famous Door
Page 40a: LC-GLB13-0716 DLC
Page 40b: LC-GLB13-0893 DLC
Page 41: LC-GLB23-0368 DLC
Page 42: LC-GLB23-0841 DLC
Page 43: LC-GLB23-0943 DLC
Page 44a: LC-GLB23-0089 DLC
Page 44b: LC-GLB23-0390 DLC
Page 45: LC-GLB23-0434 DLC
Page 46: LC-GLB23-0767 DLC

Hickory House
Page 50: LC-GLB23-1392 DLC
Page 51b: LC-GLB23-0845 DLC
Page 52a: LC-GLB23-0180 DLC
Page 52b: LC-GLB23-0648 DLC

Jimmy Ryan's
Page 54: LC-GLB23-0669 DLC
Page 55: LC-GLB23-0054 DLC
Page 56a: LC-GLB23-0916 DLC
Page 56b: LC-GLB13-0087 DLC
Page 57: LC-GLB23-0203 DLC
Page 59a: LC-GLB23-0295 DLC
Page 59b: LC-GLB23-0682 DLC
Page 60: LC-GLB23-0412 DLC
Page 61: LC-GLB23-1614 DLC

Kelly's Stable
Page 63: LC-GLB23-0789 DLC
Page 65: LC-GLB23-0084 DLC

Onyx
Page 72a: LC-GLB23-0355 DLC
Page 72b: LC-GLB23-0201 DLC
Page 73: LC-GLB23-0441 DLC
Page 76a: LC-GLB04-1141 DLC
Page 76b: LC-GLB04-1125 DLC
Page 77: LC-GLB04-1185 DLC

Spotlite
Page 83: LC-GLB23-0399 DLC
Page 83: LC-GLB13-0197 DLC
Page 84a: LC-GLB23-0226 DLC
Page 84b: LC-GLB23-0027 DLC

Three Deuces
Page 85: LC-GLB23-0091 DLC
Page 86a: LC-GLB23-0685 DLC
Page 86b: LC-GLB23-0688 DLC
Page 87: LC-GLB23-0745 DLC
Page 88a: LC-GLB23-0687 DLC
Page 88b: LC-GLB04-1136 DLC
Page 89: LC-GLB23-0818 DLC
Page 90a: LC-GLB23-0400 DLC
Page 90b: LC-GLB23-0707 DLC
Page 91: LC-GLB23-0191 DLC
Page 92a: LC-GLB23-1337 DLC
Page 92b: LC-GLB13-0844 DLC

Aquarium
Page 95: LC-GLB23-0732 DLC
Page 96: LC-GLB23-0730 DLC
Page 97: LC-GLB23-0237 DLC
Page 98a: LC-GLB23-0230 DLC
Page 98b: LC-GLB23-0008 DLC
Page 99: LC-GLB23-0419 DLC
Page 101: LC-GLB23-0047 DLC
Page 102a: LC-GLB13-0025DLC
Page 102b: LC-GLB23-0022DLC
Page 103: LC-GLB23-0755 DLC
Page 104: LC-GLB23-0046DLC
Page 105: LC-GLB13-0383 DLC
Page 106:LC-GLB13-0382DLC
Page 107: LC-GLB13-0183 DLC

21 Club
Page 110: LC-GLB04-1127 DLC

Leon & Eddie's
Page 112b: LC-GLB04-1140 DLC

Club 18 / Dixon's / Club Troubadour
Page 113: LC-GLB23-0216 DLC
Page 114a: LC-GLB23-1079 DLC
Page 114b: LC-GLB23-0121 DLC
Page 115: LC-GLB23-0134 DLC
Page 116: LC-GLB23-0303 DLC

Pages 11 and 48: Photos courtesy of New York City Municipal Archives
Page 19: Photo courtesy of Beyond my Ken
Page 79: Photo courtesy of Leonard Gaskin
Page 111/112(top): Photos courtesy of George Miller

SOURCES

During my research for this book I drew from many secondary and primary sources, such as *DownBeat* magazine, the *New York Times*, the *African-American* newspaper, *Growing Up with Jazz: Twenty-Four Musicians Talk about Their Lives and Careers* by W. Royal Stokes, *52nd Street: The Street That Never Slept* by Arnold Shaw, *Come In and Hear the Truth: Jazz and Race on 52nd Street* by Patrick Burke, *Dizzy Gillespie: The Bebop Years, 1937–1952* by Ken Vail, and *The Birth of Bebop: A Social and Musical History* by Scott DeVeax.

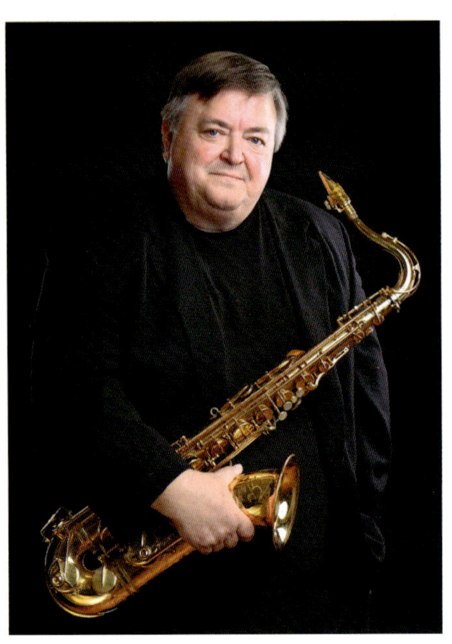

THE AUTHOR

Leo T. Sullivan has been working professionally for over forty years as a saxophonist, flutist, composer, and webmaster and has played on many CDs with various artists. He has also recorded numerous soundtracks for major television shows. Leo has played with the Manhattan Transfer, Johnny Mathis, Rosemary Clooney, the Temptations, Toni Tennile, Charo, Don Rickles, Carl Fontana, Bob Newhart, and the Osmond Brothers, just to name a few. In recent years, Leo has been involved in developing over sixty-five jazz websites. They can be viewed at www.jazzwebsites.org. Leo is also the author of *Birdland, the Jazz Corner of the World: An Illustrated Tribute, 1949–1965.*